ACCOUNTANTS' PROFESSIONAL NEGLIGENCE

ACCOUNTANTS' PROFESSIONAL NEGLIGENCE

Developments in Legal Liability

Jonathan R. H. H. Pockson, M.A., F.C.A.

HOLMES & MEIER PUBLISHERS, INC.
IMPORT DIVISION
IUB Building
30 Irving Place, New York, N.Y. 10003

346.73
P 739

First published 1982 by
THE MACMILLAN PRESS LTD
London and Basingstoke
Companies and representatives
throughout the world

ISBN 0 333 27845 3

Typeset and printed in Hong Kong

CONTENTS

ACKNOWLEDGEMENTS

I would like to thank Mr Michael Mumford of the University of Lancaster for the guidance and support he has given me during the initial stages of the research for the book. Both his advice and that of Professor Edward Stamp have been of invaluable assistance. I also wish to thank the many people who commented upon my initial findings and advised me of directions to follow. In this respect I am particularly grateful to Professor Denzil Y. Causey and Professor H. R. Jaenicke, with whom I corresponded initially.

I am very grateful to the Librarian of the Institute of Advanced Legal Studies for permitting me to use the facilities of the Institute, and also to the Social Science Research Council for their financial assistance.

Finally Val Wilson and Janet Hyde deserve my thanks for the expert way they transferred my oftentimes illegible text into type-script.

J. R. H. H. P.

The author and publishers wish to thank the following who have kindly given permission for the use of copyright material:

The Controller of Her Majesty's Stationery Office for tables from the Reports of the Department of Trade and Industry Investigations.

McGraw-Hill Publications Company for a chart from *Business Week*, 16 November 1974 © 1974 by McGraw-Hill Inc. All rights reserved.

LIST OF TABLES

LIST OF SCHEDULES

TABLE OF CASES

UNITED STATES

1 THE 'LITIGATION EXPLOSION'

I INTRODUCTION

In the past decade the United States has undergone social political and economic changes which have affected every facet of its society. The late 1960s and early 1970s were periods of expansion for 'conglomerate' corporations. Some of the less respectable conglomerate operators[1] took advantage of the rising stock market in this period to expand their operations through take-over policies. Many 'high-flying' or 'glamour' stocks had rapid rises on the exchanges and even more dramatic failures,[2] involving reorganisation or qualified audit reports.

A change which has affected society over the past decade has been the rise of consumer pressure groups, and the advent of 'consumerism' has involved almost every class of US society in litigation.[3] The professional classes have been directly affected, accountants and lawyers being enjoined in many legal actions.[4] In a business context, the investor seeking a remedy for a loss of investment or decline in stock price is likely to bring an action not only against the corporation and its directors but also its professional advisers, the accountants and lawyers. One reason for this is the involvement of the corporation's advisers in the preparation of the financial reports or prospectuses upon which the investor relied. Moreover, these advisers, independent yet connected with the corporation, may be the only defendants with sufficient resources to provide a wronged investor with a pecuniary remedy,[5] particularly when the corporation is in liquidation.

Many writers in legal and accounting journals have commented upon the causes and effects of this recent 'litigation explosion'[6] – the extent of litigation is now recognised as a major problem facing the American accounting profession.[7]

II THE EXTENT OF LITIGATION IN THE UNITED STATES

It is difficult to quantify exactly the extent of litigation involving accountants. Various commentators have estimated that currently there are approximately 1000 cases pending.[8] In one recent survey[9] the trend in auditors' litigation was thought to be consistent with the general upward trend in business litigation. Table I illustrates the

TABLE I   The rise in business lawsuits

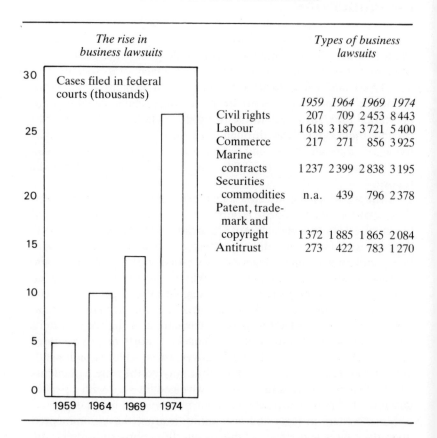

The rise in business lawsuits				*Types of business lawsuits*			
				1959	1964	1969	1974
			Civil rights	207	709	2453	8443
			Labour	1618	3187	3721	5400
			Commerce	217	271	856	3925
			Marine contracts	1237	2399	2838	3195
			Securities commodities	n.a.	439	796	2378
			Patent, trade-mark and copyright	1372	1885	1865	2084
			Antitrust	273	422	783	1270

SOURCE: *Business Week*. November 1974, p. 104,[10] using the data of the Administrative Office of the US Courts.

magnitude of the change in private lawsuits involving businesses up to 1974. Liggio has estimated[11] that by 1974 cases pending against accountants were between 500 and 1000, and over 200 cases had been decided. These figures represent a staggering increase in litigation compared with the mid-1960s, when cases were practically non-existent.[12]

Arising out of this increased litigation is a further problem for accountants. As more court actions are brought, a wider interpretation of the established law is evident.[13] Both in statute and common law the accountant faces considerable uncertainty as to his legal position. Today, established precedent[14] in important areas such as liability to third parties is being challenged by the courts and by legal commentators in the light of present social needs and pressures.[15] Accountants can no longer hide behind the protective immunity offered by privity of contract, which had for so long barred the third party from bringing an action.

III THE EXTENT OF LITIGATION IN THE UNITED KINGDOM

Having recognised that a problem faces the American accounting profession, the main objective of this book is to analyse whether it is likely that the situation currently occurring in the United States could arise in the United Kingdom. Could the British accounting profession be faced with a comparable 'litigation explosion'?

It is possible to reason, *a priori*, that because of the similarities of the two nations the situation occurring in the US will arise in the UK. Both nations have directly comparable accounting professions and similar business systems and structures.

All publicly quoted companies in America are required by statute to submit audited financial statements to shareholders and regulatory authorities. In Britain, disclosure of audited financial statements is required for all companies with a share capital.[16] These statements must be audited by legally recognised professional accountants.[17] The standards (or recommended standards) of auditing are laid down by professional institutes, together with the accounting principles involved.[18] Both in the US and the UK the purpose of the audit report is to express an opinion on the published accounting representations of the financial condition of the company.[19]

The philosophy in both countries behind this independent assessment procedure is to ensure that outsiders who need to use the statements will be able to place greater reliance upon the information disclosed. A major objective has been to promote efficiency and certainty in the stock markets for shares in quoted companies.

Accountants in both countries must normally be members of professional institutes or state societies, having satisfied examination requirements and obtained suitable experience.[20] The development of the American accounting profession was undoubtedly influenced by British practice.[21] At the turn of the century most of the major firms were British[22] and these firms provided many of the 'founding fathers' of the American profession, such as Arthur Lowes Dickinson and George O. May. The British presence at that time was so strong that Carey has termed it 'The British Invasion'.[23]

Benston has the following observations to make: 'On the whole, the similarities between the accounting standards of the United States and the United Kingdom outnumber their differences. Because of this similarity, an accountant from either country could relocate in the other without feeling too much out of place and without needing special glossaries to interpret line descriptions in financial statements. Accounting professors often hold visiting appointments during which . . . they can teach both the theoretical and applied aspects of auditing and accounting. The bond between countries is further evidenced by the fact that accounting periodicals are read and contributed to by practitioners and professionals on both sides of the Atlantic.'[24]

In law, as in accounting, there are important areas of similarity. Many American laws have their origins in Britain. This is noticeable in statutory company law, and even more so in the common law.[25] Even the procedural aspects of the legal systems have similarities, although the differences are often significant.[26] This book is concerned with the legal environment of accounting rather than accounting or auditing practices themselves; and therefore in subsequent chapters similarities and differences in the law are analysed in greater detail.

In his research into the accounting principles of various nations Zeff wrote: 'That countries learn from one another is clear. . . . Perhaps because of its more developed securities market, the aggressiveness of its financial press, and the accounting philosophy of the SEC, the US has tended to face problems earlier than other countries.'[27] Although this reference was made in connection with the development of accounting principles, it provides a lesson for other aspects of accounting, including legal aspects. The English accountant may be able to learn something from the legal predicament the American accountant now faces.

From an analysis of British professional journals and other financial reporting sources, there is no evidence of litigation comparable to that of the US. Reasons for this are brought out by the reports concerning Tremletts' case. This case never reached the courts and yet its settlement was widely reported.[28] If accountants in Britain were undergoing a comparable spate of litigation to that in the US, the financial press would surely have been similarly quick to report such a situation.

The Tremletts' case is analysed now in this respect for two reasons: (i) it is comparable to cases which have led to court action in the US; (ii) it indicates some of the reasons why the accountant in England has not been subjected to extensive court action.

In March 1974 Tremletts Limited made a takeover bid for Tower Assets Limited, a timber and furniture group. After the takeover the directors of Tremletts claimed that one of Tower's subsidiaries, the Dutch Fijnhout Group, was in serious financial difficulties. The directors alleged that Tower's financial advisers and directors must have been aware of this at the time of the bid. In October 1974 Tremletts therefore sued Tower's directors and financial advisers (the merchant bankers, Dawnay Day, and the accountants, Arthur Young McClelland Moores & Company) for misrepresentation, negligence and breach of duty for a damages claim of £6 million.

A week before the trial was to take place (27 January 1976) the parties agreed to a settlement. Two factors are said to have encouraged the settlement. Firstly, just prior to the proceedings the Bank of England and certain merchant banks put pressure upon the parties to settle so as to avoid a case which 'promised to be one of the most embarrassing the City had seen for years'.[29] The City did not wish to be shown up in bad light, especially after the several Department of Trade investigations which had commenced into companies in the previous years.[30]

The second reason for settlement, and probably more significant, was the question of costs of the extensive legal case. Neither the plaintiffs, Tremletts, nor the defendants, Dawnay Day, were in a strong financial position. Legal expenses were running at an estimated £1000 per day, and an Arthur Young partner estimated that further costs could run to over £1 million. On the costs estimate alone, the final settlement of £550 000 (of which the greater part, £500 000, was paid by the accountants) would seem to have been the best business decision in the circumstances.[31]

This case reveals the main deterrent to court action in Britain – legal costs. Despite the fact that the accountants in the above case were reported as having a good defence, they still preferred to settle to avoid the possibility of expenditure far in excess of the settlement figure.

The events of the Tremletts' case have been repeated in the London and County Securities case where the defendants Harmood Banner (now part of Deloittes) preferred to settle for £900 000 (without admitting negligence) rather than risk possible liability of £10 million. The London and County case is considered at greater length in future chapters.

IV DIFFERENCES BETWEEN UK AND US

As little litigation has been brought against accountants in England there would appear to be some substantial differences between the US and the UK which have created this situation.

Five possible reasons have been advanced, all of which are analysed in further chapters.

(i) Class actions suits (Chapter 7)

Since 1966 the class action has become a major procedural device encouraging the litigation in the US. Although there is a legal device in England which is comparable (in fact the American class action originally derived from English procedure) the cost system amongst other factors prohibits its widespread use in the UK.

(ii) Contingent fees (Chapter 7)

Lawyers in the US are able to offer their services under an arrangement whereby no fee will be charged unless the plaintiff in an action wins the case. The fee is contingent upon a successful result. This system employed with the class action suit is recognised as a powerful weapon in the hands of the investor. In England no contingent fee system is allowed. In the US contingent fee lawyers act as a leading pressure group against the practices of management and accountants.

(iii) Costs (Chapter 7)

The indemnity system of costs in the UK acts as a deterrent to bringing actions (as witnessed in the Tremletts' case). In the non-indemnity system, whereby a party to an action may be certain of his financial commitment as he will not have to indemnify the other party in the event of losing an action, there is no equivalent deterrent to filing a court action.

(iv) The Securities and Exchange Commission (Chapter 2)

In the UK there is no institution with comparable power to that of the US Securities and Exchange Commission. The SEC has pursued a policy of enforcement against professionals whereby suits by investors and the SEC itself are encouraged. The commencement of an SEC investigation will probably lead ultimately to some court action. If the SEC does not bring its own action, its findings are likely to be used in a private action. The SEC may even appear as *amicus curiae* on behalf of plaintiffs.

(v) Wider legal interpretation (Chapter 4)

Traditional American statute law has been interpreted increasingly widely by the courts. Chapters 4, 5 and 6 show that the movement beyond establishment precedent has resulted in more cases being brought under the common law in order to test the extent of accountants' liability to third parties. In England the law has not been subject to this wider interpretation. English courts are wary of overruling established precedent; American courts are more willing to overrule cases no longer considered relevant to its society.

V SUMMARY

(i) Third party aspects of the law

The research for this book has centred upon third party aspects of accountants' legal liability. This is because a significant amount of US litigation has been brought by investors, creditors or financiers who occupy a third party relationship to the accountant. In the past the accountant would not have been liable to anyone but the client with whom he had contracted.[32] Innocent third parties have demanded a wider definition of the accountants' duty of care. The American courts have upheld these demands.[33]

(ii) Common law and statute law

The book analyses the common law actions in the US as opposed to the actions brought against accountants under statute. Chapter 3 shows that the federal securities laws are not directly comparable with English statute law. However the common law is very similar in many respects, is directly comparable and cross-citation of cases appears frequently.[34]

(iii) Misrepresentation

In addition to the third party aspects of accountants' liability at common law, the book considers the legal aspects of misrepresentation. The area of negligent and fraudulent misrepresentation is significant because third parties rely upon the financial statements which the accountant has audited and signed; also there are numerous cases in this area in the US, and the law of misrepresentation has undergone important change.[35]

The book is divided into a further seven chapters as follows:

Chapter 2 expands upon some of the institutional aspects relevant to accountants' liability. In particular the role of the SEC is analysed in depth with emphasis upon its enforcement machinery and the influence it has upon creating litigation. The Department of Trade and Industry and the regulatory aspects of the English stock exchanges are the closest institutions to the SEC and are compared with it. This chapter also analyses the disciplinary effectiveness of the American Institute of Certified Public Accountants and the Institute of Chartered Accountants in England and Wales.

Chapter 3 compares the common law and statute law of the US and the UK relevant to accountants' third party liability. From this chapter it is evident that further analysis of the common law cases is beneficial because of the heavy reliance of each nation upon legal precedent of the other.

Chapter 4 outlines the methodology employed to establish the American common law cases which are analysed in both this chapter and Chapter 5. Chapter 4 also explains the summary schedules of cases and the reasons for their presentation in a schedule format.

Chapters 5 and 6 analyse recent common law cases with respect to liability for negligence in the US and the UK respectively.

Chapter 7 evaluates major legal differences between the two countries to explain important reasons why litigation has occurred in America and has not occurred in this country.

Finally, Chapter 8 itemises the conclusions of the 'litigation explosion' in the United States. The chapter raises suggestions for further research and also considers future trends of litigation for the accountant in the United Kingdom.

NOTES

[1] For examples of the dubious practices of a number of conglomerate enterprises see A. Briloff, *Unaccountable Accounting: Games Accountants Play* (New York: Harper and Row, 1972).

[2] One noted example is the National Student Marketing Corporation, whose rise and fall is depicted in A. Tobias, *The Funny Money Game* (London: Michael Joseph, 1972). See also SEC influence in 'Securities Act Release' no. 5275 – 'The Obligations of Underwriters, Brokers and Dealers in Distributing and Trading Securities, particularly of New High Risk Ventures'.

[3] In his 15 August 1972 speech to the American Bar Association in San Francisco, Chief Justice Burger decried the 'unprecedented explosion of litigation' in the past ten years. He proposed that 'every piece of legislation creating new causes of action' be accompanied by a 'court impact statement' for the purpose of having 'congress consider the needs of the courts in relation to the needs of the country for new legislation'. See E. E. Pollock, 'Class Actions Reconsidered: Theory and Practice under amended Rule 23', 28 *Business Lawyer* 741, 742 (1973). See Table I *infra*.

[4] Liggio in one article stated that 'substantial amounts of litigation have been commenced against the accountants in recent years. Current pending cases number somewhere between 500–1000. Incidentally, this has not been limited to the accountants. Other professions – especially the lawyers – have found themselves in the same quandary'. C. D. Liggio, 'The Expectation Gap: the Accountants' Legal Waterloo?', *CPA Journal*, July 1975, p. 23. The naming of attorneys as defendants in complaints alleging violations of the securities law appears to be 'increasingly fashionable today'. See J. H. Cheek, 'Potential Liability of Counsel named in a Prospectus', *Securities Law Review*, 203 (1975).

[5] What is now termed the 'deep-pocket theory'. For a full analysis see H. R. Jaenicke, 'The Impact of the Current Legal Climate on the Accounting Profession', a background paper prepared for the Commission on Auditor's Responsibilities, July 1976 (Cohen Commission) p. 5/6.

[6] The expression 'litigation explosion' is from Earle's article of the same name in *Journal of Accountancy*, March 1970, p. 65, originally published in Peat, Marwick, Mitchell & Co's journal *World*. Earle is general counsel for Peat. Another effect of the increase in litigation against the major accounting firms in the US is that they now employ their own full-time counsel. Liggio (see note 4, *supra*) is general counsel for Arthur Young.

[7] There have been a number of conferences in the US specifically on the problem. These are widely reported in the press and commentaries will usually be included in law journals. One recent example is the January 1975 *Vanderbilt Law Review*, vol. 28, no. 1, the whole issue being devoted to accounting problems and the federal securities laws. Participants included lawyers in the legal and accounting professions and members of the Securities and Exchange Commission. The AICPA recognised the problem by appointing the Cohen Commission, see note 5 *supra*.

[8] For example, Arthur Andersen & Co, Annual Report (1973). C. D. Liggio, 'The Accountant's Legal Environment for the Next Decade', paper presented at the 10 May University of Kansas Accounting Colloquium, 'Institutional Issues in Public Accounting'. See also Jaenicke, note 5 *supra*, pp. 1, 2. Data from insurers of the larger accounting firms indicate that there are approximately 300 claim files now open that involve potential demands for coverage of losses in excess of deductible amounts. See C. H. Griffin, 'Beleaguered Accountants', 174 *Accountant* 735 (1976).

[9] Peat, Marwick, Mitchell & Co, *Research Opportunities in Auditing* (New York, 1976).

[10] 'How Companies Fight Soaring Legal Costs', *Business Week*, November 1974, p. 104, cited by Peat, Marwick, Mitchell & Co., note 9 *supra*.

[11] C. D. Liggio, 'Expanding Concepts of Accountant's Liability', 12 *California CPA Quarterly* 18, 19 (Sep. 1974). Quoted by Jaenicke, note 5 *supra*, p. 2.

[12] See Jaenicke, note 5 *supra*, p. 2.

[13] Earle has stated, 'what we have been witnessing in the United States in recent years is an ever increasing resort to courts. The greater volume of litigation in turn produces a broader scope of judicial subject matter and a broader range of targets for suit. The result is more judge-made law, some of it in previously unexplored fields, of a new and often times startling nature', note 10 *supra*, p. 65.

[14] *Ultramares Corporation* v. *Touche* 255 N.Y. 170, 174 N.E. 441 (1931).

[15] This is fully analysed in Chapters 4 and 5 *infra*.

[16] UK: The Companies Act 1948 ss. 124, 127 and 158. The Companies Act 1967 ss. 24 and 47. The requirement is for *all* companies falling under the jurisdiction of the Companies Acts 1948 and 1967 having a share capital and limited liability.

US: The Securities Exchange Act 1934 s. 12, re reports to the SEC. SEC also has considerable control over the published reports sent to shareholders under this section. See H. Rappaport, *SEC Accounting Practice and Procedure* (New York: Ronald Press, 1972) (3rd ed.), Chapter 30.

[17] UK: The Department of Trade and Industry's annual report of companies

lists those accountancy bodies whose members are qualified to audit. See Companies Act 1947 s. 161 and Companies Act 1967 s. 13. In addition the DTI can (and does) register a small number of other accountants for the purpose. US: SEC Regulation S-X, Article 2, Rule 2-01(a).

[18] UK: The ICAEW provides recommendations with respect to auditing standards, see Members Handbook Part III. The profession is currently in the process of issuing auditing standards. Statements of Standard Accounting Practice have been issued since 1974. See 'Accountants launch campaign for better Auditing Standards', *The Financial Times* 9 Feb. 1976. US: The AICPA has re-coded its auditing standards as Statements of Auditing Standards No. 1. Since then other SASs have been produced. The procedure is the same for Generally Accepted Accounting Principles. See generally, M. Moonitz, 'Obtaining Agreement on Standards in the Accounting Profession', A.A.A. *Studies in Accounting Research*, Vol. No. 8.

[19] UK: See The Companies Act 1948 s. 156(3) also the Ninth Schedule for matters to be expressly stated in the Auditor's Report. US: See SEC Regulation S-X, Article 2 (Certification) Rule 2-02 *et seq*. Unlike the UK the content of the auditor's report has developed under the auspices of the American Institute, often in connection with governmental agencies and the New York Stock Exchange. See, 'The Independent Auditor's Reporting Standards in Three Nations', Accountants International Study Group, 1969, para. 18.

[20] UK: Britain has lagged behind the American practice in looking at the educational needs of the accountancy profession. In Britain greater emphasis is placed on practical experience rather than university experience in granting qualification. There are currently four major examining bodies recognised for the legal audit of companies: The three Institutes of Chartered Accountants (in England and Wales, in Scotland and in Ireland) and the Association of Certified Accountants. US: There are 54 jurisdictions granting CPA certificates with a single examining body regulated by the AICPA. See generally D. Solomons, *Prospectus for a Profession*, Advisory Board of Accountancy Education (London: Gee, 1972) Summary pp. 2 and 3.

[21] See R. Brown (ed.), *History of Accounting and Accountants* (London: Frank Cass & Co. Ltd., 1968). S. A. Zeff, *Forging Accounting Principles in Five Countries* (Illinois: Stipes Publishing Co., 1971). L. Carey, *The Rise of the Accounting Profession* (AICPA, 1979).

[22] Including the two largest firms: Price Waterhouse & Co., and Peat, Marwick, Mitchell & Co.

[23] L. Carey, note 21 *supra*, p. 27.

[24] George J. Benston, 'Accounting Standards in the United States and the United Kingdom: Their Nature, Causes and Consequences', 28 *Vanderbilt Law Review* (1975) p. 236.

[25] See Chapter 3, *infra*.

[26] See Chapter 7, *infra*.

[27] Zeff, note 21 *supra*, p. 311.

[28] See: Press release by Arthur Young McClelland Moores & Co., 20 Jan. 1976; *The Times* 20 Jan. 1976 'Tremletts settles for £500,000'; *The Times*

21 Jan. 1976 'Accountants to pay £500,000'. *Sunday Telegraph* 25 Jan. 1976 'Why Tremlett's Traumas didn't get to the High Court', City 4.
[29] *Sunday Telegraph*, ibid.
[30] Ibid.
[31] Ibid.
[32] Chapter 4, *infra*.
[33] Chapter 5, *infra*.
[34] Chapter 3, *infra*.
[35] Chapters 4, 5 and 6, *infra*.

2 INSTITUTIONAL COMPARISONS

I INTRODUCTION

The purpose of this chapter is to analyse the powers of the regulatory institutions in both the US and the UK in order to assess their influence upon litigation. This analysis is confined to a description of the enforcement powers of each of the institutions over an accountant or accounting firm and the ways in which those powers are enforced. The chapter also highlights the differences between the two countries.

Certain institutions which have some influence over the independent accountant are listed below in the order in which they are analysed in the text.

II. The Securities and Exchange Commission
III. The Department of Trade and Industry
IV. The Stock Exchange
V. The American Institute of Certified Public Accountants
VI. The Institute of Chartered Accountants in England and Wales

II THE SECURITIES AND EXCHANGE COMMISSION

J. C. Burton, the chief accountant of the SEC from 1973 to 1976, recently stated:

> . . . the Commission [SEC] has bought in recent years to focus its enforcement efforts at key points where maximum impact can be achieved. For this reason, enforcement efforts involving professionals, such as accountants and lawyers have been important even though the number of cases[1] in which professionals were so involved has not been great.[2]

The SEC has recognised that independent accountant's functions in industry are vital to the smooth functioning of the securities markets. Therefore by a rigid control[3] of these accountants the SEC is assured that the companies which are reported upon and audited will in turn be tightly controlled. By concentrating upon 'key points' the whole corporate structure is controlled. Burton continued that ' . . . professionals are an essential element in providing access to the market place, since the sale of securities cannot take place without their involvement, professional responsibility at these points of access can prevent many questionable activities before they occur'.[4] The enforcement philosophy of the SEC is therefore to deter rather than to punish wrongdoers.

(i) The SEC's quasi-judicial authority

The SEC is authorised to undertake enforcement activities against a corporation or its accountants where 'it appears that there may be violation of the Acts administered by the Commission or the rules and regulations thereunder'.[5] In such circumstances a preliminary investigation will generally be made.[6] The Acts over which the SEC has administrative power include:[7]

The Securities Act of 1933
The Securities Exchange Act of 1934
The Public Utility Holding Company Act of 1935
The Trust Indenture Act of 1939
The Investment Company Act of 1940
The Investment Advisers Act of 1940
The Securities Investor Protection Act of 1970

The Commission also serves as adviser to Federal courts in corporate reorganisation proceedings under Chapter X of the National Bankruptcy Act.[8]

(ii) The SEC's investigation procedure

While virtually all the SEC cases are civil in character, on occasions[9] a case may be regarded as sufficiently serious that it should be referred to the Department of Justice for consideration for criminal prosecution.[10] The SEC may pursue after investigation any one of three possible courses:[11]

1. Civil injunction. The Commission may apply to an appropriate US district court for an order enjoining those acts or practices alleged to violate the law or Commission's rules. (Injunctive proceedings)
2. Criminal prosecution. If fraud or other wilful law violation is indicated the Department of Justice may be notified. Through local district attorneys the evidence may be presented to a Federal grand jury to seek an indictment against the offenders. (Criminal proceedings)
3. Administrative remedy. This is a censuring remedy whereby the SEC may bar individuals or firms for practising before it, or institute other less stringent sanctions. (Rule 2(e) proceedings)

According to Burton[12] referrals to the Department of Justice when accountants have been involved have only been made when the evidence indicated that the accountant certified statements which he knew to be false.[13] In no event will cases be referred to the Department of Justice when the wrong occurred through faulty judgment alone however serious the fault. The SEC requires the *scienter* element therefore found in common law deceit actions.[14]

Table II represents the investigation procedure which the Commission will generally follow from the time it receives notice of a violation of one of the statutes it administers to the final action it takes.[15] The table indicates that the SEC has a very thorough and lengthy process of investigation. Investigations are further complicated when a professional is involved, such as an accountant or attorney, because in initial proceedings the investigatory team will not be certain if the professional is not himself involved in the violation and therefore may be enjoined in any action.

The office of the Chief Accountant has close control over cases involving accountants and before any cases proceed to civil or criminal action the Chief Accountant will personally review the testimony of the enforcement division. He will also meet with the accountants involved.[16]

One criticism of the lengthy procedure outlined in the table is that much of the impact of the SEC investigation is lost because of the time taken to complete it. The process may take as long as five years to run its course before Rule 2(e) proceedings[17] commence. In the SEC action against Peat, Marwick, Mitchell and Company, set out in A.S.R. 173, settlement occurred some seven years after the first offence was committed by the firm.

However, to ensure that no unfair sanctions are handed down the

TABLE II The SEC's enforcement 'program'

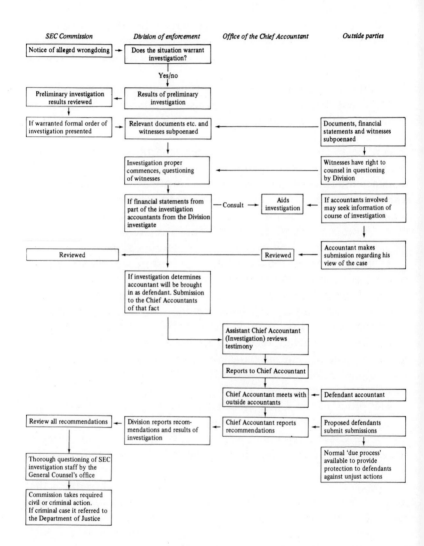

SEC Commission	Division of enforcement	Office of the Chief Accountant	Outside parties
Notice of alleged wrongdoing →	Does the situation warrant investigation?		
	Yes/no		
Preliminary investigation results reviewed	Results of preliminary investigation		
If warranted formal order of investigation presented	Relevant documents etc. and witnesses subpoenaed ←		Documents, financial statements and witnesses subpoenaed
	Investigation proper commences, questioning of witnesses ←		Witnesses have right to counsel in questioning by Division
	If financial statements from part of the investigation accountants from the Division investigate	— Consult → Aids investigation ←	If accountants involved may seek information of course of investigation
Reviewed ←		Reviewed ←	Accountant makes submission regarding his view of the case
	If investigation determines accountant will be brought in as defendant. Submission to the Chief Accountants of that fact		
		Assistant Chief Accountant (Investigation) reviews testimony	
		Reports to Chief Accountant	
		Chief Accountant meets with outside accountants ←	Defendant accountant
Review all recommendations ←	Division reports recommendations and results of investigation ←	Chief Accountant reports recommendations	Proposed defendants submit submissions
Thorough questioning of SEC investigation staff by the General Counsel's office			Normal 'due process' available to provide protection to defendants against unjust actions
Commission takes required civil or criminal action. If criminal case it referred to the Department of Justice			

SEC needs to be entirely certain that future action is warranted. This is one reason why the commission is content to leave court action to individuals after the completion of their investigations.[18]

(iii) The SEC's enforcement measures and performance

The procedural elements of the SEC enforcement measures centre upon three areas in auditing practice:[19]

1. The effect on auditing standards.
2. Quality control procedures.
3. Improving auditing standards.

The enforcement programme has one fundamental aim: the improvement of the confidence of the public and the investors in the functioning of the securities market.[20]

With the threat of an injunctive action or the risk of private civil actions the SEC hopes that those accountants pursuing unprofessional auditing standards will cease such practice.[21] The SEC when administering the securities laws has the power to bring an injunction action.[22] Under such an action the SEC alleges that a company or individuals have violated the federal securities laws or the Commission's rules and regulations. Based upon these allegations, the SEC seeks to enjoin the company or the individuals from further violations. This 'civil injunction' procedure is carried out by the application of the Commission to an appropriate United States District Court for ratification of such an order.[23]

Usually the party involved in the action will consent to the entry of the injunction but without admitting or denying the truth of the SEC's allegations, so as to put an end to the proceedings with the Commission.[24] It is not uncommon to find that following the consent decree numerous civil actions will be filed against those consenting – usually investor class action suits.[25]

The SEC therefore is aided in its enforcement programme through civil involvement after an SEC investigation. The Commission seeks out and investigates the wrongs done by companies but leaves final retribution to those concerned private plaintiffs and public interest securities lawyers who have directly suffered as a result of the wrongs.[26]

The SEC recognises the importance of this secondary power, and it does not discourage private actions.[27] The SEC publishes details of all the injunction proceedings which have taken place in its 'docket' series, so any actions which have not been picked up by the financial press are available to the investors.

Jaenicke states in support of this argument that 'the consequences of an injunction may extend far beyond an admonition to "do right" in the future. The injunction can be useful to plaintiffs in subsequent civil suits for damages; the same language in the injunction may appear in the private damage suit'.[28]

(iv) The SEC's sanctions

The SEC employs various sanctions against companies and firms which it considers have fallen short of the requirements or violated the statutes it administers.

(1) Informal measure
If the SEC considers that an audit has been marginally sub-standard it may require the individual partners of the firm involved to attend informal meetings with the Commission. These meetings are intended to indicate to the accountants that the SEC has reviewed the audit and considers it sub-standard. From such a meeting the SEC will hope to be assured that no further work of similar nature will occur again. This procedure saves considerable time and expense on the part of the SEC.

(2) Formal measure – Rule 2(e) SEC Rules of Practice
In 1971 the SEC amended[29] its Rules of Practice, Rule 2(e). An expert such as an accountant is likely to be denied the privilege of appearing or practising before the SEC if, after 1971, he is enjoined from violating the Federal securities laws or regulations.[30]

The Chief Accountant and the office of the Chief Accountant of the Commission is responsible for all cases and investigations dealing with the independence and qualifications of public accountants who practise before the Commission.[31] The Chief Accountant reviews all the cases where disciplinary proceedings involve accountants under Rule 2(e) of the Commission's Rules of Practice. (See flow chart on investigation system – Table II).

For the purposes of this Rule, 'practising before the Commission' includes the preparation of any statement, opinion or other paper by an accountant, filed with the Commission in any Registration statement, application, report or other document with the consent of such statement.[32]

Rule 2(e) states with respect to suspension and disbarment that:

(1) The Commission may deny, temporarily or permanently, the privilege of appearing or practising before it in any way to any person who is found by the Commission after notice of and opportunity for hearing in the matter (i) not to possess the requisite qualifications to represent others, or (ii) to be lacking in character or integrity or to have engaged in unethical or improper professional conduct, or (iii) to have wilfully violated, or wilfully aided and abetted the violation of any provision of the federal securities laws . . . , or the rules and regulations thereunder.

(2) . . . any person whose license to practise as an accountant . . . has been revoked or suspended in any State, Territory, District, Commonwealth, or Possession, or any person who has been convicted of a felony, or of a misdemeanour involving moral turpitude, shall be forthwith suspended from appearing or practising before the Commission.

(3)

 (i) The Commission, with due regard to the public interest and without preliminary hearing, may by order temporarily suspend from appearing or practising before it any . . . accountant . . . who, on or after July 1, 1971, has been by name

   (A) permanently enjoined by any court of competent jurisdiction by reason of his misconduct in an action brought by the Commission from violation or aiding and abetting the violation of any provision of the federal securities laws . . . or of the rules and regulations thereunder; or

   (B) found by any court . . . in an action brought by the Commission to which he is a party or found by this Commission in any administrative proceeding to which he is a party to have violation or aided and abetted the violation of any provision of the federal securities laws . . . or of the rules and regulations thereunder (unless the violation was found not to have been wilful).

(ii) Any person temporarily suspended from appearing and practising before the Commission in accordance with paragraph (1) may, within thirty days after service upon him of the order of temporary suspension, petition the Commission to lift the temporary suspension. If no petition has been received by the Commission within thirty days after service of the order by

mail the suspension shall become permanent.
(iii) Within thirty days after the filing of a petition in accordance
with paragraph (ii), the Commission shall either lift the
temporary suspension or set the matter down for hearing . . .
and after opportunity for hearing, may censure the petitioner
or may disqualify the petitioner from appearing or practising
before the Commission for a period of time or permanently . . . [33]

The effect of this Rule therefore is significant with respect to those
involved in injunction proceedings for securities law violations, as this
will give the SEC grounds for disallowing the party or parties involved
from practising before the Commission. Thus even if an accounting
firm consents to an injunction action (the so-called consent decree),
although admitting neither innocence nor guilt, then the SEC may still
disbar the party.

The hearings before the Commission put onus heavily upon the
petitioner to show cause why he should not be censored or disqualified. In addition if in previous judicial or administrative proceedings a
person consented without admitting the allegations he will have been
assumed to have been enjoined for the reasons alleged in the
complaint.[34]

Under Paragraph 3(1) of the Rule only those persons referred to
'by name' in proceedings will be bound by the Rule. This will preclude
therefore accounting partnerships and corporations unless they have
been included 'by name' in their entirety. Partners of a disqualified
individual in an accounting practice, according to Rappaport, 'may
not permit such persons to participate to any extent in matters coming
before the Commission, to participate in profits from their SEC
business, or to hold himself as entitled to practise before the SEC.
Partners and associates of a disqualified firm may not practise before
the SEC so long as they remain members of it associated with the
firm'.[35]

The powers of this Rule are very wide. The SEC has the jurisdiction
to cripple the workings of any accounting firm should the situation
warrant it. If a permanent injunction is brought against an accountant
his only recourse will be to leave the profession or to deal only with
less significant work within the firm.[36] Perhaps the greatest punishment he must bear is the stigma of SEC suspension with the considerable loss of respect attached to it.[37]

Despite the considerable hardship which the SEC could institute by a full exercise of the Rule, the number of proceedings it has published has remained comparatively small when looked at in relation to the number of accountants who prepare reports for the commission.[38] There has been resentment from some commentators[39] at the fact that the SEC does not fully undertake its powers in this regard. One particular weakness in the SEC's enforcement procedure is its reliance upon the consent decree. As Gapay writes:

> [The] weakness lies in the agency's reliance upon its favourite disciplinary tool, the 'consent decree'. Usually in a consent decree the defendant individual, corporation or broker-dealer consents to SEC findings in violations while neither admitting nor denying guilt. Often there isn't any penalty except that the consent has the effect of the SEC entering a sort of black mark against the defendant's name. The advantages of consent decrees are that they reduce the SEC's backlog while saving money for defendants who don't want to fight their case to a time-consuming conclusion.[40]

So although the SEC has the power to pursue cases to stringent ends it appears unwilling to do so. In one example, the Faberge case, which occurred at the beginning of 1973, the SEC allowed two broker-age firms and three mutual fund managers to consent to the agency's findings of misuse of inside information about Faberge Inc. stock. The SEC stopped short however, of censuring them even though their conduct violated securities laws and SEC rules and was 'censurable'. The agency did not ask for the refund of any profits made on the basis of the inside information.

(v) Accounting Series Releases

Of the proceedings against accountants which the SEC made public, through the publication of Accounting Series Releases, Tables III and IV summarise the conclusion of the disciplinary proceedings against them. The tables highlight a number of significant factors. Table III shows that the SEC has practically doubled its public disclosure of proceedings against accountants from 1970 to July 1976 when compared to the number of proceedings in the 1960s. Also the number of firms involved in SEC sanctions has increased considerably.

Table IV shows the importance the SEC has attached in the 1970s to other sanctions rather than the traditional suspension or dis-qualification proceedings. One reason for this is that major accounting firms have been involved, namely:

ASR 144 (1973)   Laventhol Krekstein Horwath and Horwath
ASR 153 (1974)   Touche Ross and Company
ASR 157 (1974)   Arthur Andersen and Company
ASR 167 (1974)   Westheimer, Fine, Berger and Company
ASR 173 (1975)   Peat, Marwick, Mitchell and Company

The following sections analyse some of the other sanctions the SEC has imposed upon these and similar accounting firms.

TABLE III   SEC proceedings against accountants or accounting firms

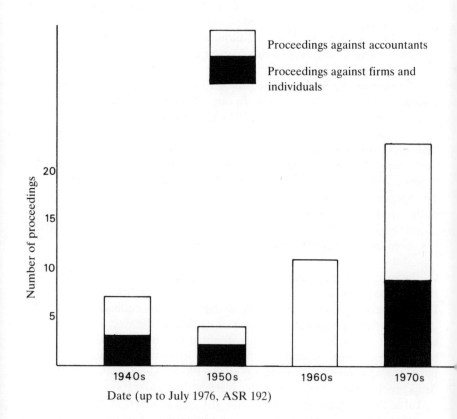

Date (up to July 1976, ASR 192)

SOURCE: Examination of SEC Accounting Series Releases.

(vi) Other sanctions

(1) Quality control review and inspections
Enforcement actions by the SEC may be instituted to encourage firms to undertake or improve 'quality control procedures'.[42] Such procedures may incorporate many aspects of accounting practice including:

TABLE IV Details of SEC sanctions against accountants

	1940s	1950s	1960s	1970s
1. Permanent disqualification	II		II	III
2. Resignation to avoid further Rule 2(e) proceedings.			IIIIII	IIIII
3. Suspension				
10 days		FI		
15 days		FI		
1 month	F	I		
2 months			I	
3 months	II			I
12 months	FI		I[41]	
22 months				I
Permanent (right to reapply)				IIII
4. Censure				IFFF
5. Investigations into firm				FFFFFF
6. Consent to SEC findings				FF
7. New clients prohibited				FFFFF
8. No merger with another firm allowed				F
9. Implement quality control procedures				FF
10. Local peer reviews				FF
11. Professional education				III
12. Proceedings dismissed	F	I	I	

SOURCE: SEC Accounting Series Releases.

In each column the number of instances where a particular sanction has been implemented by the SEC may be greater than the number of cases in the graph preceding. This is because in some instances more than one sanction has been imposed.

F =firm sanction
I =individual sanction

Recruitment
Training
Promotion
Reviews
Internal audit
Continuing post-qualification education.

The SEC may require firms to provide evidence that they are spending money on improving such procedures if the SEC through investigations consider they are warranted.[43] In connection with this the AICPA issued Statement of Auditing Standards No. 4 in December 1974 entitled 'Quality Control Consideration for a firm of Independent Auditors'. This statement outlines aspects of the SEC requirements.[44]

Throughout the investigatory stage the SEC may require firms to submit its procedures to the staff of the SEC or other firms for review. After this initial inspection the firm may be required to submit its procedures to periodic peer reviews for a specified period of time.[45] Burton admits that although 'this sanction has a number of variants tailored to particular situations, it certainly is not a panacea, and may not be appropriate in every case.'[46]

(2) Limiting new firm business

This sanction is linked with the powers vested with the SEC under Rule 2(e) in that through suspension of a firm from acting before it, it does in effect limit the firm from new business.[47] However the SEC has discretionary powers in this respect, and although it may not bar a firm from total practice before it, it is in a position to suspend firms from taking on new clients.

In July 1975 the SEC barred Peat, Marwick, Mitchell and Company (PMM) from accepting new clients for a period of six months.[48] This sanction was announced at the same time as a settlement between PMM and the SEC following an investigation into the firm's auditing practices. According to a report in the *Wall Street Journal*,[49] this sanction by the SEC is believed to have been the 'toughest treatment ever imposed by the SEC on a major accounting firm'. PMM consented to the settlement (which did not censure them) involving numerous accounting controversies dating back to 1968. These controversies include many corporate collapses including: Penn Central, Stirling Homex, National Student Marketing, Talley Industries and Republic National Life Insurance Co.[50] According to Walter Hanson, PMM's senior partner, the firm wanted 'to put an end to the situation where (the firm was) litigating with the agency with which (it was) in almost daily professional contact'. Hanson also noted that PMM had had nearly 10 000 engagements with the SEC since 1968. The number of occasions upon which the accounting and auditing practices proved to be inadequate were minute in comparison with this number of dealings.[51] The SEC had also stated (something unprecedented) that overall the audit practices and procedures employed by the firm were conducted in a competent and professional manner.[52]

To conclude this section on the SEC it is worth re-emphasising the enforcement philosophy as laid down at the beginning of this chapter. The SEC stated in ASR 157, involving Arthur Andersen and Company, and repeated in ASR 173:

The Commission and its staff do not and cannot investigate representations made to it, but must be able to rely on their completeness if this process is to work. The objectives of the securities laws can only be achieved when those professionals who practise before the Commission, both lawyers and accountants, act in a manner consistent with their responsibilities. Professionals involved in the disclosure process are in a very real sense the representatives of the investing public served by the Commission, and, as a result their dealings with the Commission and its staff must be permeated with candor and full disclosure. It cannot resemble an adversary relationship more appropriate to litigants in court, because the Commission is not an adverse party in this context. All who are familiar with the Commission's policies know that too much importance is attached to the word of the professional, to permit his or her word to become the subject of question. A professional's word is often the functional equivalent of his or her reputation. Conferences with the staff of the Commission serve a vital role in the administration of the securities laws, and such conferences are predicated, for the most part, upon full disclosure by the professionals involved. It must be understood by all who practise before the Commission, lawyers and accountants alike, that the Commission and its staff cannot tolerate less than full disclosure.

III THE DEPARTMENT OF TRADE AND INDUSTRY[53]

The impact of the SEC upon the accounting profession, and its part in the increase in litigation in the US, both provide interesting comparisons with the enforcement philosophy of the Department of Trade and Industry (DTI). Although there is no institution in the UK of similar stature to that of the SEC, due largely to the desire in this country to maintain self-regulation wherever possible, the DTI is the closest approximation.

(i) The DTI's quasi-judicial authority

The DTI's authority to enforce sanctions or undertake court proceedings are laid down by statute. Various Acts of Parliament give the Department this jurisdiction, including the Companies Acts of 1948 and 1967 and the Prevention of Fraud (Investments) Act of 1958.[54] This section will consider only those aspects covered by the Companies Acts emphasising the points at which the Acts specifically affect accountants.[55]

The DTI may appoint inspectors to investigate the affairs of a company where:

1. Two hundred or more members of a company or members holding not less than 10 per cent of the shares of the company make application; or
2. One-fifth in number of the registered persons of a company without share capital make application.

The applicants must provide sufficient evidence to the Department to show that an investigation is warranted.

3. The company itself declares through special resolution or court order that it sought to be investigated.
4. It appears to the Department that circumstances suggest the business is being conducted with intent to defraud its creditors or for a fraudulent or unlawful purpose or in a manner oppressive of any part of its members or that it was formed for such a purpose. Also because the Department considers the members have not been given all the information with respect to its affairs which they might reasonably expect.[56]

This section of the Companies Act 1948 appears to authorise an investigation even though the company's shareholders have received all the information as required by the Companies Acts.[57] Under this section it would also appear that misleading information provided in a company's accounts may qualify for investigation.

An inspector has the power to investigate any company which is a subsidiary or sub-subsidiary of the company being investigated or its holding company,[58] or any related company. The accountants or auditors of any company under investigation shall be under a duty to produce to the inspectors all books and documents relating to the company, and give all assistance to the investigation which they may be able to give.[59]

An auditor may be examined under oath,[60] and if he refuses to produce any book or document or refuses to answer any question with respect to the company's affairs, the inspector may refer the case to the court. The court may, upon investigation and after hearing witnesses, punish the auditor in like manner as if he had been guilty of contempt of court.[61]

Any person under examination by an inspector may not refuse to answer questions. If questions of an incriminating nature are put to an officer or agent of the company, the inspector must grant that person the right to study the testimony against him by other persons. And the officer or agent has the right to cross-examine those persons and also the right to answer any allegations against him.[62] Under section 167(5) of the 1948 Act an 'agent' includes *inter alia* a company's bankers, solicitors and auditors. Any answer given under oath to an inspector may be used in evidence against an officer or agent in subsequent civil or criminal proceedings.[63]

Table V shows the number of investigations the DTI has carried out under the relevant sections of the Companies Act 1948 and 1967. The table indicates the use the Department has made of its wider powers under section 109 of the 1967 Act whereby companies books and papers may be subpoenaed without the need for formal public inquiry procedures to be implemented. Criminal proceedings may also follow from a section 109 inquiry.[64]

(ii) The inspector's report and subsequent proceedings

The inspector after the investigation will issue a report and furnish copies to the parties initiating the investigation (the court, minority shareholders, the company, etc.).[65] It is normally the practice that no

TABLE V Department of Trade and Industry investigations – company investigations

Applications	1967	1968	1969	1970	1971	1972	1973	1974	1975
Outstanding at end of previous year	8	28	44	52	65	72	70	123	101
Received	240	338	390	400	432	403	408	438	456
Approved, of which under:	44	55	75	68	117	115	93	158	177
i. s. 164, 1948 Act								1	3
ii. s. 172, 1948 Act								2	2
iii. s. 165, 1948 Act	18	8	13	7	14	6	⎱2	25	16
iv. s. 334, 1948 Act							9		6
v. s. 109, 1967 Act	26	47	62	61	103	109	81	130	150
v. s. 32, 1967 Act							1		
Not proceeded with	43	109	108	109	159	173	186	192	209
Refused by DTI	136	158	199	210	149	117	76	110	97
Outstanding at year end	25	44	52	65	72	70	123	101	74

SOURCE: DTI *Companies in 19 . .* , Annual Reports from 1967 to 1975, (London: HMSO).

report will be made available to the public if subsequent civil or criminal proceedings are to take place. However this is not a prohibition laid down by law, and at the discretion of the inspector the report may be published despite further court proceedings against parties involved in the investigation.[66]

An inspector who in the course of his investigation[67] discovers matters which to his knowledge tend to show that an offence has been committed may inform the Department without the necessity of making an interim report.[68]

(1) Civil proceedings

If the DTI considers that proceedings should be brought against any person in the public interest it may do so in the name of the company.[69] Before the 1967 Companies Act recovery for damages was limited to cases involving fraud, misfeasance or other misconduct in connection with the promotion or formation of the company or through mismanagement.[70] The limitation has now been lifted and the Department is now able to sue in the company's name in any civil proceedings, for example in a negligence action by management or other agents. The basis for bringing a civil action of this nature rests upon the principle that the company itself would have brought the action, and that the action ought to be brought in the public interest.[71]

The Department has further power under section 169 of the 1948 Act to petition for a winding up of the company. In addition the Department has power to seek relief under section 210 when the affairs of a company are being executed in 'a manner oppressive' to part of the shareholders. This remedy is provided particularly for the benefit of minority shareholders who would be unable to institute their own proceedings due to the voting advantage of the majority.[72]

Although this sanction has rarely been used by the Department,[73] the possibility of such an action provides sufficient incentive to management and its officers to avoid illegal action. Minority shareholders either through the restriction of the rule in *Foss* v. *Harbottle*[74] or because of the costs involved in bringing an action[75] also benefit from the Department's power to sue directors and officers essentially on their behalf.

The DTI's power to institute civil proceedings on behalf of the company is in direct contrast with the powers of the SEC, where proceedings are brought in its own name and usually *against* the company and its officers.[76] The DTI does not publish details of the civil proceedings it has instituted under the increased statutory power it has had since 1967. Its annual report is restricted to prosecutions under the 1948 Act and civil proceedings in the High Court by the Registrar of Companies in respect of defaults in submitting accounts and returns.[77]

It was stated in the previous section[78] that the influence of the SEC is aided by the likelihood of private civil proceedings after an investigation. If the DTI institutes the necessary actions itself then recourse to private actions (even if they were financially feasible) would be unnecessary. There is no evidence to show however that accountants, for example, who have received adverse comments in DTI investigations[79] have been subjected to any subsequent legal proceedings.

(2) Criminal proceedings
The DTI has authority in criminal proceedings in a liquidation if any officer of the company has been guilty of any offence in relation to the company for which he is criminally liable.[80] The majority of proceedings by the Department itself, however, are connected with the requirements of the Companies Acts with respect to reports and returns by companies.

The responsibility of the directors in this respect is laid down by statute, and not unnaturally the majority of actions by the DTI are against them. Table VI indicates the range of offences committed by directors and companies in 1975 as reproduced from the DTI's annual report, 1975. The table represents proceedings exclusively against directors, except those under sections 187, 290 and 332 where the offences by their nature may involve persons other than directors. Two of the prosecutions under section 131 were against the company itself. In recent years criticism[81] has been growing over the inability of the DTI to impose proper sanctions against accountants. This criticism has come in the wake of a number of investigation reports issued in which the auditors have been highly criticised.[82] Mr Peter Shore (when Secretary of State for Trade) raised this criticism in Parliament. He stated that the London and Counties Securities Group report 'in common, incidentally, with other recent reports from the Department of Trade, indicate[d] clearly the need for much stronger regulating powers' and furthermore he would 'consider much more carefully the whole role of auditors in this matter'.[83]

The problem is that the Department has been highly critical of auditors in the reports but has not gone further to impose punishment upon the offending accounting firms involved. At present, the Department has no power to sanction firms from, say, taking on new clients or suspending them from auditing publicly quoted companies, powers

TABLE VI Range of offences investigated by DTI

Section	Offence	Prosecutions	Convictions	Cases dismissed	Cases not proceeded with in 1975
52	Failure to file return of allotments	2	2	—	—
107	Failure to file notice of registered office	6	3	—	3
108	Failure to publish name of company	2	2	—	—
109	Commencing business before allotment, etc.	1	1	—	—
126	Failure to forward annual return	2 635	1 540	16	1 079
127	Failure to annex documents to annual return	93	73	—	20
131	Failure to hold annual general meeting	50	36	—	14
148	Failure to lay accounts before company in general meeting	103	73	—	30
187	Undischarged bankrupt acting as a director of or concerned in the management of a company	18	16	—	2
200	Failure to file notice of directors and secretary	26	14	—	12
290	Failure of liquidator to call general meeting	4	3	—	1
328	Offences by offices of companies in liquidation	5	1	—	4
330	Frauds by officers of companies in liquidation	1	1	—	—
331	Failure to keep proper books of account	18	14	1	3
332	Fraudulent trading	7	5	—	2

SOURCE: DTI, *Annual Report 1975* (London: HMSO).

which the Securities and Exchange Commission possesses and uses to advantage.

IV THE STOCK EXCHANGE

The Securities and Exchange Commission has wide control over *all* persons involved with the functioning of the securities markets. In Britain the Stock Exchange[84] has control effectively over only two aspects of the securities exchange:

1. The membership and activities of the members of the Stock Exchange; and
2. The public listing or quotation of companies.

Unlike the SEC, the Exchange has very limited power over accountants involved with public quoted companies, and has nothing comparable to Rule 2(e) of the SEC. The only influence the Stock Exchange has directly over accountants is with respect to the reports they must submit with a company seeking a quotation on the Exchange.

(i) The governing body of the Stock Exchange

In 1948, the Deed of Settlement of the Stock Exchange, London, was amended to vest exclusive control in the Council of the Stock Exchange.[85] The Council has exclusive powers over the running of the Stock Exchange, covering every aspect of the Exchange's affairs. This power includes the facility of the Council to make and amend 'The Rules and Regulations of the Stock Exchange'. Strictly speaking, these Rules are not rules of law and the only sanctions the Council possesses with respect to them is the refusal, suspension or withdrawal of a quotation of a company's securities,[86] or of membership of the Exchange. However, companies beyond a certain size are likely to want access to the open market for capital, and so this sanction is sufficiently strong as to make the Rules in many cases as effectual as the Companies Acts.[87]

(ii) The City Code on take-overs and mergers

The need for a Code to regulate take-over and merger activity had its roots in the activity of the City in 1957.[88] In the next decade there were numerous cases where it was considered that the Stock Exchange had been manipulated by major companies in covert market operations used to obtain control of other companies.[89] This led to many criticisms of the workings of the City, as reflected in a *Times* report of 18 July 1967:

> The simplest solution would be joint action by interested parties – jobbers, brokers, the Issuing Houses Committee and the institutions – to set up a watchdog organisation on the lines of the US Securities and Exchange Commission. . . . Until a long term solution can be found in the shape of an SEC or equivalent; general supervision of the stock market might well pass to the Board of Trade.[90]

The first City Code was activated in 1968[91] but immediately met with criticism from major names in the City (including Lord Kearton of Courtaulds, and Cazenove, the City stock brokers). One criticism of the Code, and of the panel which was originated at the time to police the Code, was its limited power to sanction those who had broken its rules. At that time the only sanction it could enforce was referral to the Stock Exchange and the Issuing Houses Association.[92]

It was the Panel's inability to hand out stringent sanctions against offenders which led to calls for a body with similar powers to that of the SEC. One commentator has stated:[93]

> The Panel has demonstrated . . . that if shareholders are to be protected, a body with equal vigour, but greater power and a wider brief, is needed in the City to act both as an agent of reform and occasionally as a policeman. The history of take-over regulation has shown that the City and its satellite professions have conspicuously failed to initiate the necessary changes or to exercise the required supervision. What remains to be devised is not an authoritative City Panel on Take-Overs and Mergers, but an authoritative City Panel.

Another view is that a 'British SEC' could provide the 'background incentive' for those involved in securities dealings to maintain the public interest.[94]

(iii) Regulation and the City Code[95]

The Code does not bind parties to a take-over or merger in the same way as an Act of Parliament.[96] Neither is it comparable with professional rules which are binding upon a specific class of people, as for example the Stock Exchange Rules.[97] As the preamble to the Code signifies, there is no clearly defined body to whom the Code applies. Although accountants are not specifically mentioned in the Code, it would seem that they fall within its definition of an 'associate' and therefore are within the regulation of the Code.[98]

Under the Code's General Principles, the rules regarding the code of conduct of those involved in a take-over bid are enumerated as follows:

1. All those engaged in merger or take-over transactions should be aware that the spirit as well as the precise wording of the General Principles and Rules must be observed.   (73.1)
2. Management and advisers have a primary duty to act in the best interests of their respective shareholders. As such they must recognise that the Code may infringe upon their freedom of action.   (73.2)
3. All shareholders must be provided with all relevant information regarding the transaction.   (73.3)
4. After a bona fide offer has been communicated the Board of the Offeree Company shall not take any action without shareholder approval (at general meeting) which could effectively result in the frustration of the offer or pending offer.   (73.4)
5. Every party must endeavour to prevent the creation of a false securities market.   (73.5)
6. Outside advise must be sought in the event of an offer.   (73.6)
7. Rights of control must be exercised in good faith and the oppression of a minority is wholly unacceptable.   (73.7)
8. All shareholders of similar class to be treated similarly.   (73.8)
9. An offer made to one shareholder should be made to all others of similar class being no more or less favourable.   (74.9)
10. During the transaction all shareholders shall receive the same information from directors or their advisers.   (74.10)
11. Directors should act only and always in that capacity.   (74.11)
12. Any documents or advertisements sent out by the Board or its advisers shall be treated with the same standard of care as if it were a prospectus within the meaning of the Companies Act 1948. Especial care shall be taken over profit forecasts.   (74.12)

The accountant will be most significantly involved with the take-over or merger transactions by means of the reports or certificates he must furnish (that is, documents in the transactions circularised or advertised). Under Rule 14 all documents are the responsibility of all directors of the companies jointly and severally. Under Rule 16 attention is drawn to the requirements of profit forecasts and asset valuations. 'Notwithstanding the obvious hazard attached to the forecasting of profits, any profit forecast must be compiled with the greatest possible care by the directors whose sole responsibility they are' (Rule 16). The accounting bases and calculations used in the forecasts must be examined and reported upon by the auditors or the consultant accountants of the respective companies. The accountants' report must be contained in the documents disclosed to shareholders and a statement must be included that the accountants have given and not withdrawn their consent to publication (Rule 16).

(iv) Penalties imposed for offenders of the Rules of the City Code

The Code itself contains no provision for penalties[99] as these would be provided by the Stock Exchange, the Issuing Houses Association or the Department of Trade.[100] On this basis the only sanction against an accountant would come from the Department of Trade, as the Stock Exchange and Issuing Houses Association have no influence over the accountant but only their own members. With respect to profit forecasts, an accountants' report must be included in the circularised documents; however, the ICAEW and ICAS have issued statements to avoid possible liability by recommending that in the wording of their reports, accountants

> should take care to avoid giving any impression that they are in any way confirming, underwriting, guaranteeing or otherwise accepting responsibility for the ultimate accuracy and realisation of forecasts. Moreover, bearing in mind their special status and authority, reporting accountants should do or say nothing to encourage directors, third parties or the public to place mistaken reliance on statements as to future profits, the achievement of which must always be subject to uncertainty.[101]

An accountant, therefore, can avoid liability for his reports in a prospectus for two reasons (i) by wording his certificate in the manner recommended by the ICAEW and ICAS, and (ii) because the explicit mention in the Rules that profit forecasts are the sole responsibility of the directors would appear to exonerate him from the sanctions of the Code.

V THE AMERICAN INSTITUTE OF CERTIFIED PUBLIC ACCOUNTANTS

Although the AICPA is the main professional body with disciplinary power over accountants, there are also various state societies of certified public accountants with similar powers. Most of these state societies have adopted codes of ethics patterned after the Code of Professional Ethics promulgated by the AICPA.[102]

(i) Code of ethics

The AICPA's Code of Professional Ethics derives its authority from the bye-laws[103] of the Institute. Any member of the AICPA who violates or infringes any of the bye-laws or any provisions of the Rules of Conduct may be admonished, suspended or expelled from membership.[104] The individual rights of the member are protected in that suspension will only take place after a hearing before the Institute's Trial Board.[105]

State societies also enforce state rules and also may admonish, suspend or expel a member.[106] If a CPA is not a member of the AICPA or the state society he cannot be penalised by these organisations, and therefore in most states the CPA's practising certificate may be suspended or revoked for violation of state rules. This is a far greater deterrent than expulsion from a society.[107]

The AICPA have codified[108] five broad concepts from which the Rules of Conduct are derived.

1. Independence, integrity and objectivity. A CPA should maintain his integrity and objectivity, and when engaged in public accounting be independent of his client.
2. Competence and technical standards. A CPA should observe the profession's technical standards and strive continually to improve his competence and the quality of his services.
3. Responsibilities to clients. Clients should be served with their best interests in mind consistent with the CPA's responsibilities to

the public.
4. Responsibilities to colleagues. A CPA should conduct himself in a manner which will promote co-operation and good relations among members of the profession.
5. Other responsibilities and practices. A CPA should conduct himself in a manner which will enhance the stature of the profession and its ability to serve the public.

These five ethical principles are intended as broad guidelines as distinguished from enforceable Rules of Conduct.[108] They constitute the 'philosophical foundation' upon which the Rules of Conduct are derived.[109]

The Rules of Conduct expand upon each of the above sections providing five main rules which in turn are subdivided. The following rules[110] are those which are more relevant because they provide the grounds for disciplinary proceedings following an action by a third party reliant upon an accountant's certificate included within financial statements.

Rule 102 – Integrity and Objectivity. A member shall not knowingly misrepresent facts, and when engaged in the practice of public accounting . . . shall not subordinate his judgment to others.
Rule 201 – Competence. A member shall not undertake any engagement which he or his firm cannot resonably expect to complete with professional competence.
Rule 202 – Auditing Standards. A member shall not permit his name to be associated with financial statements unless he has complied with the applicable generally accepted auditing standards promulgated by the Institute. (In addition any departure from the Institute's Statements on Auditing Procedure must be justified by those who do not follow them. The SAPs are considered as interpretations of the auditing standards.)
Rule 203 – A member shall not express an opinion that financial statements are presented in conformity with generally accepted accounting principles if such statements contain any departure from an accounting principle . . .
Rule 204 – Forecasts. A member shall not permit his name to be used in conjunction with any forecast of future transactions in a manner which may lead to the belief that the member vouches for the achievability of the forecast.

(ii) Disciplinary action

Two factors affect the commencement of disciplinary action under the
AICPA Rules of Conduct. First, under Rule 102, it is necessary to
establish that an accountant made a statement knowing its falsity (the
common law formula in deceit actions). Negligent misrepresentation
alone would be insufficient.[111] Secondly, the reliance by a member
upon generally accepted auditing standards would absolve him from
disciplinary action. On this point one commentator has stated that
generally accepted auditing standards (GAAS) and generally accepted accounting principles (GAAP), being of such a nebulous nature,
'hardly provide a sound basis for enforcement of ethical standards'
because of the difficulty experienced in defining these standards.[112] It
is argued therefore that the AICPA rarely institutes disciplinary
proceedings upon these Rules, but rather upon the Rules of Conduct
which are more objective in nature (for example, Rules 3, 4 and 5) and
therefore provide more definite grounds.

(iii) Disciplinary action in criminal cases

Under the AICPA's Bye-laws[113] a CPA's membership will be termi-
nated without a hearing if there is filed with the Institute a judgment
for conviction of the crime defined as a felony under the law of the
convicting jurisdiction.[114] The trial board of the Institute, according to
Bye-law 7.4, may expel a member if he has been convicted of a
criminal offence which tends to discredit the profession.

This ruling by the AICPA is thought by some commentators to be
further reason why accountants are willing to settle with the SEC by
'consent decree' rather than risk their livelihoods in court action and
possible conviction.[115]

This rule of the AICPA is interesting in a situation such as that in
National Student Marketing where the AICPA itself provided an
amicus curiae brief for the defendant accountant, Natelli and
Scansaroli, who were subsequently convicted criminally. The situation
arises therefore that the AICPA has to disbar the accountants from
membership despite having supported their case throughout the
various court proceedings.[116]

One reason why the professional institutes do not effectively
implement their enforcement powers is that they are reluctant to
admit publicly that members of the profession do not always adhere
to ethical standards.[117] In the *Continental Vending* case,[118] as one
example, eight independent accountants testified for the defendant

accountant that the financial statements had been in conformity with generally accepted accounting principles. The financial statements adhered therefore to the AICPA's ethical standards, but still they failed to fairly represent the financial condition of the business. The court was then faced with the conflict between fair presentation and GAAP.

In summary it should be noted that the enforcement programme of the SEC would appear to be sufficiently powerful in that those wrong-doers brought to justice under the Commission's jurisdiction are evidently being punished. Further AICPA involvement is probably unnecessary. The AICPA's main involvement therefore centres upon those actions falling outside the Commission's jurisdiction. This position contrasts sharply with that in England where the ICAEW has no equivalent SEC aid in enforcement. In England therefore the ICAEW may find itself in the position of having to enforce its discipline upon all its members, whatever type of work they are doing.

VI THE INSTITUTE OF CHARTERED ACCOUNTANTS IN ENGLAND AND WALES

The ICAEW has been heavily criticised by the press for inadequate enforcement standards to counteract many recent accounting short-comings.[119] There is nothing new in this criticism. On every occasion in which a company comes under close scrutiny in the press, the report-ing accountants will usually come under closer scrutiny. Time and again the call is raised for the ICAEW to give a lead in reprimanding its members for allowing inadequate reports in accounts or for under-taking inadequate audits.[120]

Recognising the need for a review of its enforcement powers, the Cross Committee was appointed to consider whether the investigatory and disciplinary organisation of the ICAEW was adequate. The Committee reported in November 1977.

The Grenside Committee was appointed in December 1977 to implement the Cross Committee recommendations. This Committee reported in May 1978. The recommendations have received the approval of members of the accounting professions and an executive committee was appointed in January 1980 to run the so-called Joint Disciplinary Scheme.

Despite the fact that the Institute 'as a matter of course' enquires into DTI reports where members are criticised, there has seldom been any *public* follow-up to these enquiries.[121] The Institute rarely disciplines firms or individual accountants when a press inquiry or even a Department inquiry indicates they have been negligent in some respect.

In April 1980 two committees of inquiry were appointed to investigate the involvement of accountants in the Ozalid Company and the Burnholme & Forder Company. Both were subjects of Department of Trade Inspectors' Reports.

(i) Bye-laws of the ICAEW

According to the bye-laws[122] issued to members of the Institute, a member may be liable to disciplinary action:

> if, in the course of carrying out his professional duties or otherwise, he has been guilty of misconduct. For this purpose misconduct includes, but is not confined to, any act or default *likely to bring discredit to himself, the Institute or the profession of accountancy.*[123] (Emphasis added)

In the past decade, the practices of many companies and the ensuing investigations have resulted in considerable 'discredit to the profession of accountancy'. The bye-laws provide no definition of what is termed 'discredit' in this context. Recent criticism of accountants in the press must surely have resulted in a loss of reputation and confidence or dishonour to the profession. As a result firms or individual accountants should have been disciplined by the ICAEW.

(ii) Disciplinary procedure

The disciplinary procedure carried out by the ICAEW involves a primary investigation of any complaints before it by the Investigation Committee. This Committee however only has the power to call its own members before it, and is therefore hampered in its investigation to determine if there is a prima facie case against a member (defendant).[124]

If the Investigation Committee is of the opinion that a prima facie case has been made out, and it considers the case ought to be referred to the Disciplinary Committee, it submits to that Committee details of the evidence and representations of the case.[125]

Upon receipt of the complaint from the Investigation Committee the Disciplinary Committee appoints a tribunal of not less than three members to hear the complaint.[126] The defendant member may appear before the tribunal or be represented by legal counsel.[127]

The powers of the Disciplinary Committee are laid down in Bye-law 85(a). If the Committee is of the opinion that the complaint has been proved in whole or in part, it may make any one or more orders against the defendant as it considers appropriate having regard to 'the status of the defendant and the Committee's views as to the nature and seriousness of the complaint and any other circumstances which the Committee considers relevant'.[128] These orders are as follows:

1. that he (the defendant) be excluded from membership;
2. that he be suspended from membership for such period, not exceeding two years, as shall be specified in the order;
3. that his practising certificate be withdrawn;
4. that he be ineligible for a practising certificate;
5. that he be reprimanded, censured, or admonished;
6. that he be fined a sum not exceeding £1 000;[129]
7. that no further action be taken on the complaint.[130]

The defendant has the right to appeal within twenty-one days of the date of service of the order. An Appeal Committee after hearing the grounds for appeal and reviewing the evidence has power to vary, affirm or rescind any order given.[131] A final appeal may be made to the Council of the ICAEW and it may modify or rescind any previous orders as it regards appropriate.[132]

(iii) Joint Disciplinary Scheme

This scheme has been set up as a direct result of public pressure upon the profession to 'put its house in order' following the numerous Department of Trade reports referred to previously. The scheme sets out the procedures for investigating and regulating the professional and business conduct, efficiency and competence of members and member firms in 'circumstances which give rise to public concern'.[133]

Without spelling out in detail the machinery of setting up investigatory committees under this scheme it is important to note that there now exists the power for a Committee of Inquiry to issue an order admonishing, reprimanding or censuring *a firm* of accountants.[134] This power is new and time will tell if the ICAEW will enforce and utilise it to its full potential.

(iv) Ethics

Apart from the powers of the ICAEW to institute disciplinary proceedings outlined under Bye-law 78(a) above, it may also do so if its Code of Ethics has not been followed. Unlike the AICPA's Concept of Ethics and the Rules of Practice, the ICAEW's Code is meant as a guide and not a directive. Its purpose being to 'assist members to conduct themselves in a manner which the Council considers appropriate to the profession in general and to the members of this Institute in particular'.[135] Thus, failure to follow the guidance given by the Ethics Guide does not of itself constitute misconduct as defined in Bye-law 78(a),[136] and so, in the words of the Ethics Guide[137]

> As misconduct cannot be defined generally, but has to be determined in each individual case by the Investigation and Disciplinary Committees, it follows that the Council cannot promulgate mandatory instructions the mere breach of which amounts to misconduct. Nor can the Council say that in any given set of circumstances a member will or will not be guilty of misconduct. What the Council may do is advise that certain conduct may expose a member to the risk of disciplinary action.

Thus disciplinary action will be based upon the grounds laid down under Bye-law 78(a) for misconduct albeit that they are not defined.

(v) Results

Some indication of what is regarded as misconduct may be taken from actual disciplinary proceedings against accountants as reported in *Accountancy*.[138] At seven disciplinary hearings[139] the explanations of misconduct shown in Table VII were provided under Bye-law 78(a). From this list, the definition of misconduct would not seem to indicate the gross inadequacies over the recent past of some accounting firms as outlined in Department of Trade reports.

To take just one recent example, the case of London and County Securities Group Limited, the report devoted a complete chapter to the auditors' work.[140] The inspectors found the following defects on the part of the auditors:

Auditors' Records
Our conclusion from the examination of the auditors' records was that their audit procedures would have been more effective had they developed a better way of summarising the work carried out by

their staff and the conclusions reached by the partner in charge of
the audit. (para 13.12)

Audit Procedure
We noticed a number of cases where the auditors had failed to
follow items through in the course of the audit and to see that

TABLE VII ICAEW disciplinary actions under Bye-Law 78(a)

Offence	Number of cases
1. Failure to reply to letter from the Institute or others, in some professional capacity or make forwarding arrangements	55
2. Failure to undertake the administration of an estate or tax affairs or draft accounts preparation with due expedition	6
3. Failure to file or forward accounts or forms	4
4. Failure to satisfy judgment debt	3
5. Failure to write to preceding auditors	1
6. Failure to report discovery of misleading internal management accounts	1
7. Advertising practice	3
8. Defrauding public revenue or inland revenue	2
9. Mishandling cash in company liquidation	1
10. Imparting information of clients	1
11. False application for practising certificate	2
12. Dishonest statement in letter to Institute	1
13. Guilty of forgery	1
14. Writing letter to client in terms likely to bring discredit on the profession	1

SOURCE: *Accountancy* magazine.

agreed or necessary provisions were included in the accounts but we consider that to set out all such items would involve excessive elaboration which is not warranted for the purposes of this Report. (para 13.13)

Misleading Accounts

We consider that the accounts at 31st March 1973 of both L&C and A&D were unsatisfactory and indeed misleading, particularly with respect to the following points of which the auditors were, or should have been aware had they pursued their enquiries with reasonable diligence:

(a) the cash position, which was grossly inflated and therefore gave a wrong impression of strong liquidity;
(b) the untrue statement in note 15 in the accounts of A&D as to the advances being repayable on demand when several facility letters for advances set out longer periods for repayment;
(c) the borrowing of L&C, which were in breach of the loan trust deed at 31st March 1973 without the accounts saying so;
(d) the inclusion of excess income in the form of commitment fees and merchant banking fees charged to customer's accounts in the last three months of the financial year in what Mr McMenemy accepted was 'an unseemly scramble', with the motive of making up the shortfall of profits compared with the forecast included in the Drakes offer document;
(e) the failure to make adequate provision for bad or doubtful debts (para 13.14).

The reports highlight further deficiencies and criticisms against the auditors.[141] Surely such a statement made in a Department of Trade investigation and available to the public presents a discredit to the profession and therefore renders the auditors subject to disciplinary action. It is difficult to imagine that the deficiencies noted in this report are less serious than the failure of an accountant in his professional capacity to reply to a letter.

If the ICAEW wishes to remain as a self-regulatory body it must be seen to be forceful by its members. The London and County bank collapsed in 1973; the Department of Trade produced in 1976 a lengthy report criticising accountants; the ICAEW completed a report on the affair in 1978, this report was not made public because of the High Court action against the auditors, Harmood Banner. Now that the parties to that action have settled out of court the Institute must act. The Institute should establish a Committee of Inquiry to establish whether the affairs of London and County constitute a matter of 'public concern' but more important whether or not a firm of accountants should be admonished, reprimanded or censured. If the ICAEW allows the matter to fade it will have failed to uphold the self-regulatory principle it so much cherishes properly. It is seven years since the London and County issue first became of public concern, it is probably already too late.

VII SUMMARY

This chapter has compared the different institutions directly or indirectly concerned with the regulation of the accounting professions of the US and the UK. It is evident that some of the institutions have been effective in the role of regulator and others less so. Certainly the SEC has been a significant force behind the increase in corporate litigation in the US and part of the enforcement policy to which it is committed has directly affected American accountants and accounting firms through court action or other comparable sanction.

NOTES

[1] The cases referred to here by Burton are purely SEC cases against accountants appearing in Accounting Series Releases. See Rappaport note 25 *infra*, also Tables III and IV *infra*.

[2] J. C. Burton, 'SEC Enforcements and Professional Accountants. Philosophy, Objectives and Approach' 28 *Vanderbilt Law Review* 19, 19 (1975).

[3] Evidence of the fact that only recently has the SEC built up enforcement pressure against accountants may be seen from proceedings against accountants. There were only two criminal actions prior to 1969 and yet recently many cases have been brought including *Continental Vending*, *National Student Marketing* and *Equity Funding*. In civil actions the injunctive proceeding had not been taken against auditors prior to 1970 but since then at least seven injunctions have been filed against auditors. See note 9 *infra* and see H. R. Jaenicke, 'The Impact of the Current Legal Climate on the Accounting Profession', July 1976 Commission on Auditor's Responsibilities. Also R. J. Gormley, 'Accountants' Professional Liability – A Ten Year Review' 29 *Business Lawyer* 1205 (1974).

[4] Burton, note 2 *supra*, pp. 19–20; see also Sommer, note 21 *infra*.

[5] 17 CFR. s. 202.5 (1974), cited by Burton, note 2 *supra*, p. 19.

[6] Ibid.

[7] R. W. Jennings and H. Marsh Jr., *Securities Regulation* (3rd ed.) (New

York: Foundation Press, 1972) p. 33 citing 'The Work of the Securities and Exchange Commission' published by the SEC, Nov. 1971.

[8] Ibid.

[9] These occasions are fairly rare. Murphy cites only two cases before 1969: *US* v. *White* 124 F.2d 181. 2nd Cir. (1941) and *US* v. *Benjamin* 328 F.2d 854 2nd Cir. (1964). M. J. Murphy, 'Accounts and Accounting: The Responsibilities of CPAs: Imposed by law and by the American Institute of Certified Public Accountants'. 26 *Oklahoma Law Review* 383–95 (1973). See Jaenicke, note 3 *supra*, p. 47.

[10] For a summary of the proceedings available to the SEC see Jaenicke, note 3 *supra*, Chapter 4, pp. 46–66.

[11] Jennings and Marsh, note 7 *supra*, p. 44.

[12] Note 1, *supra*, p. 28.

[13] See for example the National Student Marketing Case: *US* v. *Natelli*, 1975 CCH *Federal Securities Law Reporter*, 95, 378, where an accountant was convicted for making false entries into a corporation's financial statements.

[14] *Scienter* suffers from being interpreted in many ways. According to the Supreme Court ruling in *Hochfelder* v. *Ernst & Ernst* (503 F.2d 1100 (1974)) the term was defined in the common law meaning of 'intend to deceive, manipulate or defraud' that is to say there must be proved to have been a 'mental state embracing the intent to deceive etc.' on the part of the defendant. See C. D. Liggio, 'The "Ernst" Ruling – Expansion of a trend', *New York Law Journal* 14 April 1976, p. 2, col. 2–3. See also Chapter 4 and 5, *infra*.

[15] This table is based upon the description of the process given by Burton, note 1 *supra*, pp. 26–8.

[16] Ibid.

[17] See text accompanying notes 32–46, *infra*.

[18] See discussion of litigation effects, text accompanying notes 25–8, *infra*.

[19] Burton, note 2 *supra*, pp. 20–3.

[20] Ibid.

[21] Sommer, a lawyer employed by the SEC, has also stated that SEC disciplinary activity has been on the increase in the early 1970s. He recently reported that over the period 1970 to 1974 injunctive actions per year increased from 111 to 182, while administrative proceedings increased from 138 to 158. See A. A. Sommer, 'Accountants: A Flexible Standard', *Journal of Accountancy*, (Dec. 1974) p. 77.

[22] See Jaenicke, note 3 *supra*, pp. 49 *et seq.* including a good summary by Sommer, ibid, pp. 37–8, as to what the SEC looks for in injunctive proceedings.

[23] Jennings and Marsh, note 7 *supra*, p. 44.

[24] Gapay, note 37, *infra*.

[25] L. H. Rappaport, *SEC Accounting Practice and Procedure* (3rd ed.) (New York: Ronald Press, 1972) pp. 27.11 and 27.12.

[26] This need not always necessarily be the case though Jaenicke, citing Sommer, *supra*, has stated that 'in some cases, the commission action follows – sometimes by quite a period of time – the commencement of private litigation: in other cases it precedes litigation', p. 50.

[27] Burton, note 2 *supra*, pp. 21–2.

[28] Note 3 *supra*, p. 49; see also 'Comment: The Effect of SEC Injunctions in Subsequent Private Damage Actions – *Rackel* v. *Hill*' 71 *Columbia Law Review* 1332 (Nov. 1971).

[29] SEC Release No. 33–5147, 10 May 1971.

[30] Rappaport, note 25 *supra*, p. 27.15.

[31] Ibid, p. 1.15.

[32] Ibid, p. 27.19.

[33] Ibid, p. 27.20.

[34] Ibid, p. 27.19.

[35] Ibid, p. 27.20.

[36] Such an action may lead to disciplinary proceedings by the AICPA. See text accompanying notes 112–16 *infra*.

[37] It has been stated that within the securities industry itself, as opposed to accounting firms, there are differing opinions as to the effectiveness of the enforcement procedures of the SEC. 'Several industry officials interviewed say most disciplines are merely slaps on the wrist and that many violators are repeat offenders. The head of one large brokerage firm says being named in an SEC case is embarrassing at the most and doesn't cost most big firms any loss of clients or revenues, although it may put tiny firms out of business. Another official says adverse publicity is the biggest sanction'. If this is the case for prestigious securities firms then arguably it will be the same for the prestigious accounting firm. See L. Gapay, 'When the SEC Slaps your Wrist', *Wall Street Journal*, 27 Nov. 1973.

[38] Rappaport states that it is not publicly known how many proceedings have been instituted by the SEC against public accountants under Rule 2(e) of its Rules of Practice. The SEC does not publicly disclose the fact that such proceedings have begun. In 1972 the SEC had made public the proceedings in 20 cases only. Note 25 *supra*, pp. 27.23 and 27.24.

[39] For example Gapay, note 37 *supra*.

[40] Ibid.

[41] ASR 92 (1962). This case is interesting in that it was the first instance in which the SEC disciplined an accountant for misconduct in connection with documents which were never filed with the Commission. The accountant in question certified a false and misleading balance sheet which was shown only to a bank. No investor or other outside party saw the financial statement. See Rappaport, note 25 *supra*, p. 27.27. The accountant appealed his case for this reason and his request for re-instatement was granted. ASR 101 (1965).

[42] See for example ASR 173 (1975).

[43] Burton, note 2 *supra*, p. 21.

[44] AICPA SAS No. 4, Dec. 1974, cited by Burton, ibid.

[45] Peat, Marwick, Mitchell and Company after an initial review in 1975 had to submit its procedures for further reviews in 1976 and 1977 (ASR 173).

[46] Note 1 *supra*, p. 25.

[47] See text accompanying notes 32–3 *supra*.

[48] ASR 173 (1975).

[49] 'SEC bars PMM from accepting new publicly held clients for six months' *Wall Street Journal*, 3 July 1975, p. 3 Staff Reporter, Washington.

[50] Four companies mentioned here had already been the subject of injunctive

actions brought by the Commission against the companies involved, other persons and PMM, *SEC* v. *National Student Marketing Corpn., et al*, Civil Action No. 225.72 (D.D.C.); *SEC* v. *Tally Industries Inc., et al*, 73 Civ. 4603 (SDNY); *SEC* v. *Republic National Life Insurance Co., et al*, 74 Civ. 1097 (SDNY); *SEC* v. *Penn Central Co., et al*, 74 Civ. 1125 (E.D. Pa). The fifth company (Stirling Homex) had been the subject of an investigation. (See ASR 173, p. 336).

[51] Note 49, *supra*. Reiling and Taussig discuss the desire by the major firms to put an end to protracted litigation by the use of the consent device. See 'Recent Liability Cases – Implications for Accountants', *Journal of Accountancy*, Sep. 1970, p. 43.

[52] ASR 173 (1975). The SEC wrote: 'In determining to accept PMM's settlement offer, we have taken into account the fact that these controversies relate to audit engagements for five clients out of a large number of audit engagements conducted by PMM over the years in question going back to 1968 and that, based upon information submitted by PMM and otherwise known to us, their overall audit practice appears to be conducted in a competent and professional manner. Moreover, we believe that the provisions of the settlement offer will provide PMM and the Commission with independent assurance of the quality of PMM's audit practice before the Commission'.

[53] Under the Secretary of State for Trade and Industry order 1970 (S.I. 1970 No. 1537) it is provided that the Secretary of State will exercise with the Board of Trade and the President of the Board responsibility for all the respective functions of the Board and the President. This order in council enables the Secretary of State and his Department to exercise the powers conferred by the Companies Acts and other legislation upon the Board of Trade. Throughout this section reference is made to the Department and not to the Board. See Boyle and Sykes, *Gore-Browne on Companies* (42nd ed.) (London: Jordan & Sons Ltd., 1972) p. iv.

[54] Amended by the Protection of Depositors Act 1963.

[55] The Prevention of Fraud (Investments) Act 1958 is discussed at length in Chapter 3 *infra*. The DTI has authority under various Acts including: The Protection of Depositors Act 1963; Industrial and Provident Societies Act 1965; Income Tax Act 1952; The Companies (Disclosure of Directors' Interests) (Exceptions) No. 1 Regulations 1967 (S.I. 1967 No 1594) and No. 2 1968 (S.I. 1968 No. 865); Monopolies and Mergers Act 1965; Monopolies and Restrictive Practices (Enquiry and Control) Act 1948; The Companies Acts 1948 and 1967 though provide the important sections under which the DTI may act in the context of the research. For example, the right attached to appoint inspectors and investigate a company's affairs and pursue court proceedings, if necessary, are all derived from those Acts (see text).

[56] ss. 164 and 165 (1948 Act).

[57] See Pennington, *Company Law* (3rd ed.) (London: Butterworths, 1976) p. 585; also refer to Pennington, *Company Law* (4th ed.) (London: Butterworths, 1979) pp. 610–15.

[58] s. 166 (1948 Act).

[59] s. 167 (1) (1948 Act) as amended by the Companies Act 1967 s. 39.

[60] s. 167 (2) (1948 Act).

[61] s. 167 (3) (1948 Act)

[62] *McCelland, Pope and Langley Ltd.* v. *Howard*, [1968] 1 All E.R. 569. In *Re Pergamon Press Ltd* [1970] 2 All E.R. 449, [1970] 1 WLR 1075, affd. [1971] Ch. 388, [1970] 3 All E.R. 535. Companies Act 1967, ss. 50 and 109(5); *Karak Rubber Co. Ltd.*, v. *Burden* [1971] 3 All E.R. 1118. Pennington, note 57 *supra*, pp. 586–7.

[63] s. 50 (1967 Act). Pennington, note 57 *supra*, p. 587. Boyle and Sykes, note 53 *supra*, p. 806.

[64] s. 111 (1967 Act).

[65] Under ss. 168(2) or 164 and 165 (1948 Act).

[66] See though Boyle and Sykes, note 53 *supra*, p. 804.

[67] Under ss. 164 and 165 (1948 Act).

[68] s. 41 (1967 Act).

[69] s. 169 (4) (1948 Act) as amended by s. 37 (1) (1967 Act).

[70] s. 169 (4) (1948 Act).

[71] s. 37 (1967 Act). See Pennington, note 57 *supra*, p. 588 and Boyle and Sykes, note 53 *supra*, p. 807.

[72] s. 210 (1948 Act) provides that if a winding up order would prejudice the position of the minority the 'court may, with a view to bringing to an end the matters complained of make such order as it thinks fit, whether for regulating the conduct of the company's affairs in future' or other remedies regarding the reduction of the company's capital.

[73] Pennington, note 57 *supra*, p. 588.

[74] (1843) 2 Hare 461. See Chapter 3, *infra*, for a discussion of the rule.

[75] See Chapter 7 for the effects of legal costs.

[76] See text accompanying notes 29 *et seq.*, *supra*.

[77] See Tables 12 and 13 of the DTI's Annual Reports of Companies – 1975 (London: HMSO).

[78] See text accompanying note 28, *supra*.

[79] See for example 'London and Counties' investigation report. Text accompanying notes 140–1 *infra*.

[80] s. 334 (1948 Act). See generally Boyle and Sykes, note 53 *supra*, p. 1059.

[81] Recent examples include: *Guardian* 7 Oct. 1976, 'Audit Ultimatum Response' and *Accountancy Age* 8 Oct. 1976, 'Who Said What About Whom'. Also 'Dressing down for the auditors', *Accountancy Age* 10 Aug. 1979.

[82] For example: 'London and Counties Securities Group Limited' Department of Trade (London: HMSO, 1976).

[83] 'DOT Reports Pending' 87 *Accountancy* 8 (March 1976).

[84] In July 1965 the leading stock exchanges in the British Isles formed the Federation of Stock Exchanges in Great Britain and Ireland. The exchanges included within this Federation are listed in the Stock Exchange's *Admission of Securities to Listing* (revised edition) (London, 1973) p. 15 as London, Birmingham, Manchester, Glasgow, Belfast and Dublin.

[85] Clause 31. The Deed of Settlement of the Stock Exchange (as amended) 1875, London. See generally Cooper and Gridlan, *Law and Procedure of the Stock Exchange* (London: Butterworths, 1971) Chapter 2, pp. 26 *et seq.*

[86] Pennington, note 57 *supra*, p. 625.

[87] Ibid.

[88] See C. Marley, 'The City Code', Part One of Stamp and Marley, *Account-*

ing Principles and the City Code – The Case for Reform (London: Butterworths, 1970) p. 6.

[89] Marley, ibid, cites the following companies involved in controversies regarding take-over bids: British Aluminium (1957/8), Watneys (1959), Pye (1966), Courtaulds (1967) and Metal Industries (1967).

[90] Quoted by Marley, ibid, p. 18.

[91] The predecessor to the City Code was that of the voluntary code entitled 'Notes of Amalgamations of British Businesses'. This statement which first appeared in the early 1960s and was amended in 1966 and 1967 was prepared by a working party of the IHA, Accepting Houses Committee, the Association of Investment Trusts, British Ins. Assoc., the Committee of London Clearing Banks and the Stock Exchange.

[92] Marley, note 88 *supra*, p. 32.

[93] Ibid, p. 62.

[94] See Stamp, note 88 *supra*, p. 144. Stamp gave two main reasons for not establishing at that time (1970) a regulatory body on the lines of the SEC. (1) The ICAEW had set up its Standards Committee. (2) The possibility that an SEC type of body *might* be set up in the future would provide adequate persuasion already.

[95] In this analysis the revised edition (Feb. 1972) of the Code is used.

[96] Cooper and Gridlan, note 85 *supra*, p. 95.

[97] See text accompanying notes 85 and 87 *supra*.

[98] *Admission of Securities to Listing*, Stock Exchange, pp. 71–2.

[99] J. Graham, 'The New Takeover Code', *Accountancy* 451 (June 1969).

[100] Cases which are referred to the Department of Trade are meant essentially to provide sanctions against members of the Stock Exchange or the Issuing Houses Association. If an action of censure against such a member is considered insufficient in the circumstances the Department may take action under the Prevention of Fraud (Investments) Act 1958 where the Department has power to revoke the exempted dealer or the licence of a licensed dealer. The effect of such a revocation is that the individual concerned would no longer be permitted to carry on the business of a dealer in securities or to circulate any offer to buy or sell securities. See Cooper and Gridlan, note 85 *supra*, p. 96.

[101] ICAEW, 'Accountants' reports on profit forecasts'. Members handbook, 1979, 3.918.

[102] J. Kauffman, 'Legal Liability' Chapter 5 of J. A. Cashin (ed.), *Handbook for Auditors* (New York: Ronald Press, 1971) p. 5.17.

[103] AICPA Bye-law Section T.4, Kauffman, ibid.

[104] AICPA, *Code of Professional Ethics – Concepts of Professional Ethics – Rules of Conduct – Interpretations of Rules of Conduct* (March 1974 edition) p. 17.

[105] Ibid.

[106] H. J. Brown, 'Professional Ethics', Chapter 4 of Cashin (ed.), note 102 *supra*, p. 4.4.

[107] Ibid.

[108] Code of Ethics, note 104 *supra*, p. 5.

[109] Ibid.

[110] Ibid.

[111] Ibid pp. 19 and 20.
[112] D. A. Scott, 'Enforcement of ethical standards in corporate financial reporting'. Included in J. C. Burton (ed.), *Corporate Financial Reporting: Ethical and Other Problems. A Symposium* (New York: AICPA, 1972) p. 111.
[113] Bye-law 7.3.1 (as amended 20 Feb. 1969).
[114] See Reiling and Taussig, note 51 *supra*, p. 52.
[115] Note 124. *infra*.
[116] Jaenicke, note 3 *supra*, p. 49. A full reprint of the AICPA's *Amicus curiae* brief which was filed before the US Court of Appeals for the Second Circuit in *SEC* v. *Natelli* was published in *Journal of Accountancy* (May 1975) pp. 69–76. Also note 114, *supra*.
[117] See Scott, note 112 *supra*.
[118] *United States* v. *Simon*, CCA Fed. Sec. L. Rep. 1192, 511 (2d Cir. 12 Nov. 1969), cert denied (30 March, 1970).
[119] The affairs of many companies where accountants have been involved have reached the financial press including: Tremletts, Slater Walker, London and Counties, SUITS, Barrow Hepburn Group, etc.
[120] Cf. with reports in the press over the Pergammon/Leasco affair as far back as 1968–9.
[121] *Accountant's Weekly*, 24 Sep. 1976, p. 5.
[122] ICAEW, *Royal Charter and Bye-laws* Jan. 1980. Chapter VIII 'discipline'.
[123] Bye-law 78(a).
[124] Bye-law 80–82.
[125] Bye-law 82(c).
[126] Bye-law 83(b).
[127] Bye-law 84(a).
[128] Bye-law 85(a).
[129] Bye-law 85(a).
[130] Bye-law 85(b).
[131] Bye-law 89(b).
[132] Bye-law 93(a).
[133] ICAEW, *Royal Charter and Bye-laws*, Appendix A. Joint Disciplinary Scheme p. 49 (Scope).
[134] Ibid, p. 51.
[135] ICAEW, 'Ethical Guide for Members'. Section 1.2 *Member's Handbook* Para. 23, p. 6. Also published in *Accountancy* (August 1975).
[136] Ibid.
[137] Ibid.
[138] *Accountancy* magazine normally publishes every other month details of the meetings of the disciplinary committee or appeals committee.
[139] Meetings held on 22 July 1975, 4 Aug. 1975, 11 and 18 Nov. 1975, 27 Jan. 1976, 23 March 1976, 25 May 1976 and 20 July 1976.
[140] Note 82 *supra*, Chapter XIII.
[141] Ibid, Paragraphs 13, 17 *et seq*.

3 LEGAL COMPARISONS

I INTRODUCTION

This chapter is separated into two sections; the common law and the statute law. Each section analyses the comparisons between US and English law relevant to the legal liability of accountants.

II THE COMMON LAW

The link between American and English law is strongest in the area of common law.[1] This is because in the early development of American law the courts needed to rely upon established precedent. The precedent employed was predominantly that of the English decided cases. The link still remains. One eminent American jurist,[2] Warren A. Seavey, has referred to the common law as 'Anglo-American', and its principles are recognised as such. English cases are still employed as the basis for the study of American law, and as Seavey notes: '[we] recognise the older cases as authoritative and place the current cases on even terms with those in American States'.[3]

In the same way that American state jurisdictions rely upon English precedent, so too the English courts cite American cases. Two landmark cases[4] in the English courts on the legal liability of auditors for negligence are analysed below, and the opinions expressed therein indicate the relevance of American cases.[5]

(i) UK reliance on US cases

Denning, L. J. (as he then was), presenting a minority view in *Candler* v. *Crane, Christmas and Company*, expressed the view that a third party should recover damages if he had relied upon an accountant's financial statements. He stated:

> It will be noticed that I have confined the duty to cases where the accountant prepares his accounts and makes his report for the guidance of the very person in the very transaction in question. That is sufficient for the decision of this case. I can well understand that it would be going too far to make an accountant liable to any person in the land who chooses to rely on the accounts in matters of business, for that would expose him to 'liability in an indeterminate amount for an indeterminate time to an indeterminate class': see *Ultramares Corporation* v. *Touche* per Cardozo, C.J.[6]

This opinion, based upon Cardozo's 'social utility rationale', is significant in the light of recent criticism of such a rationale in America, and the doubt attached to its present-day relevance.[7]

Cohen, L. J., whilst denying recovery to the third party, referred extensively to the *Ultramares* case,[8] quoting it verbatim for four pages of the original. He concluded his opinion:

> I am glad therefore to find that the conclusion which I have reached on the basis of the English authorities seems to accord to the opinion of so eminent a master of the common law as Cardozo, C.J.[9]

Gerald Gardiner, Q.C. for the appellants in *Hedley, Byrne & Co. Ltd.* v. *Heller & Partners Ltd.*, considered American cases significant to the development of the branch of the law creating a duty of care.[10]

Lord Reid in discussing the creation of a duty of care stated that American law in the area 'appear[ed] to have gone much further than ours has yet done'.[11] In analysing the *Candler* case he stated:

I must note that Cohen, L.J. (as he then was) attached considerable importance to a New York decision, *Ultramares Corporation* v. *Touche*, a decision of Cardozo, C.J. But I think that another decision of that great judge, *Glanzer* v. *Shepard*, is more in point because in the latter case there was a direct relationship between the weigher who gave a certificate and the purchaser of the goods weighed, who the weigher knew was relying on his certificate: there the weigher was held to owe a duty to the purchaser with whom he had no contract.[12]

From the above examples, taken from the two most significant English cases, it is evident that the courts attach importance to developments in the US. They are urged by Lord Devlin to observe recent developments in American common law over the past decade,[13] although in the absence of reported cases it is not evident that they have done so.

(ii) US reliance on UK cases

In order to determine the importance of English precedent upon American common law decisions, Table VIII gives a complete analysis of the precedent cited by American courts in the important cases analysed in Chapters 4 and 5.

TABLE VIII Schedule of reliance upon English precedent in American common law cases

American case	Date	English case cited (R: reliance; C: cited; D: disputed)
1. *Thomas* v. *Winchester*	1852	33(R)
2. *Savings Bank* v. *Ward*	1879	6(R), 14(R), 28(R), 20(R), 35(R), 22(R), 26(C), 16(C), 20(R), 27(C)
3. *MacPherson* v. *Buick Motor Co.*	1916	33(D), 13(R), 12(D), 10(R), 3(C), 19(C), 32(C)
4. *Seaver* v. *Ransom et al.*	1918	34(C), 36(C), 11(C)
5. *Landell* v. *Lybrand et al.*	1919	None
6. *Glanzer* v. *Shepard*	1922	35(R), 26(R), 15(R), 5(C), 29(C), 28(C), 7(C), 14(C), 21(C), 39(C)
7. *Jaillet* v. *Cashman*	1923	None
8. *International Products Co.* v. *Erie Ry. Co.*	1927	39(C), 14(C), 2(D), 30(D), 1(D), 8(R), 9(R), 38(R), 23(R)
9. *Doyle* v. *Chatham and Phenix Nat Bank of City of New York*	1930	23(R), 8(R)
10. *Ultramares Corpn.* v. *Touche et al.*	1931	8(R), 2(R), 1(C), 3(C)
11. *Beardsley* v. *Ernst et al.*	1934	None
12. *American Indemnity Co.* v. *Ernst et al.*	1937	None
13. *O'Connor et al.* v. *Ludlam et al.*	1937	None

TABLE VIII *Cont.*

American case	Date	English case cited
14. *State Street Trust* v. *Ernst et al.*	1938	24(R)
15. *Fidelity & Deposit Co. of Maryland* v. *Atherton et al.*	1944	None
16. *Duro Sportswear Inc. et al.* v. *Cogen et al.*	1954	None
17. *CIT Financial Corp.* v. *Glover et al.*	1955	None
18. *Biakanja* v. *Irving*	1958	None
19. *Mutual Ventures Inc.* v. *Barondess*	1959	None
20. *Texas Tunneling Co.* v. *City of Chattanooga*	1962	8(R)(D)
21. *Teich* v. *Arthur Andersen & Co.*	1965	None
22. *Blank et al.* v. *Kaitz et al.*	1966	None
23. *Fischer et al.* v. *Kletz et al.*	1967	25(C)
24. *Anderson* v. *Boone County Abstract Co.*	1967	33(R)
25. *Westerhold* v. *Carroll*	1967	33(R), 35(R)
26. *Investment Corp. of Florida* v. *Buchman et al.*	1968	None
27. *Rusch Factors Inc.* v. *Levin*	1968	4(C)
28. *Canaveral Capital Corpn.* v. *Bruce*	1968	None
29. *Ryan* v. *Kanne*	1969	33(R), 37(C)
30. *Rozny et al.* v. *Marnul*	1969	33(C), 17(C), 18(C)
31. *Stephens Industries Inc.* v. *Haskins & Sells et al.*	1971	None
32. *Shatterproof Glass Corp.* v. *James et al.*	1971	None
33. *Rhode Island Hospital Trust National Bank* v. *Swartz, Bresenoff, Yavner & Jacobs*	1972	18(C), 4(C)
34. *Aluma Kraft Mfg. Co. et al.* v. *Elmer Fox & Company et al.*	1973	33(R), 37(R), 18(R), 4(C)
35. *MacNerland et al.* v. *Barnes et al.*	1973	None
36. *Bunge Corporation* v. *Eide et al.*	1974	None
37. *Hochfelder et al.* v. *Ernst & Ernst*	1974	4(C)

TABLE VIII *Cont.*

English cases relied upon

Case no.	Case	Date	Reference
1.	*Brownlie* v. *Campbell*	(1880)	5 App. Cas. 925
2.	*Burrowes* v. *Lock*	(1805)	10 Ves. 471
3.	*Caledonian Ry. Co.* v. *Mulholland*	[1898]	A.C. 216
4.	*Candler* v. *Crane, Christmas & Co.*	[1951]	1 All E.R. 426, 2 K.B. 164 (C.A.)
5.	*Coggs* v. *Bernard*	(1703)	2 Ld. Raym. 909
6.	*Collis* v. *Selden*	(1868)	Law Rep. 3 C.P. 496
7.	*Coventry Sheppard & Co.* v. *Gt. Eastern Ry. Co.*	(1886)	L.R. 11 Q.B.D. 776
8.	*Derry* v. *Peek*	(1889)	14 App. Cas. 337
9.	*Dickson* v. *Reuter's Telegraph Co. Ltd.*	(1877)	L.R. 3 Com. Pl.1
10.	*Dominion Natural Gas Co.* v. *Collins*	[1909]	A.C. 640
11.	*Dutton* v. *Poole*	(1677)	2 Lev. 211 (S.C.1 Ventris 318)
12.	*Earl* v. *Lubbock*	[1905]	1 K.B. 253
13.	*Elliot* v. *Hall*	(1885)	15 Q.B.D. 315
14.	*Fish* v. *Kelly*	(1864)	17 C.B. N.S. 194
15.	*Gladwell* v. *Steggall*	(1839)	5 Bing. N.C. 733
16.	*George* v. *Skivington*	(1869)	L.R. 5 Ex. 1
17.	*Heaven* v. *Pender*	(1883)	11 Q.B.D. 503
18.	*Hedley Byrne & Co. Ltd.* v. *Heller & Partners Ltd.*	[1964]	A.C. 465
19.	*Indermaur* v. *Dames*	(1866)	L.R. 1 C.P. 274
20.	*Langridge* v. *Levy*	(1837)	2 M. & W. 519
21.	*Le Lievre* v. *Gould*	[1839]	1 Q.B. 491
22.	*Longmeid* v. *Holliday*	(1851)	6 Ex. 761
23.	*Low* v. *Bouverie*	[1891]	3 Ch. 82
24.	*Matter of London and General Bank*	[1895]	2 Ch. 673
25.	*Pasley* v. *Freeman*	(1789)	3 T.R. 51
26.	*Peppin and Wife* v. *Sheppard*	(1822)	11 Price 400
27.	*Robertson* v. *Fleming*	(1861)	4 Macq. H.L. Cas. 167
28.	*Skelton* v. *London & North Western Ry. Co.*	(1877)	L.R. 2 CP. 631
29.	*Shiells* v. *Blackburne*	(1784)	1 H.Bl. 158
30.	*Slim* v. *Croucher*	(1860)	1 De Gex, F & J 518
31.	*Smith* v. *Land & House Property Corp.*	(1884)	28 Ch. Div. 7.

TABLE VIII *Cont.*

Case no.	Case	Date	Reference
32.	*White* v. *Steadman*	[1913]	3 K.B. 340
33.	*Winterbottom* v. *Wright*	(1842)	10 M. & W. 109

Reference material
34. *Halsbury's Laws of England*
35. *Holdsworth's History of English Law*
36. *Jenk's Digest of English Civil Law*
37. *Journal of Business Law*
38. *Law Quarterly Review*
39. *Pollock on Torts*

(iii) Enhanced relevance of American common law following *Hedley Byrne*

The American common law cases are analysed in later chapters in order to evaluate the recent development of the law. In England, the important case of *Hedley Byrne* was decided in 1963 and should have provided the precedent needed for an extension of accountants' legal liability; in fact there has been little development upon that case even though at the time of its decision there was widespread fear that it would result in a wide spate of litigation against the accountant and other professionals.[14]

American courts, on the other hand, have handed down numerous important cases in situations where the factual circumstances were similar both to *Hedley Byrne* and *Candler* (which directly involved accountants).[15] In the absence of English cases, it is important to study how these recent American cases have developed the law. In the future English decisions may proceed upon similar lines to American decisions. Since American cases have weakened the *Ultramares* doctrines of liability in negligence causing an increase in litigation it would appear that, if English law develops in a similar fashion, there will be a comparable increase in litigation in this country.

Benston, in a recent review of the legal environment in the United States and United Kingdom, provides support for the view expressed here that the common law of the two countries are substantially similar. He notes that in both the United States and Great Britain some ten years ago the primary benefit rule expressed in *Ultramares* governed the liability of accountants to third parties for negligence.[16] This is supported by other commentators.[17] Benston also indicates that there is doubt surrounding the rule in *Hedley Byrne*, especially with respect to the extent of liability. It is in just this area that the American courts have developed the law, whereas English courts have remained silent leaving the field open to varying interpretation.[18]

Benston tentatively suggests that American and British common law will support damage suits against accountants by shareholders, investors and other third parties who use published financial statements.[19] The analysis of American common law cases which follows in the next two chapters will help to define this problem.

III STATUTE LAW

Statute law actions involving accountants have not been extensively analysed because, unlike the common law, there are no direct parallels between the various statute laws of the two countries. As one commentator has stated:

> Although the systems are very similar with respect to the common law liability of accountants for fraud and negligence, the provisions of the United States Securities Acts and the ability and incentives of third parties to sue accountants are in sharp contrast to the lack of similar statutory provisions and third party incentives in the United Kingdom.[20]

Analysis of American statutory actions has little significance for this country because key provisions in the relevant Acts differ between the two countries. In addition control of the US Acts is directly under the regulation of the SEC, for which UK has no counterpart.[21] The power of the SEC and its influence over the administration of the Securities Acts cannot be underestimated.

The majority of cases involving accountants which have been brought under the Federal Securities Laws have involved one or other of two sections of those Acts:

1. Section 11, Securities Act of 1933
2. Section 10b, Securities Exchange Act of 1934

(i) Section 11, Securities Act 1933[22]

The Securities Act 1933 was designed to prevent fraud in the sale of securities and also to counteract many dubious practices by companies in America during the financial collapse of 1929 and 1930.[23] The Act, through the SEC, regulates the contents and issuance of prospectuses (registration statements), controls the financial statements included in those prospectuses, and provides that the statements shall be certified by an independent accountant.[24] The sections within the Act providing civil remedy are sections 11, 12 and 15 and only section 11 directly involves accountants.[25]

Section 11(a) contains provisions relating to the liabilities arising from untrue statements or material omissions in registration statements. Liability is imposed upon those signing the registration statement including, *inter alia*, directors and 'experts', which term includes accountants.

Whenever a registration statement becomes effective, containing:

> an untrue statement of a material fact [which has] omitted to state a material fact required to be stated therein or necessary to make the statements therein not misleading; any person acquiring such security . . . may, either at law or in equity, in any court of competent jurisdiction, sue . . . (4) every accountant, engineer or appraiser or any person whose profession gives authority to a statement made by him, who has with his consent been named as having prepared or certified any part of the registration statement, or as having prepared or certified any report or valuation which is used in connection with the registration statement, with respect to the statement in such registration statement, report or valuation, which purports to have been prepared or certified by him. . . . [26]

Prior to 1968, the number of suits brought by investors under this section was relatively small[27] but in that year the *BarChris* case[28] was decided. This was one of the most comprehensive decisions in a lawsuit involving civil liability under section 11 of the Securities Act 1933, and the case ensured that the section was to become of greater significance.[29]

The main aspects of section 11 of the 1933 Act may be analysed in eight parts:

1. Any purchaser of a security being offered may sue and recover damages from various designated persons whose liability is joint and several (section 11(f)).
2. Privity is not a requirement and the remoteness of the seller is immaterial. This lack of privity requirement was a direct result of the *Ultramares* case which had stated that extension of liability to third parties should be undertaken by legislation.[30]
3. The purchaser *need not have relied* upon the misleading statement or omission and the purchaser's loss is typically not in issue.[31]
4. Liability is imposed substantially without regard to defendants' 'intention' or 'knowledge' of the misleading statements or omissions; the purchaser is freed from proving any *scienter* element (section 11(a)).[32]
5. Certain defences are available to defendants in an action and they include concepts of 'reasonable investigation', 'reasonable grounds to believe', etc. in the material presented in the statements issued.[33]
6. The persons liable are fully stipulated in the section. They include all those who signed the registration statement, the issuer, directors and prospective named directors and also certain 'experts' involved in the issue.[34]
7. The expert must prove, for his own statement only or the parts of the registration statement he certified, that he carried out a reasonable investigation and had 'reasonable grounds to believe' and had 'belief in fact' that his statements were true and had no misleading omissions (section 11(b)). In this defence the standard of reasonable investigation is that of a 'prudent man in the management of his own property' (section 11(c)).
8. In an action the court has to determine the auditors' (as experts) belief and the grounds thereof 'at the time such part of the registration statement became effective'. That is to say if the audited accounts included in the prospectus only go up to the year ending before the prospectus was issued the auditors must also attest the period from that year end to the date of the prospectus. This is connected with the 'due diligence' defence.[35]

(ii) English law equivalent to section 11, Securities Act 1933

Turning to English law, the doctrine behind the issuing of a prospectus is laid down in the Companies Act 1948. Actions may be brought by shareholders under sections of the Act, or in tort through breach of contract.

(1) Liability under contract

An important requirement for an action by a shareholder is that he had been induced to take up shares having relied upon a misrepresentation in a prospectus. Thus under section 116 of the 1948 Act a shareholder may have his name removed from a register of members, and his money returned to him with interest, if he can show that he did not act, after discovering the misrepresentation, by claiming or recognising any rights or liabilities as a shareholder.[36]

The shareholder must act within a reasonable time of discovering the misrepresentation. The untrue statement must be material, and the subscriber must have been materially influenced by it.

If a person is induced to subscribe by a material misstatement, it is no defence to an action for rescission[37] that he had the means of discovering, and might with reasonable diligence have discovered, that the statement was untrue. The omission of facts is not a ground for rescission, unless it is of such a nature as to make what is actually stated misleading.[38]

The shareholder may bring an action for negligent misrepresentation only against the other party to the contract (the company), and thus not against the directors or agents responsible for the prospectus[39] (including the reporting accountants). However, since *Hedley Byrne* v. *Heller*[40] it is possible that directors may be liable.[41] The company's liability for damages will be the same as if the misrepresentation had been made fraudulently, save that it will be a defence to show that it had reasonable ground for believing, and did believe up to the time the contract was made, that the facts represented were true.[42] An action in tort against an accountant therefore may only be brought in deceit, and not in negligence. In such event the position of the plaintiff is particularly onerous because:

1. The onus is upon the plaintiff to show the representation was material.[43]
2. He must prove that the false representation was fraudulent, in the sense that it was made knowingly, or without belief in its truth, or recklessly, without caring whether it was true or false.[44]
3. Any numbers of shareholders may combine in an action against the defendant but one subscriber *cannot maintain the action on behalf of himself and the others who have been misled.*[45]

(2) Liability under the Companies Act

The 4th Schedule of the 1948 Companies Act requires reports by the auditors and independent accountants of the company issuing a prospectus.[46] The accountants must be named in the prospectus.[47]

Under statute law a subscriber is entitled to claim only compensation from a defendant, computed on the basis of the actual economic loss suffered.[48] Any person who is induced to subscribe for shares by an untrue statement in a prospectus may claim this compensation.[49] Reliance must have been upon the prospectus and so any shareholder (subject to limited exceptions)[50] purchasing from any other source may not bring an action.

Under section 43(1) auditors or accountants are regarded as experts and liable only for 'untrue' statements in their own reports forming part of a prospectus. 'Untrue' in this section means misleading in the form and context in which it is included (section 46(a)).

The subscriber must prove that he subscribed for the shares in reliance on a false statement in the prospectus, and that he has suffered loss in consequence.[51]

In his capacity as an expert, there are certain defences open to the accountant which if proved will exonerate him from liability.

1. If the accountant was competent to make the statement or report complained of, and believed it to be true on reasonable grounds up to the time when the shares were allotted to the subscriber (section 43(3)(c)).
2. If he withdrew his consent as to the inclusion of his report in the prospectus (section 43(3)(a)).
3. Having given sufficient notice after discovering the untrue statement he withdrew his consent as to inclusion of his report(section 43(3)(b)).[52]

On a comparative basis therefore the following significant differenes exist between the Securities Act 1933 and the Companies Act 1948 with respect to the accountants' liability for misrepresentation in a prospectus (registration statement).

a. Privity. Neither Act requires privity in the strict sense of the word but in the UK only the initial subscribers have a cause for action.

b. Reliance. In the US reliance need not be proved: in the UK evidence of reliance is needed. This means that in the US an accountant's liability could extend to purchasers of securities who may have no knowledge of the auditors' report, and may not even have known of the auditors' existence.[53]

c. Defences and the scope of work the expert accountant is responsible for. In the US the so-called 'due diligence' defence of section 11(b) has meant pressure upon accountants to expand in several ways the scope of their work as it relates to registration statements. (For example they are now responsible for a full 'S-1 review' which covers the period from the last audited balance sheet to the date the prospectus was issued.)[54] On the other hand, accountants in the UK can only be liable for certain specified reports. These reports will contain *historical* data all of which has been audited.[55]

(iii) Section 10(b) Securities Exchange Act 1934 (together with the connected Rule 10b-5 of the Securities and Exchange Commission)

The other section which is used extensively in the US for action against accountants is section 10(b) of the Securities Exchange Act 1934 (the 1934 Act).[56]

The 1934 Act deals essentially with trading in securities, as distinguished from the 1933 Act which is concerned with disclosure in the registration statement. Although there are no express provisions for civil liability in the Act, the federal courts have construed certain provisions as establishing civil remedies for any violation,[57] especially with regard to section 10(b) and the associated SEC regulation 'Rule 10b-5'.

The SEC *has* used the Rule with considerable force over the past few years as witnessed by the large number of actions brought under the section as a result of SEC investigations or injunctions.[58] The section has also been employed in civil actions. Sommer states:

> Rule 10b-5 was intended purely as an enforcement tool for the Commission. In 1946 an imaginative plaintiff's counsel and a creative court combined to yield the conclusion that Rule 10b-5 was not only available to the Commission for enforcement purposes but was available to private claimants as well who could establish they had been harmed by a violation of the Rule. Thus was opened the floodgate through which oceans of litigation have passed in the intervening twenty-six years, virtually to the point that other more explicit liability-creating provisions of the federal securities laws have been vastly over-shadowed as litigants sought the benefits of Rule 10b-5.[59]

The widespread use of the section and corresponding SEC Rule has occurred because of the vagueness of its wording, which may encapsulate any transaction however remotely connected with the trading in securities.

The SEC's Rule 10b-5 provides as follows:

> It shall be unlawful for any person, directly or indirectly, by the use of any means or instrumentality of inter-state commerce, or of the mails, or of any facility of any national securities exchange, (a) to employ any device, scheme, or artiface to defraud; (b) to make any untrue statement of a material fact or to omit to state a material fact necessary in order to make the statements made, in the light of circumstances under which they were made, not misleading, or (c) to engage in any act, practice, or course of business which operates or would operate as a fraud or deceit upon any person, in connection with the purchase or sale of any security.[60]

This Rule's significance rests on the fact that it has been interpreted to apply to routine audits and auditors' opinions. Even if the statements being audited do not form part of a prospectus or other offer of securities.[61] In the *Texas Gulf Sulphur*[62] case, the court held that a misleading *press release* issued by the company constituted a violation of Rule 10b-5.

Gormley summed up the case's implications stating:

> The court interpreted the congressional intent in the phrase 'in connection with the purchase or sale of any security' in section 10(b) of the statute as requiring only that misrepresentations by defendants be likely to cause reasonable investors to purchase or sell the company's securities in reliance upon the misrepresentations. Since 1968, therefore, the term 'in connection with' has been construed broadly enough so that audit opinions and audited or unaudited financial statements with which auditors become associated may . . . be statements 'in connection with' purchases and sales of the corporation's securities by investors. . . . [63]

The dangers of this widened interpretation of the statute law has led to criticism from the profession. There is said to be no limit to the possibility of litigation against the accountant, for even mere negligence in an audit. Some federal courts have suggested that mere negligence, as distinguished from fraud, is enough to sustain liability, other courts have differed from this view.[64]

The vagueness of the wording of the Rule 10b-5 has meant that the interpretation of that Rule has developed along the more traditional lines of the common law.

As one commentator states, 'The genius of the law of Rule 10b-5 is the genius of the common law. The federal courts in interpreting the Rule are, for the most part, developing judge-made law, not construing legislation.'[65] In terms of the legislative implications of 10b-5, however, the recent supreme court decision in *Ernst & Ernst* v. *Hochfelder*[66] is of particular significance because it has limited the civil liability aspects of the Rule.[67] In *Hochfelder* the court established clearly that *scienter* was required within the traditional common law meaning of 'intent to deceive'. The *scienter* requirement must be pled and proved by a plaintiff to state a claim for damages under section 10(b) of the 1934 Act.[68] One effect of the ruling may be to exclude accountants from actions brought under the Rule in future because of the difficulty of proving such a cause. However, the effect of withdrawing the negligence standard from this section does not exclude it from section 11 of the 1933 Act.[69]

(iv) Comparison with English statute law

In English statute law there is nothing directly comparable with section 10(b) although some similarities exist with the Prevention of Fraud (Investments) Act 1958.[70]

Under the general provisions of the Prevention of Fraud (Investments) Act 1958, section 13(1) outlines the persons who may be liable:

> Any person who, by any statement, promise or forecast which he knows to be misleading, false or deceptive, or by any dishonest concealment of material facts, or by the reckless making of any statement, promise or forecast which is misleading, false or deceptive, induces or attempts to induce another person – (a) to enter into or offer to enter into – (i) any agreement for, or with a view to, acquiring, disposing of, subscribing for or underwriting securities. . . .

Section 14(1) provides:

> Subject to the provisions of this section, no person shall – (a) distribute or cause to be distributed any documents which, to his knowledge, are circulars containing – (i) any invitation to persons to do any of the acts mentioned in [Section 13(1)].[71]

The above sections are more restrictive than section 10(b) of the 1934 Act in that the relevant representations must induce the investor to undertake a particular securities transaction. Section 10(b) on the other hand involves any 'device' in connection with securities transactions. The English Act is important in that it allows a criminal remedy where there is no civil remedy and allows it against any person involved and not just the company directors and officers;[72] in this respect it is similar to the 1934 Act.[73]

Another important distinction between the two Acts concerns the wording of the offence committed. In the English Act there is an explicit requirement of fraud and deceit under the common law definition of the terms (knowingly making false or misleading statements, or promises which are not honestly intended to be fulfilled, or forecasts which are not honestly believed in, amounts to deceit at common law).[74] This is however only implied in the American Act and as analysed above has been subject to wider interpretation by federal courts.

IV SUMMARY

Due to the differences between the main statutes under which the actions in the US have been brought this book will review the civil cases under the common law doctrines of negligence.

It is in this area that the two countries' legal systems are directly comparable. The courts in each country specifically cite precedents from the other. Evidence has also suggested that the courts in America have widened the effects of the statutes in a way which has not occurred in this country. It is also recognised that very few suits[75] have been brought under the Prevention of Fraud (Investments) Act.[76]

NOTES

[1] See opinion of Benston, text accompanying note 20 *infra*.
[2] W. A. Seavey, '*Candler* v. *Crane, Christmas & Co.* Negligent Misrepresentations by Accountants', 67 *Law Quarterly Review* 466, 469 (1951).
[3] Ibid.
[4] *Candler* v. *Crane, Christmas & Co.* [1951] 2 K.B. 164 and *Hedley Byrne & Co. Ltd.*, v. *Heller and Partners Ltd.* [1964] A.C. 465.

[5] These references are only illustrative of UK reliance; their significance re. the law are discussed in Chapters 5 and 6, *infra*.

[6] [1951] 2 K.B. 164, 183.

[7] For a full discussion of this see Chapter 5 *infra*.

[8] *Ultramares Corporation* v. *Touche et al* 174 N.E. 441 (1931).

[9] [1951] 2 K.B. 164, 207.

[10] [1964] A.C. 465, 478.

[11] Ibid, p. 488.

[12] Ibid, p. 483.

[13] The importance of English cases is also evident from a comparative analysis carried out by Bradley on *Hedley Byrne* with the American case *Texas Tunnelling*. In particular he implies that the Court of Appeals in 1964 in the Texas case overruled the district court (1962) after the *Hedley Byrne* decision. The Court of Appeals was considerably restricting the district court's opinion, E. J. Bradley, *Journal of Business Law*, 190, 190 (1966). For a brief analysis of the effect of the English legal system on American common law in a current context see V. M. Earle, 'The Litigation Explosion', *Journal of Accountancy*, March 1970, pp. 65 *et seq*.

[14] This fear was felt on both sides of the Atlantic resulting in the ICAEW seeking counsel's opinion of the exact extent of its importance and the AICPA publishing this opinion in the *Journal of Accountancy*, October 1965, p. 67.

[15] See schedules in Chapter 4 *infra*.

[16] G. J. Benston, 'Accounting Standards in the United States and the United Kingdom: Their nature, causes and consequences', 28 *Vanderbilt Law Review* 235, 257 (1975).

[17] See for example Gormley, 'Accountants' professional liability – A ten year review', 29 *Business Lawyer* 1205 (1974).

[18] See for example the differing opinions quoted by Benston, including ICAEW, 'Accountants liability to third parties – The Hedley Byrne Decision', *Journal of Acountancy* (August 1965) and M. Arden, 'A legal view of current UK Practice' in *Negligence and the Public Accountant* 24, 26 (1972). See also R. Baxt, 'The Liability of Accountant and Auditors for negligent statements in company accounts', 36 *Modern Law Review* 42 (1973).

[19] Benston, note 16 *supra*, pp. 258 and 259.

[20] Benston, note 16 *supra*, p. 263.

[21] See generally Chapter 2 section I, *supra*.

[22] For a full analysis of the effects and regulations of the Securities Act and Securities Exchange Act see L. H. Rappaport, *SEC Accounting Practice and Procedure* (New York: Ronald Press, 1972) and Jennings and Marsh *Securities Regulation* (New York: Foundation Press, 1972).

[23] See C.N. Katsoris, 'Accountants' third party liability – How far do we go?' 36 *Fordham Law Review* 191, 209 (1967).

[24] Schedule A, paras 25–6, 48 Stat. 90 (1933) as amended 15 USC s. 77aa (25) – (26) (1964).

[25] Katsoris, note 23 *supra*, p. 209.

[26] 48 Stat. 82 (1933), as amended; 15 USC s. 77 K(a) (1964). Cited by Katsoris, ibíd, p. 210 and Rappaport, note 22 *supra*, pp. 27.1 and 27.2.

27 Katsoris, ibid, p. 211.
28 *Escott* v. *BarChris Construction Corp.* 283 F. Supp. 643 (1968).
29 See for example Rappaport, note 22 *supra*, p. 28.6 and Folk, 'Civil Liabilities under the Federal Securities Acts:' The *BarChris* Case', 55 *Virginia Law Review*, 17 (1969). Reiling and Taussig, 'Recent Liability Cases – Implications for Accountants', *Journal of Accountancy*, 41 (Sep. 1970).
30 In *Ultramares* it was stated by Cardozo C.J.: 'The extension, if made, will so expand the field of liability for negligent speech as to make it nearly, if not quite, coterminous with that of liability for fraud . . . many pages of opinion were written by judges the most eminent yet the word was never spoken. We may not speak it now. A change so revolutionary, if expedient, must be wrought by legislation.'
31 See though exception: 48 Stat. 82 (1933) as amended 15 USC s. 77k(a) (1964) regarding the need for reliance if the security was acquired after the issuer had made generally available to its securities holders an earnings statement.
32 *Scienter* is actual knowledge by a misrepresentor that he is making a fraudulent or dishonest misrepresentation. See Chapter 2, text accompanying note 14, *supra*.
33 These defences formed the foundation of the defendants' case in *BarChris*, note 28 *supra*.
34 An accounting firm would usually fall within the category of 'expert' as with the case of Peat, Marwick, Mitchell & Company in *BarChris*.
35 W. J. Kenley, 'Legal decisions affecting auditors', 39 *Chartered Accountant in Australia* 952 (1969).
36 *Halsbury's Laws of England* Vol. 7 *Companies* p. 143, para. 243 (citations omitted).
37 Rescission of the contract with the company to purchase the shares, see ibid para. 239 and para. 243.
38 Ibid, paras 242 and 243.
39 Ibid, para. 253
40 [1964] A.C. 465, [1963] 2 All E.R. 575, HL.
41 Halsbury, note 36 *supra*, para 253, footnote 5 states: '*Quaere* if the directors might nevertheless be held liable under the doctrine of *Hedley Byrne* [ibid] . . . a person in a special position who takes it upon himself to give information [may be] liable [for] information negligently given'.
42 Ibid.
43 Ibid, para. 248.
44 Without fully analysing the requirements for an action in deceit, the position for the plaintiff is particularly stringent. See *Derry* v. *Peek*,(1889) 14 App. Cas. 337 and ibid, para. 249.
45 *Hallows* v. *Fernie* (1868) 3 Ch. App. 467, *Croskey* v. *Bank of Wales* (1863) 4 Jiff 314. Ibid para. 247, footnote 8. This does not exclude any form of 'class action' suit so important in America. See Chapter 7 *infra*.
46 See 4th Schedule, Part II, paras 19–21, Part III, para. 30, 1948 Act for details of what information needs to be included within the reports.
47 Ibid.
48 Halsbury, note 36 *supra*, para. 254 footnote 3.

[49] 1948 Act s. 43(1).

[50] For example an issuing house rather than the company direct. See Pennington, *Company Law* (3rd ed.) (London: Butterworths, 1976) p. 244. Refer in general to Pennington, *Company Law* (4th ed.) (London: Butterworths, 1979) pp. 236–55.

[51] s 43(1) 1948 Act. See Pennington, ibid, p. 245.

[52] For a fuller analysis see s. 43 1948 Act and Pennington, ibid, pp. 246 and 247.

[53] For a discussion of the harshness of this rule see Jaenicke, *The Impact of the Current Legal Climate on the Accounting Profession*, Paper prepared for commission on Auditors' Responsibilities, July 1976, pp. 28 *et seq.*

[54] For a fuller discussion see: Reiling and Taussig, note 29 *supra*, p. 45 and *Escott* v. *BarChris Construction Corporation* note 28 *supra*.

[55] For a full description see 4th Schedule, 1948 Act, Part II.

[56] See Rappaport, note 22 *supra*, p. 27.8.

[57] See Katsoris, note 23 *supra*, p. 217.

[58] See Section I, Chapter 2, *supra*.

[59] Sommer, 'What are the Courts saying to Auditors?', Auditing Looks Ahead (Proceedings of the 1972 University of Kansas Symposium on Auditing Problems).

[60] 17 CFR s. 240: 10b-5 (1967) quoted by Katsoris, note 23 *supra*, p. 217.

[61] See for example Gormley, note 21 *supra*, pp. 219–21 and Causey, 'Foreseeability as a Determinant of Audit Responsibility', 48 *Accounting Review*, 258, 263 (1973).

[62] *SEC* v. *Texas Gulf Sulphur Co.* 401 F.2d 833 (2d Cir. 1968) (en banc) cert. denied. 394 US 976 (1968).

[63] Note 17 *supra*, p. 122/21. Cases involving accountants include *Fischer* v. *Kletz* 266 F. Supp. 180 (1967), where the 'in connection with' interpretation has led to liability.

[64] See V. M. Earle, 'Accountants on Trial in a Theatre of the Absurd', 85 *Fortune Magazine*, 227, 228 (1972).

[65] T. J. Fiflis, 'Current Problems of Accountants' Responsibilities to Third Parties', 28 *Vanderbilt Law Review* 31, 113 (1975).

[66] *Ernst & Ernst* v. *Hochfelder* 503 F.2d 1100 (1974) on appeal.

[67] See C. D. Liggio, 'The "Ernst" Ruling — Expansion of a Trend', *The New York Law Journal*, April 14–15, 1976; also Jaenicke, note 53 *supra*, pp. 35 *et seq.*

[68] For a full analysis of the case see Liggio, ibid.

[69] Ibid. Another effect of the *Hochfelder* ruling is that more cases are likely to occur under the common law – see C. H. Griffen, 'Beleaguered Accountants – An American Defendant's Viewpoint', *The Accountant*, 24 June 1976, p. 737.

[70] See Benston, note 16 *supra*, p. 261.

[71] 6 and 7 Eliz. 2, 45 pp. 394–5.

[72] Pennington, note 50 *supra*, p. 249.

[73] Other sections of the Prevention of Fraud (Investments) Act of comparative relevance include:

s. 18: Any person who, in furnishing any information – for any of the purposes of this Act or rules or regulations made thereunder, makes any statement which, to his knowledge, is false in a material particular, shall be liable, on conviction or indictment, to imprisonment for a term not exceeding two years or to a fine not exceeding two hundred pounds or to both . . . or on summary conviction, to imprisonment for a term not exceeding three months or to a fine not exceeding one hundred pounds or to both . . . (these penalties equate with s. 111 of the Companies Act, 1967).

s. 21: The Department of Trade may make any rules or regulations for prosecuting anything which by the Act is required (cf. with similar SEC's facility) – but

s. 22: These rules must be controlled by Act of Parliament.

[74] Pennington, note 50 *supra*, p. 249.

[75] See Benston, note 16 *supra*, p. 261.

[76] For a thorough analysis of this Act see Prevention of Fraud (Investments) Act, 1958 (as amended by the Protection of Depositors Act, 1963 s. 21(1). 22 Halsburys Statutes (3rd ed.). Pennington, *Company Law*, note 50 *supra*, pp. 248 *et seq. Halsbury's Laws,* note 36 *supra*, p. 157 *et seq* (paras. 263–5).

4 ANALYSIS OF THE CASES AFFECTING ACCOUNTANTS' LEGAL LIABILITY IN THE UNITED STATES

I ESTABLISHING THE SIGNIFICANT CASES

In order to establish a corpus of cases regarded as 'authorities' in the field of accountants' liability to third parties, the main data sources employed were American law journals. The bibliography of articles was obtained from an analysis of the Index of Legal Periodicals[1], and the Accountants' Index[2] for a ten year period from 1966. These articles provided lists of cases on the subject cited or discussed by the author.

Each of the cases were then analysed from the law reports so that (i) any cases not directly connected with the subject could be discarded, and (ii) further significant cases cited in the reports could be included. This process resulted in a matrix cases.

II THE MATRIX OF CASES

The matrix of cases in Table IX includes all the cases considered of primary significance to the subject. The cases are listed in date order, and next to each case are the symbols R and C, representing the cases discussed, referred to or relied upon in judgment (R); and the cases cited to support or reject arguments (C). An approximate time-scale is reproduced on the right hand side of the matrix.

The matrix was produced in this format for a number of reasons:

TABLE IX Cases in the development of the common law with reference to accountants' liability

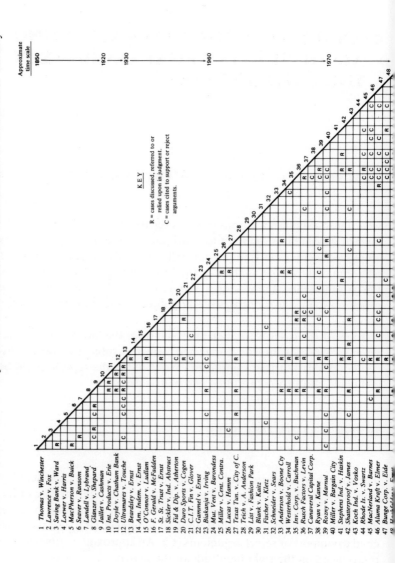

1. To indicate the cases which are relied upon by subsequent cases, thereby showing their significance. For example, *Ultramares*[3] (case 12) is relied upon by 21 out of 36 of the subsequent cases.
2. To highlight, visually, trends in the common law. It is very noticeable, for example, how the courts consistently cite *Glanzer*[4] (case 8) and *Ultramares* (case 12) following *Biakanja*[5] (case 23). The matrix also indicates a further trend in the last ten years. It is evident that *Ultramares* was the dominating authority from the 1930s to the 1960s as hardly any other precedent was needed in support of a judgment. However from the 1960s and the *Anderson*[6] case (case 33) specific reliance becomes less noticeable as various state courts cite numerous precedents, having initially compared *Glanzer* with *Ultramares*.
3. To show the time-scale of cases. In this respect the large number of cases in the late 1960s and early 1970s show to some extent that the law is uncertain. *Ultramares*, the established precedent for almost 30 years, is being questioned and weakened during this period.

III THE CASE SCHEDULES

The matrix provides 37 cases which are included in the case schedules. These schedules are separated into three parts as follows:

Schedule A: Factual analysis of all the cases.

Schedule B: Analysis of the negligence actions[7]

    Ba: *Thomas* to *Ultramares*
       From 1852 to 1931

    Bb: *Biakanja* to *Hochfelder*
       From 1958 to 1974

    Bc: Supplement to Schedule Bb. Additional factors in negligence actions.

Schedule C: Analysis of the fraud and deceit actions from 1931 to 1973.

Schedule A details the factual or undisputed aspects of each case. Schedules B and C, on the other hand, consider the judgments and court opinions in the two relevant aspects of the law of tort – negligence and deceit. The data in Schedule A was obtained from the headings and summaries of each law report. For Schedules B and C, however, the choice of data was more subjective. In particular, any aspects of the judgment not connected with the negligence or deceit cause of action were omitted.

IV DESCRIPTION OF SCHEDULES

(i) Schedule A: Factual analysis of all the cases

Schedule A is divided into various sub-sections as follows:

(1) Title of case
Each case is listed in chronological order under the title by which it will usually be referred.

(2) Date of case
Where the case has extended over a year or more (quite common in the recent cases) the latest date of final judgment relevant to the common law aspects of the case is included. If a case goes to appeal the latest report available has been used in the analysis and the date of that report employed.

(3) Jurisdiction
This section is divided into two – 'state' and 'court' – representing the state within which the case was heard and the court within that state. This indicates the state law which is employed in the case, particularly significant with respect to precedent reliance. Under the 'state' heading the symbol 'F' represents the cases appearing within the federal system.

(4) The cause(s) of action
The three sub-divisions here represent negligence (N), fraud and deceit (F) and other actions related to accountants' third party liability (O).

(5) Parties to the case
Divided into 1st, 2nd and 3rd parties, this section indicates very broad-

SCHEDULE A   Factual analysis of the major American cases

Case	Date	State	Court Action			Parties to the case			Representation	Damage		Knowledge of reliance
			N	F	O	1st	2nd	3rd			Yes	
1. *Thomas v. Winchester*	1852	NY	x				Pharmacist	Purchaser	Label	Physical	Yes	Unknown third party
2. *Savings Bank v. Ward*	1879	Col	S	x		Borrower	Attorney	Bank	Title cert.	Loan	Yes	Unknown third party
3. *MacPherson v. Buick Motor Co*	1916	NY	A	x		Manufacturer	Car dealer	Purchaser		Physical	Yes	Unknown third party
4. *Seaver v. Ransom et al*	1918	NY	A		x		Executor	Beneficiary	Promise	Estate	Yes	
5. *Landell v. Lybrand et al*	1919	Penn	S			Private company	CPA	Investor	CFS	Share value	Yes	No
6. *Glanzer et al v. Shepard*	1922	NY	A	x		Seller	Weigher	Purchaser	Weight cert.	Sale value	Yes	Copy sent to third party
7. *Jaillet v. Cashman*	1923	NY	A	x			Dow Jones	Investor	Stock Report	Share value	Yes	No
8. *International Products Co. v. Erie Ry. Co*	1927	NY	A	x			Warehousers	Importer	Insurance cert.	Goods	Yes	
9. *Doyle v. Chatham & Phenix Nat. Bank of City of New York*	1930	NY	A	x		Bond issuer	Trustee to bondholders	Bondholder	Trustees cert.	Bond value	Yes	Yes, known the serious purpose to act and rely
10. *Ultramares Corporation v. Touche et al*	1931	NY	A	x		Private company	CPA	Bank/factor	CFS	Loans	Yes	Yes, but the actual third party unknown
11. *Beardsley v. Ernst et al*	1934	Ohio	A	x		Corporation	CPA	Investor	CFS	Share value	Yes	No
12. *American Indemnity Co. v. Ernst et al*	1937	Tex	A	(X)	x	School district	CPA	Surety	CFS	Bond	Yes	Alleged by plaintiff
13. *O'Connor v. Ludlam et al*	1937	F(2)	A (C)	x		Private company	CPA	Investors	CFS/Pros.	Investments	Yes	Yes, but the actual third party unknown
14. *State Street Trust v. Ernst et al*	1938	NY	A	x		Financing wholesalers	CPA	Bank	CFS	Loans	Yes	Yes, but the actual third party unknown
15. *Fidelity & Deposit Co. of Maryland v. Atherton et al*	1944	NM	S (X)	(X)	x	County	CPA	Surety	Audit	Bond	Yes	
16. *Duro Sportswear Inc. et al v. Cogen et al*	1954	NY	S	x		Private company	CPA	Investor*	CFS	Investment	Yes	

SCHEDULE A *cont.*

Case	Date	State	Court Action	N	F	O	Parties to the case 1st	2nd	3rd	Representation		Damage	Knowledge of reliance
17. *C.I.T. Financial Corp. v. Glover et al*	1955	F(2)	A(C)	X			Manufacturer	CPA	Bank	CFS	Yes	Loan	Yes and no (two periods)
18. *Biskanjz v. Irving*	1958	Cal	S	X			Testator	Notary	Beneficiary	Will		Legacy	
19. *Mutual Ventures Inc. v. Barondess*	1959	NY	S	X	(X)		Borrower	CPA	Bank	CFS	Yes		
20. *Texas Tunneling Co. v. City of Chattanoga et al* (Appealed)	1962	F(Tn)	D	X	X		City	Engineers	Subcontractor	Drawing	Yes	Losses in digging	
21. *Trich v. Arthur Andersen & Co.*	1965	NY	S		X		Corporation	CPA	Investor	CFS	Yes?	Overpayment on share	No
22. *Blank et al v. Katz et al*	1966	Mass	S	X		X	Corporation	CPA	Directors	CFS	Yes?	Share value	No, vital factor in case
23. *Fischer et al v. Kletz et al*	1967	F(NY)	D		X	X	Corporation	CPA	Investors	CFS	Yes	Share value	Yes (actual unknown)
24. *Anderson v. Boone County Abstract Co.*	1967	Mo	S	X			Land owner	Abstractor	Purchasers	Title cert	Yes	Title	
25. *Westerhold v. Carroll*	1967	Mo	S	X			Land owners	Architect	Surety	Completion cert	No	Bond	No
26. *Investment Corp. of Florida v. Buchman et al*	1968	Fla	A	X		X	Corporation	CPA	Investor*	UntCFS	Yes	Loss of stock	Yes
27. *Rusch Factors Inc. v. Levin*	1968	F(2)	D	X	X		Corporation	CPA	Bank	CFS	Yes	Loan	
28. *Canaveral Capital Corp. v. Bruce*	1968	Fla	A	X	X		Borrower	CPA	Bank	CFS	Yes	Loan	No
29. *Ryan v. Kanne*	1969	Iowa	S	X			Corporation	CPA	Investor*	CFS	Yes	Share value	Yes, vital factor in this type of case
30. *Rozny et al v. Marnul*	1969	Ill	S	X		X	Builders	Surveyor	Purchaser	Survey	Yes	Land	Not specifically but implied in transaction
31. *Stephens Industries Inc. v. Haskins and Sells et al*	1971	F(10)	A(C)	X	X		Corporation	CPA	Investor*	CFS	Yes	Share value	Yes but insignificant in negligence actions
32. *Shatterproof Glass Corp. v. James et al*	1971	Tex	A	X		X	Corporation	CPA	(Bank)	CFS	Yes	Loan/Credit	Yes
33. *Rhode Island Hospital Nat. Bank v. Swartz et al*	1972	F(4)	A(C)	X			Corporation	CPA	Bank	CFS	Yes	Loans	Yes, *Ruach* rule applied
34. *Aluma Kraft Manufacturing Co. et al v. Elmer Fox & Co. et al*	1973	Mo	A	X		X	Corporation	CPA	Investor*	CFS	Yes	Share value	Unknown third party

SCHEDULE A   *cont.*

Case	Date	State	Court Action N	Court Action F	Court Action O	Parties to the case 1st	2nd	3rd	Representation		Damage	Knowledge of reliance
35. *MacNerland et al v. Barnes et al*	1973	Ga	A	X	X		Corporation	CPA	Investor*	UnCFS	Yes	Investment	
36. *Bunge Corp. v. Eide et al*	1974	F(N.D)	D	X		X	Corporation	CPA	Financier	CFS	No	Loans	No
37. *Hochfelder et al v. Ernst & Ernst* (Appealed) (Class action suit)	1974	F(7)	A (C)	X		X	Brokers	CPA	Brokers' clients	CFS	No	Fictitious shares	No. Direct reliance important element

ly the parties to the case. The abbreviation 'CPA' is used to depict the accountant or accounting firm throughout. Of the 37 cases analysed, 24 are concerned with accountants; and of the 27 cases since *Ultramares*, 22 involve accountants.

Generally, the relationship of the 'parties' in a case is as follows:

a. There will be a contractual relationship between the '1st' and '2nd' parties (for example, CPA as auditor of a corporation as in *Hochfelder*).

b. As a result of this contract some representation is made.

c. This representation is then allegedly relied upon by a '3rd' party in addition to the original contracting party.

d. Upon this reliance the '3rd' party suffers damage and as a result brings an action against the '2nd' party for negligent and/or fraudulent misrepresentation.

(6) Representation

This division indicates the type of representation produced by the '2nd' party. The term 'CFS' means certified financial statement. The second sub-division analyses the question: 'Did the third party rely upon the representation?'

(7) Damage

In any civil action, damages must be suffered by the plaintiff in the action. This section indicates the type of damage suffered. In early precedent, recovery in negligence for a diminution of financial estate would not have been allowed. Only if physical injury had occurred would recovery have been permitted. Evidence of a diminution in financial estate was only permitted in a fraud and deceit action for recovery (see further analysis below).

(8) Knowledge of reliance

The reliance question in this section may be distinguished from the reliance upon representation analysis above in that the question is considered from the representor's stand-point.

(ii) Schedule B: The judgments in negligence

The development of American common law for negligent or fraudulent misrepresentation may be separated into three distinct periods. The first period runs from the origins of the law to *Ultramares* in 1931. The case law trends of this period are included in Schedule Ba. The landmark case of *Ultramares* provides the dividing line between the first and second periods, because of the rigid precedent it established especially in the area of negligent misrepresentation. *Ultramares* however also had substantial influence upon the actions brought in deceit and fraud.

The *Ultramares* doctrine (that negligence so gross may in certain instances be sufficient to provide an inference of fraud) led to a movement away from negligence actions after *Ultramares* to actions brought for fraud and deceit. This movement, analysed in Schedule C, may be called the second period in the development of the law, from 1931 to the 1960s. At the beginning of the 1960s there again appeared actions against professional persons for negligence. The increase in actions at this time, whether it be a questioning of the modern relevance of *Ultramares* or consumer pressure upon the courts, provides the third period in the development. This period commences with *Biakanja*, the first significant case for almost thirty years to fully develop the *Glanzer/Ultramares* distinction. Schedule Bb, therefore, analyses the cases from 1958 to the present.

Schedule Bc, an extension of Schedule Bb, itemises under various heads additional significant aspects influencing the modern trend away from *Ultramares*.

(iii) Schedule Ba: *Thomas* to *Ultramares* (1852–1931) and Schedule Bb: *Biakanja* to *Hochfelder* (1958–1974)

(1) Privity
In any negligence action the courts will primarily consider the relationship of the parties. Under the principle that anyone outside a contractual relationship, that is having no privity of contract, could not bring an action for mere negligence, but only in fraud or deceit. This section analyses the importance of privity.

(2) Duty
Following on from the privity requirement is the concept of the 'duty owed'. If the courts could establish that one party owed, or was owed, a duty to exercise reasonable care in an engagement to another party then, even if privity was absent, an action might proceed.

(3) Fundamental purpose
This is concerned with the purpose of the representation (and is linked with the next section below). In the *Glanzer* decision it was held that if

SCHEDULE Ba   *Thomas to Ultramares*

Case No. (Sch. A)	Privity	Duty	Fundamental purpose (primary benefit)	Proximity or remoteness	Beneficial contract	Public duty	The class and foreseeability	The degrees of negligence
1.	Not relevant when the injury is physical	Foreseen danger thus duty arises to avoid causing injury						
2.	Required	Attorney has a duty to employ care and skill						
3.	Not relevant when the injury is physical	*Thomas v. Winchester* cited and relied upon						
4.	Not necessary when third party beneficiary contract is proved	Created under the rules of beneficiary contract			*Lawrence v. Fox* cited and relied upon			
5.	Required	No duty between the third party and the representor established in this case						Admitted that the accountants were careless and negligent
6.	Not relevant. Bond so close as to approach privity of contract	Duty imposed by law between buyer and seller	Certificate to the third party was the end and aim of the transaction	Significant factor	Implied. *Lawrence v. Fox and Seaver* cited	Defendants held themselves out as holding a public duty	Implied foreseeability. The 'Foreseen' third party first established	Ordinary negligence sufficient, but there was also negligent action in the case. Physical act of weighing
7.	Required. No liability without a contractual or fiduciary relationship	Duty imposed by law between buyer and seller		Relationship very remote. compared to newspaper readership				
8.	Depends upon the relationship of the parties in each case	This must be proved. Diligence owing to all parties both representor and third party		Negligent words may justify the recovery of proximate damages				*Glanzer* supported re. negligent words. English precedents refuted
9.	No duty between a trustee and a stranger about to deal with a cestui que trust	According with *Glanzer*. The very end and aim of the transaction	Certificates were the proximate cause of the loss					*Glanzer* supported re. negligent words also *Erie* cited

SCHEDULE Ba *cont.*

Case No. (Sch. A)	Privity	Duty	Fundamental purpose (primary benefit)	Proximity or remoteness	Beneficial contract	Public duty	The class and foreseeability	The degrees of negligence
10.	Distinguished with *Glanzer*. If not required it would make the law co-terminous with fraud	No duty can arise here. 'If liability for negligence … Hazards of business too great	Distinguished with *Glanzer*. The main purpose of the representation was not for the third party	The remoteness of the third party distinguished with *Glanzer*	*Lawrence v. Fox* cited but not applicable under the facts of the case. Use in *Glanzer* distinction		Allowing recovery would extend liability to indeterminate class. Fear of unlimited liability	Audit negligent, but not sufficient in itself to allow recovery. Gross negligence may create an inference of fraud

a representation had a fundamental purpose (that is to benefit a third party) then an action, even for economic loss, could be brought in negligence. This doctrine concerning the purpose of the representation became, therefore, a common law principle in a negligence action.

(4) Proximity or remoteness
Again the *Glanzer* case brought out the need to assess the proximity of the parties to the transaction. This section may also be classified as one of the 'inroads into the privity doctrine', because it analyses the erosion of the privity doctrine traditionally established at common law.

(5) Beneficial contract
Initially, attempts were made to bring actions under the law of 'third party beneficiary contract', but these attempts were rarely discussed at length after the first few cases failed (as evident from Schedule Bb).

(6) Public duty
This section is distinct from the normal duty relationship discussed above because it is concerned with a doctrine in law which makes third party recovery possible regardless of privity if a 'public' duty is established.

(7) The class and foreseeability
This is perhaps the most important section in terms of defining the limits of accountants' liability. Given the premise that the liability of the accountant is increasing through the inroads into the privity doctrine, the extent of the limitation is important. Fundamentally, the court has to define the class of persons to be included in the range of those to whom the accountant is responsible. Usually the court will apply some foreseeability standard, although the lines which may be drawn between those parties who are foreseen and those who are merely foreseeable are numerous.

(8) The degrees of negligence
This section is important for two reasons, (i) regarding the establishment of the degree to which negligence would constitute a viable action; (ii) with respect to negligence being an inference of fraud. For this latter reason the section could be included in Schedule C rather than Schedule B; where relevant the two schedules can be read in conjunction.

SCHEDULE Bb *Biakanja* to *Hochfelder*

Case No. (Sch. A)	Privity	Duty	Fundamental purpose (primary benefit)	Proximity or remoteness	Beneficial contract	Public duty	The class and foreseeability	The degrees of negligence
18.	Recognition that the doctrine of privity has been greatly liberalised. *Glanzer* cited	Implied in the judgment that a duty is owed, although not specifically discussed	*Biakanja* test (i). Was the transaction intended to affect the plaintiff?	*Biakanja* test (ii). The closeness of the connection between defendant's conduct and the injury suffered		*Biakanja* test (iii). Moral blame of the defendant and the policy of preventing future harm	*Biakanja* test (iv). The foreseeability of harm to the plaintiff	
19.	(This case was essentially concerned with the definition of the term misrepresentation and the court did not discuss the elements of a negligence action)							
20.	Not a prerequisite for the existence of a duty under tort law ...	In omitting info. the defs. failed to use the care expected of professionals. The foreseen test to establish duty		The negligence was the proximate cause of the loss of the plaintiff		Public policy can only find duty in cases of ultra-hazardous or wilfully dangerous conduct (*Ultramares*?)	Restriction of *Ultramares* foreseeability doctrine criticised. If injuries foreseen then def. not immune (see text)	
22.	Required							Reliance upon the certificate is more significant than a finding of gro... negligence
24.	Not required if the *Winterbottom* test is satisfied						Foreseeability test to act as a limit to the class	
25.	Not required if the *Winterbottom* test is satisfied	Duty based upon the foreseeability formula	Almost end and aim. This was the first case to really make the important distinction between *Glanzer* and *Ultramares*, reflected in these sections in the judgment	Approaching privity.			Foreseeability and the duty test per *Biakanja*	
26.	Required for *Ultramares*	Important to establish a duty of care. None without privity. Per *Ultramares*	Reference to *Glanzer* but no end and aim could be established here		The trial court established no beneficiary contract therefore cannot be brought under *Glanzer*			Gross negligence would be an inference of fraud. Per *Ultramares*

SCHEDULE Bb *cont.*

Case No. (Sch. A)	Privity	Duty	Fundamental purpose (primary benefit)	Proximity or remoteness	Beneficial contract	Public duty	The class and foreseeability	The degrees of negligence
27.	Not required. The social utility rationale of *Ultramares* refuted	Common law duty to inform	Again reliance upon *Glanzer* in the judgment. However, distinction made such that the court did not wish to overrule *Ultramares*			Support for the theory that there is a common law duty to inform. *Fischer*	Foreseeability to be encouraged to elevate the caution of the profession. Liability to actually foreseen and limited classes of persons	
28.	Required unless fraud can be proved							Gross negligence would create an inference of fraud. (Implied)
29.	*Ryan* test (i). Social utility rationale over 30yrs. To relax privity is the 3rd party limited	*Ryan* test (ii) Whether a duty to take care is proved, action can be brought	Reliance upon *Ruach Factors*, itself relying upon *Glanzer*	Same arguments as *Ruach Factors* and *Glanzer*			*Ryan* test (iii). Is the third party foreseen?	
30.	Privity has proved to be an unsatisfactory yardstick for the assessment of liability in negligence, therefore should be measured by the duty owed rather than the artificial concepts of privity		Purpose of the representations seen in terms of foreseeability	The unknown and unlimited doctrine of *Ultramares* should not be lightly discarded	No direct benefit therefore no 3rd party beneficiary contract			
31.	Required							
32.	Trend recognised that the importance of the privity doctrine is diminishing	Duty created per *Glanzer*					Foreseen if a limited class	Gross negligence criticised as a basis to assess an inference of fraud
33.		Duty to foresee and limited class of persons		A known reliance is the factor to create the action				
34.	The *Winterbottom* test analysed. The known/unknown 3rd party distinction. Rule re. privity stated	Professional standards of care referred to	*Glanzer* and *Ultramares* distinguished. If the purpose is to supply information to a known 3rd party then privity not required				Foreseeability	

SCHEDULE **Bb** *cont.*

Case No. (Sch. A)	Privity	Duty	Fundamental purpose (primary benefit)	Proximity or remoteness	Beneficial contract	Public duty	The class and foreseeability	The degrees of negligence
35.	Required. Reliance upon *Ultramares*	No duty created in this situation, as the accountant was not independent of management	*Glanzer* not mentioned in the judgment					
36.	New test established for State of Dakota						Actually foreseen and limited class of persons	
37.	Extension of liability to foreseen, known or unknown. Per *Glanzer*	Duty at common law still needs to be established	*Glanzer* and *Ultramares*	Distinguished. The social utility rationale doctrine of *Ultramares* discussed.			Foreseeability and limited class	

(iv) Schedule Bc: Additional factors in negligence actions

The cases brought for negligence since the early 1960s have high-lighted further factors which are relevant to the developing trend of the law. These factors are included in Schedule Bc which covers the cases from *Biakanja* in 1958 to the present.

(1) Restatement (Second) of Torts
By 1965 the American Law Institute had interpreted its Second Restatement of the Law of Torts. Partly reliant upon the English decision in *Hedley Byrne*,[8] this Restatement had interpreted the law of negligent misrepresentation to third parties more broadly than previously. The full effects of the restatement are discussed in Chapter 5.[9]

(2) Professional standards
Directly influenced by the controversy surrounding accounting practice in the 1960s, the courts began to include within opinions lengthy discussions upon the adherence to standards laid down by the profession. The importance attached to the pronouncements of the AICPA had not previously received such notice by courts.

(3) Ultramares criticised
Again indicating the pressure upon the courts and also the power of *Ultramares*, the trend in recent issues has been towards a lengthy criticism of *Ultramares*. Usually the courts will rely upon authoritative legal writers and reviewers when discussing the *Ultramares* precedent, especially when they are seeking to weaken its position. For this reason recent decisions, unlike previous cases, have cited at length from law journals. Some of these writers are noted under the heading 'Reliance upon legal writers and reviewers'.

(4) Other matters
The final section itemises other related factors in cases which have been emphasised as important by the court.

SCHEDULE Bc Additional factors in negligence actions

Case No. (Sch. A)	Restatement (second) of torts	Professional standards	Ultramares criticised	Reliance upon legal writers and reviewers	Other matters
19.	Reference				
20.	Reference to the Restatement of Torts 1938 version		Re. privity and its foreseeability	Prosser, Hawkins, Richardson	
21.					A 'case by case' approach should be adopted
23.	Reference to 1st Restatement § 551				
24.	The 1st Restatement should be used in order to evaluate the 'class'			Prosser	Statute law could have extended liability but was not. Conflict of actions between states argued
25.				Prosser, Holmes, Bohlen	Case by case approach, The 'overall policy' test
26.	Reference made to the 1st Restatement but not accepted by the court				
27.	Full reliance upon the Restatement. Actually foreseen and limited class		*Ultramares* criticised	Seavey (re. *Ultramares* criticism)	
29.	Reliance upon the Restatement	Importance to fully distinguish in auditors' report re. audit work done	*Ultramares* criticised	*Marquette Law review* (re. *Ultramares* deficiencies)	
30.	Reliance upon the Restatement	Importance of the certificate wording, re. guarantee, etc., and informing when an error had been found	*Ultramares* criticised re. undesirability of the third party suffering	Katsoris, Levitin, *et al.* Prosser	The 'small group' exposure to liability. (What is small?)
31.	Implied that the court here would not accept Restatement, but it was analysed	Discussion of the standards of audit practice	Criticism of *Ultramares* in the case not accepted		
32.	Reliance upon Restatement re. the foreseen and limited class. Law in Texas	Auditing standards discussed		Hallet, Hawkins, Collins	
33.	Reliance here in addition to the *Rusch* test, some doubt re. class limits	The accountants' letter and opinion very significant			Reference to the State 'Public Accountancy' Act
34.	Cited re abandoning of doctrine of privity	Code of ethics and the standards of the profession important			

SCHEDULE Bc *Cont.*

Case No. (Sch. A)	Restatement (second) of torts	Professional standards	Ultramares criticised	Reliance upon legal writers and reviewers	Other matters
35.		Importance established of the AICPA standards	The criticism in *Ultramares* recognised, but no precedent for the disclaimed opinion		
36.	Considered a better rule than previously applied in similar cases	AICPA standards also recognised			

(v) Schedule C: Fraud and deceit

The rules or formulae for a successful action in fraud and deceit have been laid down and applied without controversy ever since *Derry* v. *Peek*[10] (as reiterated in *Ultramares*). This schedule heads the main rules in the deceit actions, namely, intent to deceive, wilful and recklessness, pretension of knowledge. The section 'inference of fraud' stems from the opinion in *Ultramares*. Again a miscellaneous section, 'other matters', is included where the court has stressed a particular doctrine considered significant.

Actions against accountants alleging fraud and deceit are brought less frequently than actions alleging negligence; consequently no further analysis of these types of actions has been included.

V REASONS FOR PREPARING THE SCHEDULES IN THIS FORMAT

1. An analysis of the most important cases over time highlights the trends and developments in the law.
2. It is easier to discern the elements of any action considered significant by the courts.
3. The analysis establishes the major elements which can then provide a solid base for comparison with English developments.
4. The format also draws attention to aspects in a case which could easily be overlooked in a written discussion.
5. One particular aspect of the law can be inspected and analysed without recourse to the complete range of cases.
6. Schedule A highlights immediately facts which would not have been appreciated from a written analysis, for example the number of suits in the last decade when compared with the whole period of common law development.
7. The schedules, apart from pointing out the elements relied upon in a judgment, also indicate factors *not* considered by the court. In *MacNerland*[11] as an example, no mention was made of *Glanzer*, since *Ultramares* was blindly followed. This is significant considering the case was decided in 1973 and many judgments around that time had already weakened the *Ultramares* precedent.

SCHEDULE C Fraud and deceit

Case No. (Sch. A)	Intent to deceive	Wilfulness and recklessness	Pretension of knowledge	Inference of fraud	Other factors
10.		The accountants certified in their opinion something as fact . . .	. . . to their knowledge if false then cannot be exonerated. Reasonable ground for belief test. *Derry v. Peek*	Negligence does not preclude an inference (*Derry v. Peek*). See the degrees of negligence	
11.			Certification made knowingly or pretense of knowledge when there is none. Then action can be brought		Specific disclaimer in report therefore no pretense of 'knowing'
12.	Intent and knowledge and false representation can maintain an action of fraud	See intent	See intent		
13.	Presupposes both an untrue statement and fraudulent intent	Proof needed that false representation has been made either knowingly or without belief in its truth or in a reckless disregard of whether it be true or false. Honest belief needed			Distinction is needed between 'opinion' and knowledge. Only 2nd is actionable in deceit if false
14.	Found in this case when covering letter sent after accounts 30 days later	This may take the place of the need to prove deliberate intention		If negligence was gross, or blindness not equal to fraud may result in an inference of fraud	Representations do not have to be the sole inducing cause
16.		Refusal to see the obvious or to investigate the doubtful. (*State Street Trust* relied upon)		If gross negligence then can infer . . .	cf. with faulty judgment
17.					No evidence was produced that the statements were false. Needed in deceit action
21.		Was the plaintiff induced to buy on reliance?			What was the materiality of the alleged concealment

SCHEDULE C   *cont.*

Case No. (Sch. A)	Intent to deceive	Wilfulness and recklessness	Pretension of knowledge	Inference of fraud	Other factors
26.				Gross negligence may be an inference of fraud	
27.	Loss should be placed on the shoulders of the misrepresentor if intent	See inference		Heedless conduct may create an inference of fraud	Action in fraud if more flexible may deter future harm
35.				An honest blunder is no inference of fraud	

VI US COMMON LAW ANALYSIS – THE PAST

(i) Introduction

The fact that in the US accounting is a relatively new profession is witnessed from the lack of established legal authority in the area of accountants' legal liability. For example, one commentator[12] wrote in December 1936 that the 'extent a public accountant is liable for failure to portray through the audit report the true financial position of the subject is not definitely established'.

Compare this with the position in England where much of the law. regarding the extent of an auditor's liability had already been established by the end of the nineteenth century.[13]

This factor has had two important influences upon the development of American law. Firstly it had to rely in its infancy upon English precedent and, secondly, the law developed in a more modern and realistic environment.

The law of torts in relation to accountants' liability to third parties is still not resolved.[14] It could be argued that the uncertainty is due to the American system, where the doctrine of *stare decisis* so rigidly adhered to in England is not faithfully followed.[15] The accountant is currently facing twin evils; an explosion of litigation and uncertainty in the law by which he is being tried.[16]

(ii) The origins of the law of torts in the US:
Effects of English precedent

In 1905 the Supreme Court of New York[17] established that the public accountant was a member of a skilled profession, and as such subject to the same rules of liability for negligence as members of other skilled professions. The court established the basis of liability as being that:

> Every man who offers his services to another . . . assumes the duty to exercise in the employment such skill as he possesses with reasonable care and diligence. In all those employments where peculiar skill is requisite, if one offers his services, he is understood as holding himself out to the public as possessing the degree of skill commonly possessed by others in the same employment and, if his pretensions are unfounded, he commits a specie of fraud upon every man that employs him in reliance on his public profession.[18]

Two main elements therefore are present; firstly, the accountant is recognised as a possessor of certain skills at a certain standard, and secondly he assumes a duty to perform such skills to that standard.

The law of torts in the area of liability to third parties recognises that a duty owing is a fundamental prerequisite. When undertaking an audit or accounting engagement the accountant will be under a contract to the client engaging him. He owes a duty to his client and any breach of this duty will allow the injured party cause for action either through tort or breach of contract. If he owes no duty to the party who seeks to hold him liable, he cannot be liable in damages, no matter how negligent he may have been and no matter what damage the other party may have sustained.[19] This is an ancient legal doctrine recognised on both sides of the Atlantic and still upheld.[20] Forming a contract normally establishes a duty, and this presents the foundation for an action. Unfortunately, the origin of a duty is harder to establish in the relationship between an accountant and a third party.

The third party is someone outside the contractual relationship. In order to bring an action for negligence the privity requirement was essential. Anyone who had passed no consideration or who had no other legal relationship was without privity of contract. The third party therefore having no cause for action, in negligence, could only bring an action under fraud and deceit doctrines – which were harder to prove and less likely of recovery.[21]

The first major inroads into the doctrine of privity concerned the damage suffered. In England, *Winterbottom* v. *Wright*[22] had effectively curtailed action by third parties, regardless of the damages suffered. In America, however, the importance of allowing recovery to injured third parties who had obviously been wronged was the first major break from English authority. In *Thomas* v. *Winchester*,[23] the court held that an original vendor of negligently labelled drugs should be liable for the injuries suffered by a plaintiff. The law, for the first time in the State of New York, thus imposed upon a wrong-doer a duty to avoid acts in their nature likely to endanger the lives of others.[24] In *MacPherson* v. *Buick Motor Co.*[25] the *Thomas* principle was extended beyond items – such as poison and explosives – which 'in their normal operation are implements of destruction'. The defective motor vehicle in *MacPherson* was not an implement of destruction but if negligently manufactured would in all probability become an implement of 'danger', and likely to place life and limb in peril. In addition to the element of danger the court considered there should also be knowledge that the thing would be used by persons other than the purchaser;

and then, irrespective of contract, the manufacturer of this article of danger would be under a duty to make it carefully.

At the time of *MacPherson* the limits of the doctrine it established were still uncertain in England. *Winterbottom* v. *Wright* is often cited.[26] The defendant undertook to provide a mail coach to carry mail bags. The coach broke down from latent defects in its construction. The defendant, however, was not the manufacturer. The court held that he was not liable for injuries to a passenger. This decision was criticised in *Heaven* v. *Pender*[27] because it did not suggest a duty aside from the special contract which was the plaintiff's main reliance.[28]

From the analysis of the recent English case of *Hedley Byrne* it is interesting to note that the House of Lords still had to consider the physical/economic injury distinction.[29] In America *MacPherson* had already commenced to break down the distinction's importance in negligence actions.

In *Landell* v. *Lybrand*, which was the first American case involving independent accountants,[30] the court was unwilling to extend liability where the damage suffered involved the diminution of financial estate. Despite proof that the accountants had produced misrepresentations and had undertaken a careless audit no action was allowed in negligence. As the judges of the Supreme Court of Pennsylvania stated: 'There was no contractual relations between the plaintiff and defendants, and, if there is any liability from them to him, it must arise out of some breach of duty, for there is no averment that they made the report with intent to deceive him';[31] here the duty and privity doctrines are equated, and for an action to succeed by a third party, a case would need to be brought for fraud and deceit requiring proof of an intent to deceive.

At the beginning of this century therefore a pattern of the law of torts developed as depicted in Table X. The table shows the importance courts attached to the damages suffered. If the damage was 'physical' (danger to life and limb) then this fact would constitute an exception to the privity doctrine and an action was maintainable in negligence. If the loss was financial, as will usually be the case for those relying upon an accountant's financial statements, there was reluctance to allow recovery in a negligence action. Up to the 1920s therefore the only remedy for a third party against an accountant would have been to prove him fraudulent, mere negligence was inadequate.

In 1922 a further extension of the law of negligent misrepresentation took place. In that year the courts handed down the case of

Glanzer v. *Shepard*,[32] which although it remained dormant for some time after *Ultramares* had weakened its impact, was to prove a very significant precedent in the 1960s and 1970s.[33]

TABLE X   The law of torts

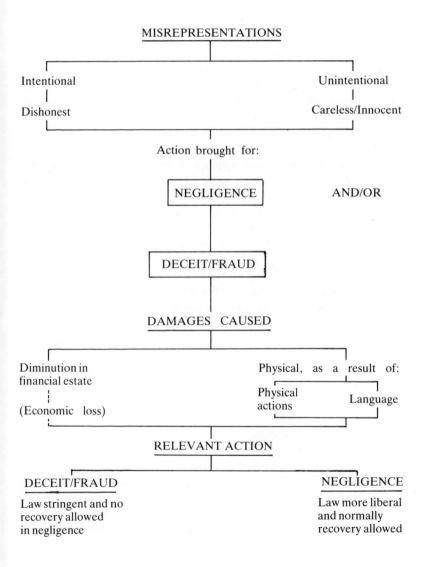

(iii) *Glanzer* v. *Shepard* – Recovery by a third party for financial loss

The plaintiffs purchased some merchandise from a merchant, payment for which was to be dependant upon a certificate of weight produced by the defendant, a 'public weigher'. The defendant certified the weight and forwarded to the plaintiffs, as well as the merchant who had contracted for the certificate, copies of the certificate of weight. The certificates proved incorrect and the plaintiffs overpaid as a result. They sued the weigher for negligence in order to recover the amount overpaid. This was a representative third party case where reliance upon a misrepresentation had caused financial loss (overpayment on the purchases). Relying upon previous precedent the plaintiff would have had no case, unless fraud could have been proved. The court, however, allowed recovery. The significant aspects of the case are discussed under three headings.

(1) Duty

In a negligence action it has been seen[34] that for recovery there must be proved to be a duty owing to the parties in the case. On the basis that duty was coterminous with contractual privity, there was no duty owing because the purchaser of the goods was outside the contract the weigher had with the wholesaler. However, Cardozo, C.J., presiding over the case, considered that in such cases the law should impose a duty.[35] The contract to weigh the goods resulted in a certificate which was the very 'end and aim' of the transaction; indeed, the contract would not have taken place if the weigher had not produced the certificate. In addition, the weigher had knowledge that the third party was going to rely upon the certificate, and had in fact sent him a copy for this very purpose. The duty, it was held, did not need to be looked at in terms of contract or privity. Given the transaction and the relation between the parties the duty of care was imposed by law,[36] even though that duty had an origin which was not exclusively contractual.

(2) Proximity and the class

The doctrine of proximity or remoteness was also a significant factor closely related to the creation of a duty. In *Glanzer* the actual identity of the third party was known by the parties from the commencement of the contract. When compared with *Savings Bank* v. *Ward*,[37] previous authority, the defendant had no knowledge that a report was to be used by certain third parties, and recovery was not permitted.

Glanzer therefore endorsed the doctrine of the 'foreseen' third party; a party so 'close' as to imply a contractual relationship. This doctrine was compared by Gardozo to the 'third party beneficiary contract' doctrine but was distinguished from it.[38] The case was not founded on the fact that the third party was a 'beneficiary' but on the basis that he was 'foreseen' as being affected by the representations.

(3) Negligence
A further distinction analysed in this case has been advanced as weakening its importance, and has been relied upon by those courts wishing to follow a more traditional *Ultramares* line.[39] The public weigher was considered to have been guilty not only of negligent words (a factor that had not been grounds for recovery of damages up to that time in tort law) but also of negligent actions (that is to say the physical act of weighing, a factor which did have precedent).[40] This was a fine distinction to make because in any vocation where the production of a certificate is the end product (that is words or written representations) there is certain to have been some 'action' necessary in the production of the certificate. The auditor, for example, will produce a report based upon the physical act of testing the books of account and physically comparing them to the financial statements. It is uncertain whether this distinction was introduced so as to soften the impact of the new law established in the case; Cardozo himself admitted that the line between these diverse liabilities was difficult to draw: '[it] does not lose for that reason its correspondence with realities. Life has relations not capable always of division into inflexible compartments. The moulds expand and shrink'.[41]

(iv) Reliance on *Glanzer*

In *International Products Co.* v. *Erie Railway Co.*[42] the court admitted that it was committed to a rule for negligent language; however, it wanted to establish a more distinct test for liability than by letting 'every casual response' give rise to a cause of action. The court therefore decided that primarily there must be a duty to give correct information. This in turn involved the following considerations:

1. There must have been knowledge, or its equivalent, that the information was desired for a serious purpose.
2. He to whom it was given must have intended to rely and act upon it.
3. If the information was false or erroneous, he would because of it

have been injured in person or property.

4. Finally, the relationship of the parties, arising out of contract or otherwise must have been such that in morals and good conscience the one had the right to rely upon the other for information and the other giving the information owed a duty to give it with care.[43]

Cardozo stated that in one respect the *International Products Co.* case was in advance of anything decided in *Glanzer*. 'The latter case suggest[ed] that the liability there enforced was not one for the mere utterance of words without due consideration, but for a negligent service, the act of weighing, which happened to find in the words of the certificate its culmination and its summary. . . . The rule in the case of the Erie Railroad show[ed] that the rendition of a service [was] at most a mere circumstance and not an indispensable condition. The Erie was not held for negligence in the rendition of a service. It was held for words and nothing more.'[44]

(v) The *Ultramares* case

In 1931 the New York Court of Appeals heard the case of *Ultramares Corporation* v. *Touche et al.*[45] Defendants were co-partners in a firm of certified public accountants, Touche, Niven & Co. They had been hired by a company (Stern) to prepare and certify a balance sheet exhibiting the financial condition of Stern as of 31 December 1923. From experience, the accountants knew that Stern used these certified financial statements to obtain finance for its operations, and so, on certifying the statements, the accountants provided thirty-two copies of the report and accounts. The certified balance sheet showed Stern with a net worth of over one million dollars when in reality the concern was insolvent. The Ultramares Corporation, who were bankers and factors, received a set of the accounts from Stern and relied upon them in advancing loans.

Ultramares was first approached for loans in March 1924 and continued throughout the year to advance money to Stern, the final loan of $165,000 being made in December. Stern was declared bankrupt in early January 1925. Ultramares sued the accountants for common law deceit and negligence.[46]

Confining, in this section, the discussion to the negligence action the following arguments were advanced (again by Cardozo) as to why the accountants could not be liable even though a jury had proclaimed them guilty of negligence in the audit and the preparation of their report.

(1) The duty

The court recognised the common law duty owing to the accountants' clients and also the duty to third parties to whom Stern showed the certified financial statements. This secondary duty, however, had to be limited to a duty to make representations without 'fraud' since there was notice in the circumstances of the transaction that the Stern company was not intending to keep the certificates to itself. In answering the question: 'Did the accountants owe a duty to the third party to make it without negligence?' Cardozo stated:

> If liability for negligence exists, a thoughtless slip or blunder, the failure to detect a theft or forgery beneath the cover of deceptive entries, may expose accountants to a liability in an indeterminate amount for an indeterminate time to an indeterminate class. The hazards of a business conducted on these terms are so extreme as to enkindle doubt whether a flaw may not exist in the implication of a duty that exposes to these consequences.[47]

Cardozo, therefore, dismissed the theory that a duty was owing. His opinion was based purely on a pragmatic policy decision so as to avoid the possibility of making business transactions any more hazardous and exposing accountants to a wider liability. It was thought that a widened liability may have threatened the continued existence of the accounting profession.[48]

(2) Privity and Glanzer distinguished

Having re-established that the duty owed to third parties could only be based upon an action in fraud, the court then turned to the privity doctrine. Recognition was given to the trend of recent years which had created exceptions to the privity requirements. However the inroads being made were in each case considered to be as a result of 'physical force generating physical injury'.[49] In establishing that similar inroads could not be made in the instant case (where no physical act took place) the court distinguished the facts with those of *Glanzer* (amongst other precedent).

In *Glanzer* the transmission of the certificate was the 'end and aim' of the transaction, and the case could have been covered by the *Lawrence* v. *Fox*[50] doctrine or even by the terms of contract law. The bond was so close as to approach that of privity. In *Ultramares* however there was no contractual relationship as no one could assess the indeterminate class of persons who might rely upon the certified accounts of Stern. Further the service provided in *Glanzer* was primarily for the benefit of the third party, whereas in *Ultramares* the benefit was primarily for Stern.

Another distinction was that *Glanzer* allowed recovery not because of the mere utterance of words but for negligent actions. In *Ultramares* negligence could be inferred from the negligent transmission of words and nothing more.[51]

The logic or validity of the various distinctions made by Cardozo has been questioned[52] by a number of recent court opinions and legal writers in the US. One can sense from a study of *Glanzer* the desire to expand the liability of those producing negligent misrepresentations to all parties who can reasonably be foreseen as being affected by them (as with physical injury). The social desirability of making the representor, rather than the injured and innocent third party, suffer because of his negligence would seem justifiable. *Glanzer* could have been a step in that direction, had not the decision in *Ultramares* implied a 'social desirability' of *not* extending liability to an indeterminate class.

The fear of extending liability to accountants, envisaged under *Glanzer*, was considered a dangerous 'social' precedent by the court, essentially because the accountants' reports were available (it was thought) to such a wide variation of third parties. It could be argued that the accountant knows that his report forming part of a company's financial statements will be sent out to all the shareholders, who are therefore foreseen as receiving the statements. Logically, the decision in *Ultramares* could have been that the shareholders (at the very least) were a determinate class, and a duty should extend to them just as much as to the client – even if the duty does not extend to creditors and other third parties.

One commentator, reviewing the case immediately after its decision, considered that the 'pragmatic business policy' of refusing an extension of duty was justifiable. To allow such claims as would arise under a broader definition of care would amount to the 'abdication of the court's power where it was needed most. . . . It could not push the matter over to a jury upon the ritual of a 'foreseeability formula' because there was no legal rule or formula to really guide it'. The court 'was at large in a world of intricate business relations and charged with the obligation of marking the boundaries of governmental control over business practices'.[53]

The restrictive judgment in *Ultramares* is based therefore on a fear of extending liability to unprecedented limits. This extension of liability could have reflected upon the accounting profession's ability to continue and develop, remembering that in 1931 it was still a relatively new profession whose importance was recognised by industry and the courts alike.[54]

Another reason why the negligence action was not granted was because it would move the doctrine of negligence so close to that of fraud as to make the law in the two separate doctrines coterminous. Precedent had always maintained the barrier between fraud and negligence, and it was considered *Ultramares* did not justify the destruction of such a barrier.[55]

VII SUMMARY

Although *Ultramares* provided the precedent for negligence and deceit actions for at least thirty years, it is evident from the above analysis that uncertainties in the law were still prevalent. The next chapter analyses the law of negligence in the light of the American cases which have occurred since the early 1960s. It is during this current period that major criticism has been voiced against the *Ultramares* decision and its hold has been gradually weakened.

NOTES

[1] *The Index of Legal Periodicals* (New York: H.W. Wilson Company, in co-operation with the American Association of Law Libraries, 1966–76).

[2] AICPA, *The Accountants' Index* 1966–76.

[3] *Ultramares Corporation* v. *Touche et al.* 255 N.Y. 170, 174 N.E. 441 (1931).

[4] *Glanzer* v. *Shepard* 233 N.Y. 236, 135 N.E. 275 (1922), affirming 194 App. Div. 693, 186 N.Y. Supp 88 (1921).

[5] *Biakanja* v. *Irving* 49 Cal. 2d 647, 320 P.2d 16 (1958).

[6] *Anderson* v. *Boone County Abstract Co.* 418 S.W.2d 123 (1967).

[7] There were no significant cases in negligence between 1931 and 1958.

[8] *Hedley Byrne & Co. Ltd.* v. *Heller & Partners Ltd.* [1964] A.C. 465.

[9] See Chapter 5, text accompanying notes 90 to 104 *infra*.

[10] *Derry* v. *Peek* (1889) 37 Ch. D. 341, 14 App. Cas. 337.

[11] *MacNerland* v. *Barnes* 129 Ga App 367, 199 S.E.2d (1973).

[12] W. R. MacMillan, 'Sources and Extent of Liability of a Public Accountant', 15 *Chicago-Kent Law Review* 1,1 (Dec. 1936).

[13] *Leeds Estate, Building and Investment Co.* v. *Shepherd* (1887) 36 Ch.D. 787. (An auditor is not bound to do more than exercise reasonable care and skill in the audit.)

Re Kingston Cotton Mill Company (No. 2) [1896] 2 Ch. 279, 65 L.J. Ch. 673, 74 L.T.R. 568. (The approach an auditor should take in carrying out an audit – also the position regarding contracts and stocktaking.)
Re London and General Bank (No.2) [1895] 2 Ch. 673 (Auditors' duty to report.)
Derry v. *Peek* (1889) 37 Ch.D. 341, 14 App. Cas. 337 (Auditors' position in negligence and in fraud.)

[14] W. L. Prosser, a leading authority on the law of torts, wrote in March 1966 'the case [*Ultramares*] . . . was one of misrepresentation causing pecuniary loss to a third person who acted in reliance upon it, but to whom it was not made. It is in this area that the assault upon the citadel [of privity] has made, during the intervening thirty-five years, the least headway, and has broken down into a tangle of more or less unconnected struggles which are apparently making no great progress in any definite direction'. 'Misrepresentation and third persons', 19 *Vanderbilt Law Review* 231, 231 (1966).

[15] See the comments in the American case *Westerhold* v. *Carroll* 419 S.W. 2d 73, 79 (1967).

[16] See Chapter 1, text accompanying notes 8 to 12.

[17] *Smith* v. *London Assurance Corporation* 96 N.Y.S. 820 (1905).

[18] The court quoted 3 *Cooley on Torts* (4th ed.) 335, s 473. This quote also appears in MacMillan, note 12 *supra*, Prosser, note 14 *supra*, D. Y. Causey, *Duties and Liabilities of the CPA*' (rev. ed.) (The Bureau of Business Research, University of Texas, 1976).

[19] See *Landell* v. *Lybrand* 264 Pa 406, 107 A 783 (1919) and *Ultramares Corp.* v. *Touche*, note 3 *supra*.

[20] For the importance of this doctrine see the analysis of the *Hedley Byrne* decision in Chapter 6, *infra*.

[21] *Derry* v. *Peek* (1889) 37 Ch.D. 341, 14 App.Cas. 337.

[22] *Winterbottom* v. *Wright* (1842) 10 M. & W. 109. The Court of Exchequer denied the plaintiff any right of recovery on the ground that there was no privity of contract between the parties, the agreement having been made by defendant with the postmaster general alone. 'If the plaintiff can sue' said Lord Abinger, 'every passenger or even any person passing along the road who was injured by the upsetting of the coach might bring a similar action. Unless we confine the operation of such contracts as this to the parties who enter into them the most absurd and outrageous consequences to which I can see no limit would ensue.' (Cf. with Cardozo C. J. in *Ultramares*.) Cited in *MacPherson* v. *Buick*, note 25 *infra*.

[23] *Thomas* v. *Winchester* (1852) 2 Seld 297

[24] Cardozo, C.J. in *MacPherson* v. *Buick Motor Co., infra*, analysed the trend in this aspect of the law of torts from its origins. He cited a number of cases where physical damage had been incurred and recovery was allowed, including: *Loop* v. *Litchfield* 142 N.Y. 494, 1 Am.Rep. 513 (defective circular saw), *Losee* v. *Chute* 51 N.Y. 494, 10 Am.Rep. 638 (steam boiler), *Devlin* v. *Smith* 89 N.Y. 470, 42 Am. Rep. 311 (scaffolding), *Statler* v. *Ray Mfg. Co.* 195 N.Y. 478, 88 N.E. 1063 (coffee urn).

[25] *MacPherson* v. *Buick Motor Co.* 217 N.Y. 382, 111 N.E. 1050 (1916).

[26] See for example *MacPherson* 111 N.E. 1050, 1054.

[27] *Heaven* v. *Pender* (1883) 11 Q.B.D. 503.

[28] *MacPherson* 111 N.E. 1050, 1054. Other English cases cited by the court were *Earl* v. *Lubbock* [1905] 1 K.B. 253 which reflected *Winterbottom*, *supra*, and a later case *White* v. *Steadman* [1913] 13 K.B. 340, 348 which followed and cited *Thomas* v. *Winchester* as did *Dominion Natural Gas Co.* v. *Collins* [1909] A.C. 640, 646. The underlying principle of *Devlin* v. *Smith* that one who invites another to make use of an appliance is bound to exercise reasonable care was followed in two further English cases, *Caledonian Ry Co.* v. *Mulholland* [1898] A.C. 216, 227 and *Indermaur* v. *Dames* (1866) L.R. 1 C.P. 274.

[29] Chapter 6, *infra*.

[30] K. I. Solomon, 'Ultramares Revisited: A Modern Study of Accountants' Liability to the Public', 18 *De Paul Law Review* 56, 62 (1968).

[31] *Landell* v. *Lybrand* 264 Pa 406, 107 A 783 (1919).

[32] 233 N.Y. 236, 135 N.E. 275 (1922), affirming 194 App. Div. 693, 186 N.Y. Supp. 88 (1921).

[33] See Chapter 5, and the Matrix of Cases (Table IX).

[34] Text accompanying notes 18 *et seq, supra*.

[35] *Glanzer* v. *Shepard* 135 N.E. 275, 275 (1922).

[36] 135 N.E. 275, 275–6.

[37] *Savings Bank* v. *Ward* 100 U.S. 195 (1879).

[38] 'Third party beneficiary contracts' were established in *Lawrence* v. *Fox* 20 N.Y. 268 (1859).
This case permitted a third party to maintain an action on a contract made between other persons for his benefit. In *Seaver* v. *Ransom* (1918) 224 N.Y. 233, 120 N.E. 639, 2 AL.R. 1187, which relied upon *Lawrence*, the general rule was stated that privity between a plaintiff and a defendant is necessary to the maintenance of an action on the contract, the consideration being furnished by the party to whom the promise was made. The right of a beneficiary to sue on a contract made expressly for his benefit has been fully recognised in many American jurisdictions, and is now said to be the prevailing rule in America (*Hendrick* v. *Lindsay* 93 U.S. 143, 23 L.Ed 855, 1876). The reason for this legal doctrine is that it is just and practical to permit the person for whose benefit the contract is made to enforce it against one whose duty it is to pay (*Seaver* v. *Ransom, supra*, p. 640). In England there is no equivalent doctrine, and the law remains that a contract cannot be enforced by or against a person who is not a party (7 *Halsbury's Laws of England* 342, 343 and Jenks *Digest of English Civil Law* s. 229, cited by *Seaver* v. *Ransom* ibid).

[39] See Schedule Bb, *supra*.

[40] See Table X, *supra*.

[41] *Glanzer* v. *Shepard* 135 N.E. 275, 276–7 (1922).

[42] *International Products Co.* v. *Erie Railway Co.* 244 N.Y. 331, 155 N.E. 662 (1927).

[43] 155 N.E. 662, 664.

[44] *Ultramares*, 174 N.E. 441, 446.

[45] 255 N.Y. 170, 174 N.E. 441 (1931).

[46] 174 N.E. 441, 441–3.

[47] 174 N.E. 441, 444. These lines can be directly attributed to Lord Abinger in

Winterbottom v. *Wright*, a case which Cardozo did so much to discredit with respect to cases involving physical damages. See Solomon, note 30 *supra*, p.66. For case details see note 22 *supra*.

[48] This pragmatic business policy is termed by some commentators as the 'social utility rationale'. See for example T. J. Fiflis, 'Current Problems of Accountants' Responsibilities to Third Parties' 28 *Vanderbilt Law Review* 31 (1975).

[49] 174 N.E. 441, 445.

[50] *Lawrence* v. *Fox*. 20 N.Y. 268 (1859).

[51] This is open to dispute, however, due to the fact the trial term jury found the auditors negligent in their audit as well as their report.

[52] Reference can be made to the schedules reproduced in this chapter, especially Schedule Bc, 'Ultramares criticised'. See also Chapter 5, *infra* for a fuller analysis of the present position of *Ultramares*.

[53] L. Green, 'The Judicial Process – *Ultramares Corp.* v. *Touche*' 26 *Illinois Law Review* 49, 50 (1931).

[54] See Chapter 5, for further discussion.

[55] 174 N.E. 441, 448–9.

5 US COMMON LAW ANALYSIS –
THE PRESENT

. . . the *Ultramares* decision, after a long and active life, may now be obsolete.

I INTRODUCTION

As noted in the introductory chapters,[1] the American accountant is at present subjected to an unprecedented amount of litigation brought mostly by third parties.[2] This is despite the efforts of the AICPA to reform auditing standards[3] and accounting principles.[4] Estimates have been made since 1966[5] to establish the extent of this litigation. According to the 1973 Annual Report of Arthur Andersen & Co., there were 500 companies with litigation or claims in process involving auditors at 31 March 1973.[6] Further estimates in 1974 by Liggio,[7] general counsel for Arthur Youngs, put cases pending against accountants somewhere between 500 and 1000.

This chapter analyses the shifting trend in American common law with respect to negligent misrepresentation from the foundations laid in the 1930s.[8] Although a significant portion of the cases outstanding or recently decided will have been class action suits brought under sections of the Federal Securities Laws, there have been comparable developments in the common law resulting in increased litigation against the accountant.[9]

A factor becoming increasingly apparent from the study of recent cases is that the common law doctrines providing the basis for accountants' legal liability to third parties are by no means uniform in the various jurisdictions in the United States.[10] As Solomon notes:

It is generally agreed upon by jurists and legal commentators that the law of accountants' liability to third parties, although giving the surface impression of well-settled doctrine, is still far from being crystal clear even at this late and crucial date.[11]

As the previous chapter has shown, much of the current uncertainty of the law, which is analysed in this chapter, is attributed to legal decisions of the 1930s.[12]

II THE QUESTIONING OF *ULTRAMARES*[13]

The previous chapter noted that the 'social utility rationale' or public policy was one major doctrine established by Cardozo, C.J., restricting actions in negligence[14] against accountants. This doctrine has been criticised on a number of grounds.

(i) Compared with previous precedent

Solomon has analysed the illogicality[15] of the social utility rationale by comparing it with Cardozo's decision in *MacPherson*.[16] *MacPherson* rejected the rationale of *Winterbottom* v. *Wright*[17] in that an action could not be brought by a third party outside the contract. In Lord Abinger's words:

> Unless we confine the operation of such contracts as this to the parties who entered into them, the most absurd and outrageous consequences, to which I can see no limit would ensue.[18]

In *MacPherson*, Cardozo concluded:

> There is nothing anomalous in a rule which imposes upon A, who has contracted with B, a duty to C and D and others according as he knows that the subject matter of the contract is intended for their use.[19]

Solomon contended[20] that the *MacPherson* decision did not 'jibe' with the decision in *Ultramares* where Cardozo expressed fear of exposing accountants to a liability to an 'indeterminate class'.[21] Following on from *MacPherson* Cardozo should have held in *Ultramares* that 'the *identity* of future users of the financial statements and reports prepared by accountants need not be foreseeable to those accountants as a precondition to the imposition of liability for their own negligent conduct'.[22]

(ii) The need for a 'social utility rationale'

The *Ultramares* decision needs to be considered in terms of the needs of society at the time it was decided.[23] In the 1930s the American accounting profession was different in concept. The purpose of an audit was to enable the owners of companies to detect fraud within the company or to detect other director or employee irregularity. Those likely to be affected by an auditor's negligence were therefore already in a contractual relationship. The auditor's role and responsibility has now shifted. It can no longer be held true that the auditor has only incidental responsibility to third party users of financial statements.[24] In the 1930s[25] the profession was in its infancy and the *Ultramares* decision was laid down to protect the profession's growth.[26]

The profession is now fully established and a multi-million dollar industry.[27] The negligence formula which has protected the accounting profession since the 1930s has begun to be questioned. Commentators[28] ask why the profession should not be held liable, if it fails to comply with its standards of care. Why should an innocent third party suffer as a result of relying upon the statements of an accountant? They consider that the accounting profession should now take on the responsibilities of the modern industrial system of which it forms so important a part. These arguments have meant that the social utility rationale established in *Ultramares* is now losing its importance in the place of most significance – the courts.[29]

In *Rusch Factors* v. *Levin*[30] the court asked: 'Why should an innocent reliant party be forced to carry the weighty burden of an accountant's professional malpractice?'[31] It considered that the risk of loss could more easily be distributed and jointly spread by imposing it upon the accounting profession, which is able to pass the cost of insuring against the risk to its clients, who in turn can pass on this cost to the entire consuming public.[32] This, it was thought, would be a more equitable solution than that where an innocent third party has to suffer the total financial burden and is unable to pass on any cost whatsoever.[33]

The social utility rationale has also been questioned by courts when dealing with other professions.[34] In *Rozny* v. *Marnul*[35] which was concerned with an inaccurate title certificate prepared by a surveyor, the court agreed that the 'unknown and unlimited liability factor, so ably stated by Mr Justice Cardozo . . . is not to be lightly discounted.'[36] However, the defendant might reasonably have foreseen that third parties would rely upon his certificates in the purchase of surveyed property. Under such circumstances the situation is not 'one fraught with such an overwhelming potential liability as to dictate a contrary result, for the class of persons who might foreseeably use this (certificate) is rather narrowly limited, if not exclusively so, to those who deal with the surveyed property as purchasers or lenders.'[37]

The doctrine in *Ultramares* concerning the social utility rationale is doubted therefore from two standpoints: (i) *the need* for such a rationale no longer exists, and (ii) the risk of unlimited liability no longer remains a valid argument. In the accounting context the risk of indeterminate liability is unwarranted. The shareholders receiving financial statements are known by name and address and their numbers are limited. If the statements they receive cannot be relied upon for investment purposes, as is implied by the doctrine, then surely the financial statements serve little purpose? Solomon[38] has gone further than this in his analysis of *Ultramares*. As he pointed out, Cardozo might easily (relying upon his own precedent) have said:

> After all, since the accountant knows that his report and certified financial statements are normally included as part and parcel of his client's annual report *to stockholders, creditors, potential investors and financial analysts*, this class of ultimate readers of his report and statements is certainly foreseeable to him even though the identity of the specific members of this class is not known to him. Hence, those users of financial statements are beneficiaries of a duty of care owed to them by the accountant; and, if he should be negligent, he must, in fairness and right, compensate those who have been injured by his wrongful act or conduct.[39] (Emphasis added)

The discussion concerning the responsibility of the accountant to those beyond the traditional client/accountant relationship leads to a third factor giving rise to criticism of *Ultramares*.

(iii) *Ultramares* and the primary benefit doctrine

When distinguishing the facts of *Ultramares* with *Glanzer* v. *Shepard*[40] Cardozo stated that ' . . . the service was primarily for the benefit of the Stern Company, a convenient instrumentality for use in the development of the business, and only incidentally or collaterally for the use of those to whom Stern and his associates might exhibit [the financial statement] thereafter. Foresight of these possibilities may change with liability for fraud. The conclusion does not follow that it will change with liability for negligence.'[41]

This doctrine encapsulates one fundamental aspect of accountants' liability – the extent of the accountants' responsibility. In the sense that *Ultramares* stated in the 1930s that the accountant's function was primarily for the benefit of his client, so in the 1960s and 1970s the accountant's function has been considered[42] *only* relevant in a third party context. Today it would be naive to consider the accountant only responsible to the party who pays him – the accountant has a much heavier burden.[43] One could say the profession is unique in that its responsibilities extend from the client and stockholders, to creditors, government agencies and potential investors, in fact to everyone within the economic environment.[44]

This position is recognised by the profession. The 1974 Code of Ethics published by the AICPA states that:

A distinguishing mark of a professional is his acceptance of respon-sibility to the public. . . . The ethical Code of the American Institute emphasises the profession's responsibility to the public, a responsi-bility that has grown as the number of investors has grown, as the relationship between corporate managers and stockholders has become more impersonal and as government increasingly relies on accounting information.[45]

It is interesting to compare the sentiments behind this Code with that of the English Institute who revised their 'Ethics Guide' in August 1975. The first paragraph of the UK code reads:

A member of a profession owes duties to the public, including those who retain or employ him, to the profession itself and to the other members of it.[46]

Although it is recognised that the accountant owes a duty to the client it is also imperative that he remain independent of that client, in every way, when undertaking the auditing obligations. The very basis of independence is that the public (the third party) may rely upon the reports of the accountant which form an important part of the company's financial statements.

The insistence upon independence and the trend which made the accounting profession recognise its duty towards the public did not develop, however, until after the *Ultramares* decision was handed down.[47] In the present economic environment some would consider the public is the accountant's most important 'client'.[48] The importance of the public (that is to say the third party) was even evident a very short time after *Ultramares*.[49]

These sections have analysed the reasons why the *Ultramares* decision, which for over thirty years was ruling law in the field of accountants' liability to third parties, has begun to be questioned. Surprisingly, it is only in the last decade that the weight of public opinion and criticism has filtered through to court opinion and changes in the law. 'Hence' as Fiflis states 'the *Ultramares* decision, after a long and active life may now be obsolete.'[50] One cannot however state emphatically that *Ultramares is* obsolete. The case still has considerable weight and may even be the only case the present-day accountant can profess knowledge of with confidence.[51] The following sections of this chapter will analyse the trend in legal development away from *Ultramares*, influences upon that development and the present standing of the law.

III ANALYSIS OF THE MATRIX AND THE DECLINE OF PRIVITY

(i) The matrix analysis

In the matrix of cases reproduced in Chapter 4[52] certain trends are discernible after Case 33 decided in 1967. This part of the matrix is reproduced as Table XI. The following points are highlighted:

1. The courts in nine out of fifteen cases from Case 33 have distinguished the doctrines of *Glanzer* ('A') and *Ultramares* ('B'). *Glanzer* has become a much more significant precedent.
2. The courts have moved away from blind reliance upon *Ultramares* and have tended to cite and rely upon very recent cases regardless of whether the actions were from the same state or federal jurisdiction. This is evident from the area of the matrix in the bracket marked 'C'.

TABLE XI A section of Table IX

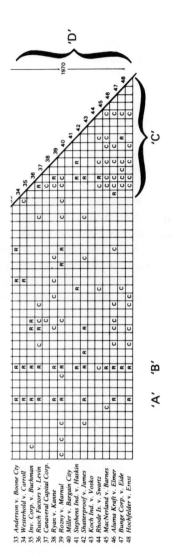

3. Connected with point 2 and the uncertainty of the law following the questioning of *Ultramares* different states come to different conclusions. If the law in the area was certain many fewer cases would have gone to appeal (see 'D'). This is reflected in the cases bracketed 'D' in relation to the rest of the matrix.

In the same way that the matrix indicates the increase in activity in this area of the law, the schedules Ba and Bb also provide an overview of certain trends. These schedules reproduced in Chapter 4 may be referred to as they directly link with the remainder of this chapter.[53]

(ii) Privity

The case analysis indicates increasing uncertainty of the validity of the privity doctrine which had precluded actions against accountants since *Ultramares*.[54] Table XII numerates the thirteen cases since *Biakanja* (1958) on the requirement of privity. This table is meant to represent only the general opinion from a study of the cases in question. It can only act as an indicator of the trend away from privity. (It is obviously not possible to isolate the entire argument of an opinion into one succinct heading, as used in the table.)

TABLE XII Privity (since 1958)

	Cases
Required per *Ultramares*	4
Not required if the '*Winterbottom* test' satisfied[55]	3
An 'unsatisfactory yardstick' (liability per duty owed)	1
Not required if third party member of limited class	1
Not required	4

In an action for fraud, privity of contract is no defence. This rule was stated in *Ultramares* and has been followed ever since. The doctrine is that an *intentionally* misrepresenting accountant is liable to all those persons whom he should reasonably have foreseen would be injured by his misrepresentation.[56] In such a case neither actual knowledge by the accountant of the third person's reliance nor quantitative limitation of the class of reliant persons is requisite to recovery for fraud.[57]

This rule also prevails when the misrepresenting accountant's conduct is heedless enough to raise an inference of fraud.[58]

In negligence, however, liability has not gone to this extent for two reasons: (i) for fear of making negligence coterminous with fraud and (ii) because of the public policy reasons expounded in *Ultramares*. In *Rusch Factors* the court considered that an accountant should take on a greater duty to the public. In that case it was asked: 'Wouldn't a rule of foreseeability elevate the cautionary techniques of the accounting profession?'[59] The importance of privity has declined.

The absence of a privity requirement has led the courts to establish different criteria for establishing liability. Since *Rusch Factors* which was supported by *Ryan* v. *Kanne, Rhode Island Hospital*,[60] and *Shatterproof Glass*,[61] the accountant is considered as owing a responsibility to a wider range of parties. As stated in *Fischer* v. *Kletz* it is evident from recent decisions, involving investors and other persons who extend credit to corporations, that the courts have replaced privity and primary benefit with the concepts of good faith and common honesty.[62]

Having recognised that certain jurisdictions have abandoned the privity of contract requirements in third party actions it needs to be stated that there is still a substantial split of authority on the question.[63]

A number of recent decisions have not allowed recovery, the courts taking a traditional *Ultramares* line. One fundamental reason for this traditionalist line is simply the fear of the court overruling established state precedent (under the rule of *stare decisis*). In *Stephens Industries Inc.* v. *Haskins & Sells*[64] (heard in Colorado) the court stated that jurisdictions facing the question had followed the rule and reasoning of *Ultramares*. However, despite considering *Rusch Factors* and *Ryan*, the court stated:

> While success in a case such as this does not necessarily depend on proving that a preponderance of jurisdictions support appellant's view of the law, there must be substantial evidence showing that Colorado would align itself with the developing trend.[65]

In *Investment Corporation of Florida* v. *Buchman* the court stated:

> In Florida no court has been asked to pass upon the question . . . which is, in the absence of fraud, are certified public accountants liable to a known third party for negligence in the preparation of a certified financial statement. . . . [66]

In *MacNelland* v. *Barnes*,[67] (which applied Georgia law), the court
cited both these cases in not allowing recovery to a third party. This
court in fact explicitly stated that the *Ultramares* case seemed to
comport with Georgia law. To support this view further the court cited
cases in Georgia involving attorneys and concluded that 'the necessity
for the attorney-client relationship to be present has been recognised.'[68] After citing cases where the courts had moved from *Ultramares* the court stated:

> We have, nevertheless, found no persuasive authority upholding
> liability where there was both lack of privity and an uncertified
> statement or more particularly an express disclaimer. *Ultramares*
> stands as the majority rule and we see no reason to depart from its
> rationale.[69]

The question of privity remains therefore a doctrine open to dispute.
One can expect that the various state jurisdictions which have not yet
had to tackle the issue with respect to accountants will have to refer
the cases to higher courts. This will mean the law in this area will be
subject to further amendment. The question whether *Ultramares*
will remain as the majority rule when the various states have had
to deal with these cases may then be answered. However the evidence from these cases supports the view that the need for privity is
divided.[70]

The increase in the number of recent cases against accountants may
be directly attributed therefore to the testing of the privity doctrine in
the various American states.

IV THE MOVEMENT BEYOND PRIVITY

(i) Duty and foreseeability

The demise of privity has meant the emergence of other parameters to
assess liability. This has led courts to establish whether there was a
duty owing the third party by the accountant. In *Rozny* v. *Marnul* for
example the judge opened his opinion by stating:

> This process of adhering to or eliminating the privity requirement
> has proved to be an unsatisfactory method of establishing the scope

of tort liability to third persons. Because of the difficulties in applying the rule, courts created exceptions deemed necessary to achieve desirable results which were not always reconcilable. To eliminate any uncertainty still remaining . . . we emphasize that lack of direct contractual relationship between the parties is not a defence in a tort action in this jurisdiction [Illinois]. Thus, tort liability will henceforth be measured by the scope of the duty owed rather than the artificial concepts of privity.[71]

In early cases duty was clearly linked with the privity doctrine as evidenced from *Landell* v. *Lybrand*[72] in 1919: 'There were no contractual relations between the plaintiff and defendants, and, if there is any liability from them to him, it must arrive out of some breach of duty . . . and as no duty rested upon them to him, they cannot be guilty of any negligence of which he can complain.'[73] This rule was strengthened by *Ultramares* where no duty was owed under the social utility rationale of Cardozo.[74] Contrary to these judgments was the view in *Glanzer* where it was held that in the situation present in that case 'the law imposes a duty toward buyer and seller'.[75] The opinion continued that the duty need not be stated in terms of a contractual or privity requirement but growing out of the contract and the relationship of the parties a duty was created.[76]

The trend to determine the duty owing instead of privity restrictions has meant courts have had to rely upon another yardstick to provide the limits of this duty. Does the accountant owe a duty to every third party who might read his certificate, or to a certain defined class of persons? With the objective measure of privity abandoned, the subjective measure of foreseeability has replaced it. This has led to uncertainty.

In *Glanzer* the doctrine of the foreseen third party was established. In *Ultramares* negligence liability was disallowed because of the foreseeability problem of unlimited liability.[77]

In *Texas Tunneling Company* v. *City of Chattanooga, Tenn*, the judge stated that the 'trepidation expressed by the New York court at the unlimited areas of liability . . . may be no more than a tilting at windmills'[78]; the court emphasised this by stating that there were methods for limiting liability for negligent misrepresentation which were 'less artificial and less drastic' than the *Ultramares* rule.[79]

Table XIII represents the extent of the ranges of foreseeability from *Glanzer* to the present from the analysis of cases. The table shows the various descriptions of foreseeability given by the courts so

TABLE XIII Foreseeability in negligence actions to establish duty and responsibility

Class of persons falling within the definition	Case	Description of foreseeability	Cases relying or relied upon
Third party being a 'primary beneficiary' i.e. identity known[80]	Ultramares	No duty owing to anyone who might foreseeably rely on accountants' negligent misrepresentation. Liability should not be imposed for merely negligent misrepresentation to a plaintiff whose reliance thereon the defendant could not specifically anticipate or where the injury to him was not foreseeable	Investment Corpn MacNelland
Identified third party	Anderson	Liability to be extended to identified third party. The representor has special reason to expect that he may act in reliance. (Based upon Prosser, *Torts* analysis)	Biakanja
Known class (identified third parties)	Restatement, Torts (1938) 552[81]	'One who in the course of his business or profession supplies information for the guidance of others in their business transactions is subject to liability for harm caused to them by their reliance upon the information if.... (b) the harm is suffered (i) by the person or one of the class of persons for whose guidance the information was supplied....'	Shatterproof Glass
Unknown third party	Westerhold	Liability extends to a third person although not identified, when the author of the report or certificate knows the recipient intended to supply the information, although the exact identity of the third person receiving the information was not actually known. (Akin to but not as liberal as *Rusch Factors*[31])	Aluma Kraft

Class of persons falling within the definition	Case	Description of foreseeability	Cases relying or relied upon
Known class (unidentified third parties)	*Glanzer*	One who follows a common calling may come under a duty to another whom he serves, though a third party may give the order or make the payment. Liability being limited to a foreseeable class of actual purchasers	*Rusch Factors* and cases following it
Limited class (unidentified third parties)	Restatement, Torts[82] (2d) (1966) 552	'One who, in the course of his ... profession ... supplies false information for the guidance of others in their business transactions, is subject to liability ... (to plaintiffs) relying upon the information. ... [T]he liability is limited to loss suffered (a) by the person or one of the persons for whose benefit and guidance he intends to supply the information, or knows that the recipient intends to supply it ...'	*Rusch Factors, Ryan, Rozny, Rhode Is., Bunge*[83]
Foreseeable but limited class	*Rusch Factors*[86]	Accountant should be liable in negligence for careless misrepresentations relied upon by actually foreseen and limited classes of persons. The dictum in this case was analysed by some commentators to mean that liability should be co-extensive with liability for physical torts, i.e. liability to all those whose reliance is foreseeable, following the principle that 'the risk reasonably to be perceived defines the duty to be obeyed'[84]	*Ryan, Rhode Is., Hochfelder,*[85] *Bunge*
Unknown injury, known class of injuries. Unknown class of persons or individual[88]	*Harbin*[87]	The unforeseeability of a particular injury does not affect the responsibility of the defendant who causes it, at least not if the injury was of a type or class of injuries which could have been foreseen as a potential result of the defendants' conduct[88]	

as to establish a duty owing beyond the privity requirement. The dimensions get progressively more extensive further down the table, thus *Ultramares* represents the most conservative decision.

The table is divided into the following sections:

(1) Class of persons falling within the description
It was noted above that once the measure of privity is removed the range of possible plaintiffs to an action needs to be limited in some way. This section indicates the likely range of individuals or class of persons falling within the foreseeability description.

(2) Case
This section notes the case (or in two cases the Restatement position) which established the doctrine.

(3) Description of foreseeability
A synopsis of the foreseeability doctrine established by the case in section two gives a fuller description of the extent of foreseeability. It can be seen that there is a fairly narrow shift between the divisions after *Ultramares*. In any area of common law it is dangerous to compartmentalise; however from an analysis of the cases and by the reliance of subsequent cases the above divisions seem applicable.

(4) Cases relying or relied upon
This section lists some cases which have followed the formula established by the case in section 2. In some instances (*Anderson*, for example) the case has adapted an earlier case to establish the foreseeability formula.

It would seem that recent cases involving accountants are leaning towards the *Rusch Factors* decision of foreseeability. Some writers[89] have concurred with this view and they consider that the extension of liability as outlined in *Rusch Factors* and its supporting cases is sound and a logical development from the rigidity of *Ultramares*. On that basis liability of the accountant may now extend to plaintiffs who are members of a limited class, who have relied upon the misrepresentations and suffered damage as a result. This position concurs with the Second Restatement position: However, as noted in the table, *Rusch Factors* has been interpreted to extend liability beyond the Restatement.

Because of the considerable influence of the Restatement in case law discussion and because it has the weight of the American Law Institute behind it, it is worth discussing in greater detail.

(ii) The Restatement (Second) Torts

The American Law Institute in 1965 and 1966 issued 'tentative drafts' of the law, styled 'The Restatement (Second) of Torts'.[90] One influence upon the Restatement has been recognised[91] as coming from the English case of *Hedley Byrne* v. *Heller*[92] decided in the House of Lords in 1963 in addition to other authorities.

The significance of the Restatement rests upon the following factors:

1. It has been cited and relied upon in many recent landmark cases.[93]
2. The scope of the latest Restatement was wider than the previous Restatement issued in 1938.[94]
3. The reliance of the Restatement upon English precedent.[95]
4. The timing of the Restatement gave courts at a critical period (1966) the strength to move from the confines of *Ultramares*.

The Tentative Draft No. 12 issued in 1966 provides as follows:

(1) One who, in the course of his business, profession or employment, or in a transaction in which he has a pecuniary interest, supplies false information for the guidance of others in their business transactions, is subject to liability for pecuniary loss caused to them by their justifiable reliance upon the information, if he fails to exercise reasonable care or competence in obtaining or communicating the information.

(2) Except as stated in Subsection (3), the liability stated in Subsection (1) is limited to loss suffered.
   (a) by the person or one of the persons for whose benefit and guidance he intends to supply the information, or knows that the recipient intends to supply it; and
   (b) through reliance upon it in a transaction which he intends the information to influence, or knows that the recipient so intends, or in a substantially similar transaction.

(3) The liability of one who is under a public duty to give the information extends to loss suffered by any of the class of persons for whose benefit the duty is created, in any of the transactions in which it is intended to protect them.[96]

In order to illustrate the extent of the draft the Restatement provided the following hypothetical example of the rule:

A is negotiating with a bank for a credit of $50,000. The bank requires an audit by certified public accountants. A employs B & Company, a firm of accountants, to make the audit, telling them he is going to negotiate a bank loan. A does not get his loan from the first bank but does negotiate a loan with another bank, which relies upon B & Company's certified statements. The audit carelessly overstates the financial resources of A, and in consequence the second bank suffers pecuniary loss. B & Company is subject to liability to the second bank.[97]

The illustration indicates that the interpretation of the Restatement is such that liability will not extend to the very large class of persons who may obtain a copy of the auditor's certified statements, but to the limited class of people or businesses which the auditor knew or should have foreseen would be provided with a copy of the statements by his client.

Employing the above illustration it can be seen that this rule goes much further than the rule in *Ultramares*. In that case the auditor was specifically requested to provide thirty-two additional certified statements for the client to obtain finance. Under the Restatement position of today the accountants in that case would certainly have been liable.

Schedule Bc[98] indicates the cases which had cited the Restatement in judgment giving an indication of its importance in all state jurisdictions. Unlike particular state case law precedent which may be ignored by other state jurisdictions, the Restatement has influence over all the state and federal systems. Table XIV analyses the actual reliance or statements by courts concerning the Restatement and indicates its importance in developing the trend in common law.

In all except for two cases the Restatement has been accepted in some form in the state law. The two exceptions are *Investment Corporation* which was committed to following other authority, and *Stephens Industries* which analysed the fundamental ruling in its opinion but did not explicitly state that the Restatement would be accepted in Colorado.

If the Restatement has given courts the opportunity to move away from *Ultramares*, the rule has in the same way left some doubt as to the exact extension of liability. For the cases cited above the Restatement has been employed to extend liability to parties of a limited class who were actually known to the representing accountant (for example, *Rusch Factors* and *Rhode Island*). The extension to a wider range of third parties is implied in *Shatterproof* but here again the limit is set

TABLE XIV Reliance upon the Restatement position

Date	Case	Reference	Restatement	State	Opinion
1962	Texas Tunneling	204 F. Supp. 821, 830 (1962)	1938	Texas	Relying upon the 1938 Restatement. The court held it supported the doctrine that an action should be allowed for negligent misrepresentation with regard to business transactions when damages proximately occur from justifiable reliance thereon.
1967	Fischer v. Kletz	266 F. Supp. 180, 185 (1967)	1938	N. York	The court held that there was no reason why an accounting firm should not have a duty to disclose after acquired information to investors it knows upon its representations. 266 F. Supp. 180, 185 (1967).
1967		266 F. Supp. 180, 185-6 (1967)	1938		The court also ruled upon the definition of 'business transaction' which is also included in 552. The court held that the act of certification by an accountant was similar in its effect to a representation made in a business transaction; both supply information which is naturally and justifiably relied upon by individuals for decisional purposes. There is no distinction therefore between accountants and parties to a business transaction.
1967	Anderson	418 S.W. 2d 123, 129 (1967)	1938	Missouri	Although no Missouri case had passed directly on the matter, the Missouri courts would, if called upon, accept the Restatement as the law of this state.
1968	Investment Corporation	208 S.O. 2d 291, 295-6 (1968)	1938	Florida	The court held that the Restatement appeared to be in conflict with the precedent it was relying upon in judgment and although the court realised there were public policies in support of the arguments advanced by the parties to the action it felt obliged to follow the established authority.
1968	Rusch Factors	284 F. Supp. 85, 91 (1968)	1966 (No. 12)	Rhode Is.	Used to support argument that the *Glanzer* principle had been applied to accountants.
1969	Ryan	170 N.E. 2d 395, 402 (1969)	552 (No. 11)	Iowa	The court held that the position announcement in the Restatement may be accepted to the extent that it extends the right to recover for negligence to persons for whose benefit and guidance the accountant *knows* the information is intended, especially when the party to be benefited is identified before the statement or report is submitted by the accountant. The test whether the accountant owes a duty of care is adopted therefore when the recipient is actually foreseen and a member of a limited class of persons.
1969	Rozny	250 N.E. 2d 656, 663 (1969)	552 (No. 12)	Illinois	The court held the Restatement was opposite to the situation in the case. While the draft was recognised as not yet adopted, it apparently recognised liability to a nebulous group whose reliance on a certificate was something more than foreseeable but something less than identifiably known.
1971	Stephens Industries	438 F. 2d 357, 360 (1971)	Not specified	Colorado	A vital element of the rule is that liability is contingent upon the failure 'to exercise that care and competence in obtaining and communicating the information which its recipient is justified in expecting'. The accountants in this case did not fall in this regard. Court also stressed that Colorado has not as yet accepted the Restatement.
1971	Shatterproof	466 S.W. 2d 873, 46 A.L.R. 3d 968 (1976)	552 (No. 12)	Texas	Relying upon the analysis of Professor Hawkins the court welcomed a shift to the negligence doctrine enunciated in the 1938 Restatement. It recognised that with slight textual change the Second Restatement was very similar in its wording and was identical in meaning to the First Restatement. The court held that the Second Restatement should be adopted as law in Texas. Court held further that within the scope defined in the Second Restatement an accountant may be held liable to third parties who rely upon financial statements, audits, etc., prepared by the accountant in cases where the latter fails to exercise ordinary care in the preparation of such statements, audits, etc., and the third party because of such reliance suffers financial loss or damage.
1972	Rhode Island Hosp.	455 F. 2d 847, 851 (1972)	1938 & 1966	Rhode Is.	Both Restatements were cited to support the finding that accountants should be liable in negligence for careless financial misrepresentations relied upon by 'actually foreseen and limited classes of persons'. (per *Rusch Factors*)
1973	Aluma Kraft	493 S.W. 2d 378, 382-3 (1973)	552 (No. 12)	Missouri	Relied upon in the judgment here such than when an accountant knew the audit was to be used by a third party plaintiff for its benefit and guidance, etc., he has a claim in negligence against the accountant who rendered an unqualified opinion upon which the plaintiff relied to his detriment. This would indicate support for *Anderson* above in Missouri.
1974	Bunge Corpn	372 F. Supp. 1058, 1062-3 (1974)	1966	N. Dakota	The Restatement the court noted represented a compromise between *Ultramares* and an allowance of recovery to third persons under the common law theory of negligence. In the courts view the Restatement was a better rule and yet it still recognised the fears expressed in *Ultramares* of imposing liability upon accountants to third parties under a theory of negligence but nevertheless it applied a limited form of negligence in some accountant third party cases.

'within the scope defined in the Second Restatement'.[99] Perhaps of greater significance is the use in *Fischer* of the First Restatement, section 551. In that case the accountants did not specifically *know* the numerous defendants who were investors relying upon financial statements. In fact, as the case was a class action suit,[100] the plaintiffs involved would include all the stockholders of the company who had received the relevant financial statements and who had not specifically wished to be excluded from the suit.[101] No court yet has interpreted the rule to include such a class, and thus at present the law would seem to be that an accountant may be liable in negligence to third parties relying upon misrepresentations to their detriment, the parties involved being specifically foreseen and known to him.

According to one writer[102] the notes accompanying the Restatement admit dissatisfaction with the definition of the limits of the class of third persons involved. From a further hypothetical example the notes raise the query 'whether there is any limitation in terms of the size of the group to whom the defendant knows that the recipient intends to communicate the information.'[103] As with *Fischer* above, of major concern will be a situation where two large public corporations decide upon a merger. An accountant in such a case will be required to furnish a certificate of one of the corporations in order for the other to evaluate the merger. In such event 'will a merely negligent overstatement of the financial condition of the audited company . . . subject the accountant to liability to the entire group of stockholders?'[104] The auditor will be aware of the business transaction involved and the parties will be foreseen as reliant upon them. The requirements of the Rule are satisfied and the exposure of liability could be immense.

This example has not yet arisen in practice and the Restatement has not been amended further. With more courts citing the Restatement, however, it would seem that the required interpretation will be left in the hands of the judges. It is possible, therefore, that judges may extend established law when more cases are heard in the future.

NOTES

[1] See Chapter 1, text accompanying notes 8 to 15.
[2] K. I. Solomon, 'Ultramares Revisited: A Modern Study of Accountants' Liability to the Public', 18 *De Paul Law Review* 56, 56 (1968).
[3] Codification of Auditing Standards by the AICPA into SAS No. 1 (1973).
[4] Creation by the AICPA of the FASB in 1973.

5 Heinemann 'Accountant's Role Undergoing Test,' *New York Times*, 27 March, 1966 Sec. 3. p. 1. Col. 3. Also *Wall Street Journal*, 15 Nov. 1966 p. 1. Col. 6.

6 Quoted by H. Jaenicke, 'The Impact of the Current Legal Climate on the Accounting Profession', a background paper prepared for the Commission on Auditors' Responsibilities, July 1976, p. 1.

7 C. D. Liggio, 'Expanding concepts of accountants' liability' 12 *California CPA Quarterly*, (Sept. 1974), pp. 18–19. Quoted by Jaenicke, ibid, p. 2.

8 As analysed in Chapter 4.

9 Jaenicke, *supra* note 6, p. 2. The measure of the increase in litigation is also reflected in estimates of malpractice insurance premiums and related costs incurred by auditing firms. Jaenicke quotes estimates of these costs payable by the seventeen largest accounting firms at $80 million per annum. In total, American accounting firms are paying around $100 million, this being a conservative estimate (ibid. p. 2).

10 See T. J. Fiflis, 'Current Problems of Accountants' Responsibilities to Third Parties', 28 *Vanderbilt Law Review* 31, 102 (1975). See also *Fischer* v. *Kletz* 266 F. Supp. 180 (S.D.N.Y. 1967): 'The law in this area is in a state of flux due to the inroads being made into the old doctrine of *caveat emptor*' (266 F. Supp. 180, 184) (nondisclosure of information). See also W. L. Prosser, 'Mis-representation and Third Parties', 19 *Vanderbilt Law Review* 231 (1966); also E. J. Bradley, 'Auditors' Liability and the Need for Increased Accounting Uniformity', 30 *Law and Contemporary Problems* 898, (1965) and E. J. Bradley, 'Liabilities to Third Persons for Negligent Audit', *Journal of Business Law*, 190, 193 (1966).

11 Note 2 *supra*, p. 57.

12 Ibid p. 66 referring to the *Ultramares* decision.

13 *Ultramares Corpn.* v. *Touche et al* 255 N.Y. 170, 174 N.E. 441 (1931).

14 See Chapter 4, text accompanying notes 47 *et seq*.

15 Also recognised by A. J. Marinelli, 'The Expanding Scope of Accountants' Liability to Third Parties', 23 *Case Western Reserve Law Review* 113, 117 (1971).

16 *MacPherson* v. *Buick Motor Co.*, 217 N.Y. 382, 111 N.E. 1050 (1916).

17 *Winterbottom* v. *Wright* (1842) 10 M & W. 109.

18 Ibid.

19 217 N.Y. 382, 393.

20 Note 2 *supra*.

21 174 N.E. 441, 444.

22 Solomon, note 2, *supra*, p. 66. Emphasis in original.

23 See Fiflis, note 10, *supra* p. 105. In *Texas Tunneling Co.*, v. *City of Chattanooga* 204 F. Supp. 821 (1962), 329 F.2d 402 (6th Cir. 1964) the judge stated: ' . . . it may be observed in this connection that there have been significant changes in the American society during the thirty years that have elapsed since the decision in the *Ultramares* case. The continued growth and expansion of industry, the growth of population, the urbanisation of society, the growing complexity of business relations and the growing specialisation of business functions all require more and more reliance in business transactions upon the representations of specialists' (204 F. Supp. 821, 833).

[24] See *Rozny* v. *Marnul* 43, Ill. 2d 54, 250 N.E. 656, 661 (1969).

[25] Fiflis, note 10, *supra* p. 107.

[26] In this regard Fiflis, ibid, has noted: 'The unlimited publicity that misleading financial statements might obtain was viewed as a potential cause of widespread reliance and loss, and a change in the law to liability for such loss was considered too radical for judicial reform like that which altered the law of physical *torts* in *MacPherson* v. *Buick Motor Co.*' (p. 104). *Ultramares* did suggest however that the legislature should impose such reform and not the courts. Other commentators have noted 'it is generally agreed that privity and intent were required in third party actions because it was feared that the auditing profession would be eliminated if auditors were held liable to all who would reasonably be expected to rely on their certification of financial statements'. D. D. Hallet and T. R. Collins, 'Auditors' Responsibility for Misrepresentation, Inadequate Protection for Users of Financial Statements', 44 *Washington Law Review* 139, 180 (1968).

[27] Wise, 'The Auditors have Arrived', *Fortune* (Nov. 1960) p. 151.

[28] For example Levitin, 'Accountants' Scope of Liability for Defective Financial Reports', 15 *Hastings Law Journal* 436, 445 (1964). Seavey 'Mr. Justice Cardozo and the Law of Torts' 52 *Harvard Law Review* 372, 400 (1939). Notes: 'The Accountants' Liability – for what and to whom?', 36 *Iowa Law Review* 319, 327–8 (1951), Notes: 52 *Marguette Law Review* 158 and 18 *De Paul Law Review* 56.

[29] See for example *Westerhold* v. *Carroll* 419 S.W.2d 73 (1967); *Aluma Kraft Manufacturing Company* v. *Elmer Fox* 493 S.W.2d 378 (1973); *Fischer* v. *Kletz* 266 F. Supp. 180 (S.D.N.Y. 1967); *Ryan* v. *Kanne* 170 N.W.2d 395, (1969 Iowa); *Rusch Factors Inc.*, v. *Levin* 284 F. Supp. 85, 91 (1968). See Schedule B of Chapter 4, *supra*.

[30] *Rusch Factors Inc.* v. *Levin* 284 F. Supp. 85 (1968).

[31] 284 F. Supp. 85, 91 (1968).

[32] Ibid.

[33] See Hallet, note 26 *supra*, p. 180.

[34] Notaries: *Biakanja* v. *Irving* 49 Cal. 2d 647, 320 P. 2d 16 (1958). See Wade 'The Attorneys' Liability for Negligence' 12 *Vanderbilt Law Review* 755 (1959).

Abstractors: *Anderson* v. *Boone County Abstract Co.*, 418 S.W.2d 123 (1967). Surveyors: *Rozny* v. *Marnul* (note 24, *supra*).

[35] Note 24, *supra*.

[36] 250 N.E.2d 656, 662 (1969).

[37] Ibid.

[38] *Supra*, note 2, p. 67. This quotation is footnoted with the comment that such a forthright statement would have abandoned privity just as the California supreme court repudiated that doctrine in the case of a notary in *Biakanja* v. *Irving*, *supra* note 34.

[39] The question and ·extent of foreseeability is considered further in this chapter. See text accompanying notes 71 *et seq., infra*.

[40] *Glanzer* v. *Shepard* 233 N.Y. 236, 135 N.E. 276 (1922).

[41] *Ultramares Corporation* v. *Touche* 174 N.E. 441, 446.

[42] See text accompanying notes 23 to 26 *supra*.

[43] Consider the statement in the *Matter of Touche, Niven, Bailey and Smart* 37

SEC 629, 670–671 (1957). The accountant's responsibility 'is not only to the client who pays his fee but also to investors, creditors and others who might rely on the financial statements which he certifies. . . . The public accountant must report fairly on the facts as he finds them whether favourable or unfavourable to his client. His duty is to safeguard the public interest, not that of his client.' Quoted in *Fischer* v. *Kletz* 266 F. Supp. 180, 184 (S.D.N.Y. 1967).

44 P. D. Montagna, 'Public Accounting: The Dynamics of Occupaional Change' in R.R. Sterling, (ed.) *Institutional Issues in Public Accounting* Papers and Responses from Accounting Colloquium III, (Kansas: Scholars Book Co., 1974) p. 4. In this regard the accounting profession is considered to be separate from the legal profession; the lawyer is concerned with the interest of his client alone.

45 AICPA 'Code of Professional Ethics' 2 CCH AICPA Professional Standards E.T. s., 52. 09 (1974) as cited by Fiflis, note 10, *supra* p. 106.

46 ICAEW *Members' Handbook*. Section 1.2.

47 See Fiflis, note 10 *supra* p. 106, Solomon, note 2 *supra* pp. 73–4 and Montagna, note 44, *supra* p. 4.

48 Montagna, note 44, *supra* p. 4, Savoie, 125 *Journal of Accountancy*, 8–10 (March 1968). See also Marinelli, note 15, *supra* p. 113, J. W. Meek, 'Liability of the Accountant to Parties other than his employer for Negligent Misrepresentation', [1942] *Wisconsin Law Review*, p. 371 and Heinemann, note 5, *supra*.

49 The American Institute of Accountants, *Audits of Corporate Accounts* (1934). See S. A. Zeff, *Forging Accounting Principles in Five Countries* (Illinois: Stips Publishing Co., 1971) pp. 124 and 125.

50 Note 10 *supra*, p. 107.

51 Liggio has noted that this was the case in the 1960s: 'If an accountant had then been asked to define the extent and scope of his liability, I believe that every accountant could have recited the holding of *Ultramares* v. *Touche* and also may have referred to a few other cases that had been decided. As a lawyer, I could have added a few sentences to that and probably would have named one or two other cases involving the accounting profession which had been decided; but nothing earth shattering would have been said. Those were the happy days!' C. D. Liggio, 'The Accountants' Legal Environment for the Next Decade' included in Sterling, note 44 *supra*, p. 99.

52 See Table IX *supra*.

53 See Chapter 4, schedules Ba and Bb.

54 See Chapter 4, text accompanying notes 44 *et seq*.

55 The 'Winterbottom test' refers to the two conditions laid down in the English case *Winterbottom* v. *Wright* (1842) 10 M. & W. 109, 152 Eng. Rep. 402.
Privity need not be required when (1) there is no fear of unlimited liability, and (2) it does not endanger the contract. Cases employing this formula include *Anderson* v. *Boone County*, note 34 *supra*, and *Westerhold* v. *Carroll*, note 29 *supra*.

56 See for example *Rusch Factors Inc.* v. *Levin*, 284 F. Supp. 85, 90.

57 Ibid.

[58] See *Ultramares*, note 13 *supra* and *State Street Trust* v. *Ernst* 278 N.Y. 104, 15 N.E.2d 416, 120 A.L.R. 120 reh. den. 278 N.Y. 704, 15 N.E.2d 851, 120 A.L.R. 1261 (1938) and *Rusch Factors*, ibid.

[59] 284 F. Supp. 85, 91. The doctrine was fully supported and quoted at length by the court in *Ryan* v. *Kanne*, 170 N.W.2d 395, 401.

[60] *Rhode Island Hospital Trust* v. *Swartz et al.* 455 F.2d 847, (1972).

[61] *Shatterproof Glass Corpn.* v. *James* 466 S.W.2d 873, 46 A.L.R. 3d 968, error n.r.e.

[62] 46 A.L.R. 968, 973. See notes 83 *et seq. infra*.

[63] See analysis of cases in 46 A.L.R.3d 989, also D. Y. Causey, *The Duties and Liabilities of the CPA* (Revised Edition) (Bureau of Business Research, The University of Texas, 1976) Chapter 6, pp. 171–92.

[64] *Stephens Industries Inc.* v. *Haskins & Sells* (1971; CA10 COLO) 438 F.2d 357 (1971).

[65] 438 F.2d 357, 360 (1971).

[66] *Investment Corporation of Florida* v. *Buchman* 208 SO.2d 291, 294 (Flo) (1968).

[67] *MacNelland* v. *Barnes* 199 S.E.2d. 564, 566 (Ga) (1973).

[68] Ibid.

[69] Ibid. Compare however with the opinion in *La Plant* v. *E.I.DuPont de Nemours & Co.* 346 S.W.2d 231 (1961). 'In fact, throughout the years so many exceptions have been engrafted upon the rule that it has been said, perhaps too broadly, that the exceptions have "swallowed the rule".' Quoted in *Westerhold* v. *Carroll* 419 S.W.2d 73, 77 (1967).

[70] See Table XI *supra*. This view is supported by 46 A.L.R. 3d. Significantly perhaps *MacNelland* v. *Barnes*, note 67 *supra* cited A.L.R. 2d dated 1958.

[71] 250 N.E. 656, 660 (1969).

[72] *Landell* v. *Lybrand et al.* 264 Pa. 406, 197Atl 783 (1919).

[73] 170Atl 783, 783 (1919).

[74] 'If liability for negligence exists. . . .' 174 N.E. 441, 444 (1931). See Chapter text accompanying note 60. Supported in *Investment Corp.* v. *Buchman*, note 66 *supra*.

[75] 135 N.E. 275, 275 (1922).

[76] 135 N.E. 275, 276 (1922).

[77] Causey states: 'The one distinction, however, is that in *Glanzer* the public weigher foresaw the specific third party and the transaction which resulted in loss, whereas in *Ultramares* foreseeability was limited to knowledge that the audit report was for the benefit "of a class of indefinite extension".' D. Y. Causey, 'Foreseeability as a Determinant of Audit Responsibility', 48 *Accounting Review* 258, 260, (1973).

[78] 204 F. Supp. 821, 833 (1962).

[79] 204 F. Supp. 821, 834 (1962).

[80] See Fiflis, note 10 *supra*, pp. 104–5.

[81] See text accompanying note 106 *infra*.

[82] See text accompanying note 102 *infra*.

[83] *Bunge Corpn.* v. *Eide* 372 F. Supp. 1058 (1974).

[84] *Palsgraf* v. *Long Island Rail Road* 248 N.Y. 339, 344, 162 N.E. 99, 100; 59 A.L.R. 1253 (1928).

[85] Cited in *Hochfelder et al* v. *Ernst & Ernst* 503 F.2d 1100 (1974) since decided in the Supreme Court see Chapter 4.

[86] *Rusch Factors, Inc.* v. *Levin* 284 F. Supp. 85(1968).

[87] *Harbin* v. *Dunn* 39 Tenn. App. 190, 282 S.W.2d 203 (1943).

[88] The *Harbin* case was not thought applicable by the district court in *Texas Tunneling* 329 F. 2d 402 (1964). Therefore the final two sections of this table which slightly shift the doctrine from a class of persons to a class of injuries may not be applicable law.

[89] See for example Marinelli, note 15 *supra* p. 122, and Fiflis note 10 *supra*.

[90] Restatement (Second) of Torts. Comments and Explanatory Notes. Tentative Draft No. 12, 1966, The American Law Institute. The object of the Restatement is to ensure the periodic revision of the law of torts to keep pace with the growth of decisions in each subject. The Restatement is a vital force in the shaping of the law of torts as it has developed through precedent. See Introduction to the Restatement (Second) of Torts, (1963).

[91] See for example Jaenicke, note 6 *supra* p. 14; R. J. Gormley, 'Accountants' Professional Liability – A Ten Year Review' 29 *Business Lawyer*, 1205, 1208 (1974); C. N. Katsoris, 'Accountants' Third Party Liability – How far do we go?' 36 *Fordham Law Review* 191, 197–8 (1967).

[92] *Hedley Byrne & Co. Ltd.* v. *Heller & Partners Ltd.*, [1963] All E.R. 575, [1964] A.C. 465.

[93] See Table XIII *infra*, text accompanying note 110 *infra*. See also Schedule Bc, Chapter 4.

[94] See Table XII *supra*. The original Restatement of 1938, s. 552 provides:
INFORMATION NEGLIGENTLY SUPPLIED FOR THE GUIDANCE OF OTHERS.
One who in the course of his business or profession supplies information for the guidance of others in their business transactions is subject to liability for harm caused to them by their reliance upon the information if
a) he fails to exercise that care and competence in obtaining and communicating the information which its recipient is justified in expecting, and
b) the harm is suffered
   (i) by the person or one of the class of persons for whose guidance the information was supplied, and
   (ii) because of his justifiable reliance upon it in a transaction in which it was intended to influence his conduct or in a transaction substantially identical therewith.

[95] Note 92 *supra*.

[96] Tent. Draft. No. 12, 1966, s. 522.

[97] Explanatory Notes, s. 552, paras. 13–16, 23–5. (Tent. Draft. No. 12 (1966)).

[98] Chapter 4 *supra*.

[99] 46 A.L.R. 3d 968, 976 (1971).

[100] The case report does not indicate the actual numbers involved but to give some indication of the size, the headnote to the report states that the original action (No. 65 Civ. 787) had been joined and consolidated with fifteen other actions.

[101] See analysis of class actions in Chapter 7 *infra*.

[102] Katsoris, note 91, *supra*, pp. 198–9.

[103] Tent. Draft. para. 16.

[104] Katsoris, note 91 *supra* p. 199. See also Bradley 'Auditors' Liability and the Need for Increased Accounting Uniformity', 30 *Law and Contemporary Problems* 898, 916 (1965).

6 THE ENGLISH COMMON LAW ANALYSIS

I INTRODUCTION

The analysis of the many recent American cases brought for negligence has highlighted a trend in American common law and established the current legal position. The analysis has also indicated the lack of uniformity between the various state jurisdictions. The accounting profession has been critical of the legal uncertainties to which it is subjected.[1]

In England the case of *Hedley Byrne & Co Ltd* v. *Heller & Partners Ltd*[2] caused concern amongst the English accounting profession in a comparable way to the concern caused in America.[3]

Hedley Byrne established precedent in England which had been law in America since *Glanzer*.[4] Unfortunately the ruling in *Hedley Byrne* has also been subject to uncertainty.[5] It seems important therefore to study the position of the law of negligent misrepresentation in England, both in the light of decided cases and also with respect to the recent important American cases analysed in the previous chapter. In this way it should be possible to establish whether American law has extended beyond the negligence law in England.

II TORT LAW FOR NEGLIGENCE PRIOR TO *HEDLEY BYRNE*

To establish[6] the law with respect to negligent misrepresentations, one need not go back further than *Derry* v. *Peek*.[7] In *Derry* v. *Peek* the plaintiff subscribed for shares in a limited company in reliance upon a prospectus issued by the directors, who included the defendants. The prospectus contained a negligent misstatement made in good faith. Although the cause of action in the case was for deceit (there being no alternative claim at that time in respect of negligent or innocent misrepresentation), the case is indirectly relevant to the law of negligence.[8] Implicit in the opinions of the *Derry* v. *Peek* judgment was the principle that, in the absence of some fiduciary or contractual relationship between the parties, there was no remedy for merely negligent misrepresentation, honestly believed, where the harm that resulted to the plaintiff was only pecuniary loss.[9]

This doctrine implied in *Derry* v. *Peek* was supported in subsequent judgments, including *Nocton* v. *Lord Ashburton*,[10] *Woods* v. *Martins Bank*,[11] *Burke* v. *Cory*,[12] *Cann* v. *Willson*,[13] *Le Lievre* v. *Gould*,[14] *Old Gate Estates* v. *Toplis*,[15] *Candler* v. *Crane, Christmas*.[16] For an action in negligence to be brought there must be a duty owing the plaintiff. Lord Haldane, L. C., in *Nocton* v. *Ashburton*, whilst examining the decision of the House of Lords in *Derry* v. *Peek* stated: 'They must indeed be taken to have thought that the facts proved as to the relationship of the parties in *Derry* v. *Peek* were not enough to establish any special duty arising out of that relationship other than the general duty of honesty.'[17] In *Low* v. *Bouverie*[18] Bowen, L. J. said '*Derry* v. *Peek* decides . . . that in cases such as those of which that case was an instance, there is no duty enforceable at law to be careful in the representation which is made. Negligent misrepresentation does not certainly amount to deceit, and negligent misrepresentation can only amount to a cause of action if there exists a duty to be careful – not to give information after careful inquiry. In *Derry* v. *Peek* the House of Lords considered that the circumstances raised no such duty.'[19]

This view of the law was supported by Cohen, L. J., in *Candler*, and it was further supported by leading textbook writers of the day. Cohen, L. J., stated 'The learned editor of *Salmond on Torts* expresses the view that with certain exceptions not material to the present case, "a false statement is not actionable as a tort unless it is wilfully false. Mere negligence in the making of false statements is not actionable either as deceit or as any other kind of tort."'[20]

III THE ANOMALY OF THE LAW

Criticism of *Derry* v. *Peek* arose as a result of the distinction the case made between physical and economic damages. This distinction was

settled in American law as early as 1922 in *Glanzer* v. *Shepard*, where
a third party was allowed recovery having suffered economic damage.
Prior to *Hedley Byrne* the legal doctrine concerning the difference
between economic and physical damage was stated by Dr Charlesworth in his book on the Law of Negligence; cited in *Candler*:

> The duty to take care is ultimately based on the possible con-
> sequences which will occur if care is not taken. What the con-
> sequences may be of any particular act or omission is often a very
> difficult problem involving inquiry into questions of causation. This
> inquiry is difficult enough in cases where physical damage is
> concerned in which the cause, whether it be defective vehicles or
> machinery or lack of care and skill in management, can usually be
> accurately traced. To regard the issue of a certificate, an opinion, or
> a report as carrying the same duty of care as the delivery of a
> defective chattel would be to introduce a most disturbing factor into
> the mutual intercourse of society.[21]

Many commentators have considered the anomaly and concluded that
there is no intrinsic reason why the rules as to liability for physical
harm should be different from those regarding liability for harm to
economic interests.[22]

Seavey, writing in 1951, considered[23] that neither Asquith, L. J. nor
Cohen, L. J. in *Candler* provided a satisfactory explanation. He
thought the reason for such a doctrine was purely historical and 'hence
one which [gave] no reason for a distinction today'.[24]

In the same way that in 1916 the American case of *MacPherson* v.
Buick[25] allowed recovery for physical damage suffered by third parties
(thus destroying the barrier created by the English case of *Winterbottom* v. *Wright*),[26] so too, the case of *Donoghue* v. *Stevenson*[27] put
English law on an equal footing with the American. *Donoghue* v.
Stevenson was seen as 'a striking victory of principles over rules'.[28] The
plaintiff's counsel in *Candler* cited *Donoghue* in their plea to get the
law for negligent misrepresentation extended to the area of economic
loss.[29] Asquith, L. J. rejected the argument by stating that 'the notion
that *Donoghue's* case was intended parenthetically or *sub silentio* to
sweep away the substratum of *Derry* v. *Peek*' seemed quite
unconvincing.[30] Having analysed various cases advanced by counsel as
providing a remedy for economic damages, (including *Cann* v.
Willson, *Le Lievre* v. *Gould*, *Nocton* v. *Ashburton*, *Heaven* v.
Pender,[31] *Old Gate Estates Ltd.* v. *Toplis*, *George* v. *Skivington*,[32]

Derry v. *Peek* and *Low* v. *Bouverie*), Asquith, L. J. stated that these cases allowed recovery purely on the basis of 'the existence of a fiduciary relationship, and subsequently the breach of duty arising'[33] and not as a result of economic injury suffered.

The main barrier in law was therefore easily recognisable. The doctrine was firmly maintained in England until the 1960s. If the damage suffered by the third party was pecuniary or economic he had no recourse against the misrepresentor in a negligence action – his only recourse was in deceit.

IV *CANDLER* v. *CRANE, CHRISTMAS & CO.*

It may be contended that the most forceful criticism against this principle in a case involving accountants was that of Denning, L. J. (as he then was) in *Candler*. It is worth analysing, at this stage, his opinion in some depth not only because it was endorsed in subsequent cases (especially in *Hedley Byrne*) but also because it was a major case directly involving the work and certificate of an accountant. In fact, Lord Denning's dissenting opinion is the reason for the continued importance of the case.[34]

Facts of the case[35]

> The managing director of a company instructed the defendants, a firm of accountants and auditors, to prepare the company's accounts and balance sheet. A clerk in the employment of the defendants (who was held to be acting throughout within the scope of his employment) prepared the accounts knowing that they were wanted for the purpose of inducing the plaintiff to invest money in the company. The draft accounts were shown to the plaintiff in the presence of the defendants' clerk, and, relying on their accuracy, the plaintiff subscribed £2,000 for shares in the company. The defendants subsequently certified the accounts in the form in which their clerk had shown them to the plaintiff. The accounts had been prepared negligently, but without any fraud on the part of the defendants or their clerk, and did not give a true statement of the financial position of the company. The company went into liquidation, and, there being no assets, the plaintiff lost the money which he had invested. In an action against the defendants for damages

for negligence, or, alternatively, for breach of their duty, in the circumstances, to give to the plaintiff accurate information.

Held: (i) (Denning L. J., *dissentiente*) in the absence of a contractual or fiduciary relationship between the parties, the defendants owed no duty to the plaintiff to exercise in preparing the accounts and giving their certificate, and the plaintiff, therefore, could not maintain against them an action for negligence.

Le Lievre v. *Gould* ([1893] 1 Q.B. 491), *applied.*

Principles in Donoghue v. *Stevenson* ([1932] A.C. 562), *discussed.*

(ii) since the plaintiff had invested the sum of £2,000 before the relationship between the defendants, as auditors, and the plaintiff, as shareholder, of the company had become operative, no damage flowed from the breach of any such duty owed by the defendants to the plaintiff in that capacity.

After considering the less important aspect of the case, whether the accountant was acting in the course of his employment,[36] Lord Denning considered the main question: 'did the accountants owe a duty of care to the plaintiff?'[37] He answered in the affirmative but recognised that his opinion would be restricted by established common law authority. His criticism rested upon the fact that, *prima facie*, authority did not recognise such a duty. He summed up this shortcoming with the words: 'A country whose administration of justice did not afford redress in a case of the present description would not be in a state of civilisation'.[38]

Although there were a number of cases supporting the situation of *Candler* each had been thought inappropriate by the court in *Le Lievre* v. *Gould*.[39] *Le Lievre* v. *Gould* in Lord Denning's opinion was 'infected by two cardinal errors'. Firstly, that no one out of contract could sue on it or anything arising out of it. This error in tort was exposed in *Donoghue*, which held that the presence of a contract did not defeat an action for negligence by a third person, provided that the circumstances disclosed a duty by the contracting party to that third person.[40] Secondly, that no action lay for a negligent statement even though it was intended to be acted on by the plaintiff and *was* in fact acted upon to his loss (*Derry* v. *Peek*). This error was exposed in *Nocton* v. *Ashburton* which held that an action did lie for a negligent statement where the circumstances disclosed a duty to be careful. In *Derry*, the particular circumstances implied no duty. Employing

Donoghue and *Norton* therefore, Lord Denning thought the law should be re-examined with respect to negligent misstatements. His re-examination concentrated upon three defences raised by counsel:

1. If such a duty arose it would overrule recognised authority.
2. A duty of care only arose where the result of a failure to take care would cause physical damage to persons or property.
3. There was no liability for negligence to third parties, the duty of care arose to the other contracting party only.

The first and third defences were dealt with by citing the authority of *Derry*, *Donoghue* and *Nocton*. The second defence (as outlined above) was the barrier upon which past cases had stumbled. Lord Denning, in seeking to overrule this defence, was unable to cite specific precedent; his opinion was based purely upon his own judgment. He stated 'I must say, however, that I cannot accept [the physical/economic argument] as a valid distinction. I can understand that in some cases of financial loss there may not be a sufficiently proximate relationship to give rise to a duty of care; but, if once the duty exists, I cannot think that liability depends upon the nature of the damage.'[41] This statement identified the factors upon which the remainder of the opinion was to be based; namely, the proximity of the parties and the establishment of a duty. This statement also pinpointed the weakness in the law at that time regarding the illogicality of the physical/economic damage distinction.

The remainder of the opinion considered the question: 'In what circumstances did a duty to use care in a statement exist, apart from the contractual duty?' This question was examined by raising three further questions:

1. What persons are under such a duty?
2. To whom is this duty owed?
3. To what transactions does the duty of care extend?

The answer to the first question was simply that those with a special skill or professional knowledge in the preparation of statements owe a duty to provide them without negligence. Therefore, a duty is owed by 'those persons such as accountants, surveyors, valuers, and analysts, whose profession and occupation it is to examine books, accounts and other things, and to make reports on which other people – other than their clients – rely in the ordinary course of business'.[42]

In reply to the second question, Lord Denning cited accountants specifically as owing a duty 'to their employer or client; and also . . . to any third person to whom they themselves show the accounts, or to whom they know their employer is going to show the accounts, so as to induce him to invest money or take some other action on them'.[43] This duty could not, however, extend to any stranger who might see the accounts without the accountant's knowledge and consent.[44] In those cases where the accountant knew all the time (even before the accounts were presented) that his employer required the accounts for a specific third party so as to induce him to invest money then a duty was owed to that third party.[45] Therefore, the test of *proximity* was: 'Did the accountant *know* that the accounts were required for submission to the plaintiff and use by him?'[46]

In answer to the third question concerning the extension of such a duty, the opinion stated 'it extends only to those transactions for which the accountants knew their accounts were required'.[47] To expand this concept further, duty could not extend to the very transaction in mind at the time of the representation.[48] With respect to the limits of the extension of duty Lord Denning stated: 'I can well understand that it would be going too far to make an accountant liable to any person in the land who chooses to rely on the accounts in matters of business.'[49] In support of this the social utility rationale in *Ultramares*[50] was cited.[51] Lord Denning reserved judgment on whether the duty should extend to a *specific class* of persons, as for example the specific class of persons who rely upon a prospectus, per sections 40 and 43 of the Companies Act 1948.[52]

In summary Lord Denning stated that if the duty was not extended the law would be failing to serve the best interests of the community.[53] If persons other than the client had no remedy for misrepresentations the very purpose for which the accounts had been prepared would be lost. The accounts served a real function in society, the accountant's certificate being the only safeguard for an investor or other third party relying on a set of financial statements. If that investor has no legal remedy the certificate ceased to fulfil its purpose and it would become simply 'a snare for those who rely on it',[54] in effect, destroying the very purpose of the independent accountant and threatening his continued existence as an independent auditor.

V COMPARISON WITH AMERICAN LAW

Lord Denning's view in *Candler* may be directly compared with American authority. Although *Glanzer* was not specifically cited, the outcome in the opinion corresponds directly with the proximity arguments of that case.[55] In *Glanzer* there was a *particular transaction* forming *the end and aim* of the contract. The third party was known to the defendant and relied upon the representation. All these factors were forceably brought out by Lord Denning in *Candler*. Interestingly, the criticism against the social utility rationale was also raised in *Candler*. Lord Denning, like present critics,[56] could not envisage that liability would extend to an indeterminate class of statement users, and he employed the specific class of persons provided by legislation as an example.[57]

The opinion is also directly comparable with the American Law Institute's 1938 Restatement of Torts as analysed in the previous chapter.[58] In the Restatement the scope of liability for negligent language was extended to cases where the information was furnished in the course of a business or profession to one of a class for whose guidance the information was supplied. The information was intended to influence a person's conduct and be relied upon.[59]

From this analysis, therefore, it is possible to establish the exact position of *Candler's* minority opinion in the 'foreseeability' table in the previous chapter.[60] It is evident that the American common law of recent years has extended beyond the confines of the 1922 position in *Glanzer* or the 1938 position of the First Restatement.[61] So, even given the reform considered necessary by Lord Denning in 1951, the law would have still lagged behind American common law. Significantly, Lord Denning has been one of the most outspoken of advocates against the rigidity of the English adherence to the doctrine of *stare decisis*.[62]

Following *Candler* it took some twelve or thirteen years for the courts in England to achieve what Lord Denning defined as a 'state of civilisation'.[63] In 1963 the House of Lords handed down a unanimous decision in *Hedley Byrne*. In that case at least two of the Lord Justices (Lords Devlin and Hodson) explicitly supported Lord Denning's opinion in *Candler*.[64] For this reason the above analysis has current validity in English law. *Hedley Byrne* unanimously overruled the majority opinion in *Candler*.[65]

VI *HEDLEY BYRNE* AND ITS IMPORTANCE

Facts of the case[66]

A bank inquired by telephone of the respondent merchant bankers concerning the financial position of a customer for whom the respondents were bankers. The bank said that they wanted to know in confidence and without responsibility on the part of the respondents, the respectability and standing of E. Ltd., and whether E. Ltd. would be good for an advertising contract for £8,000 to £9,000. Some months later the bank wrote to the respondents asking in confidence the respondents' opinion of the respectability and standing of E. Ltd. by stating whether the respondents considered E. Ltd. trustworthy, in the way of business, to the extent of £100,000 per annum. The respondents' replies to the effect that E. Ltd. was respectably constituted and considered good for its normal business engagements were communicated to the bank's customers, the appellants. Relying on these replies the appellants, who were advertising agents, placed orders, for advertising time and space for E. Ltd., on which orders the appellants assumed personal responsibility for payment to the television and newspaper companies concerned. E. Ltd. went into liquidation and the appellants lost over £17,000 on the advertising contracts. The appellants sued the respondents for the amount of the loss, alleging that the respondents' replies to the bank's inquiries were given negligently, in the sense of misjudgment, by making a statement which gave a false impression as to E. Ltd.'s credit. Negligence was found at the trial and contested on appeal; the appeal was determined, however, on the assumption that there had been negligence, but without deciding whether there had or had not been negligence.

Held: although in the present case, but for the respondents' disclaimer, the circumstances might have given rise to a duty of care on their part, yet their disclaimer of responsibility for their replies on the occasion of the first inquiry was adequate to exclude the assumption by them of a legal duty of care, with the consequence that they were not liable in negligence.

Prior to analysing the case in detail mention should be made of the difficulty of separating the *ratio decidendi* and *obiter dictum* of *Hedley*

Byrne. Many commentators[67] have discussed this difficulty which has led to uncertainty in English law.[68]

The controversy over the *obiter* and the *ratio* in the case is caused because the judgment decided *against* the third party appellants. The respondents, specifically disclaimed all responsibility for the information they supplied. The appeal failed on this factor alone.[69] Therefore all the opinions concerning the creation of a duty for negligent misrepresentation automatically became *obiter*. Sir Milner Holland is reported in 1963 as saying:

> One matter has arisen in the last few weeks which has attracted a good deal of attention. I refer to the *obiter* observations in the House of Lords in the *Hedley Byrne* Case; they were, of course, *obiter* since the decision was against liability.[70]

However, the Lords *did not* restrict their opinions to a mere overview of the law of negligent misrepresentation; each spent the major part discussing the issue to the extent of specifically overruling established authority (*Le Lievre* v. *Gould*). Lord Devlin for example devoted eighteen pages[71] of the report to the question of a duty of care and less than two to the facts of the case.[72]

The *ratio/obiter* argument has been discussed in subsequent court action. In *Rondel* v. *Worsley*;[73] Danckwerts, L. J. considered the problem.

> In my view there is a short and conclusive answer to this. Whatever be the weight which might be given to some observations of the learned Lords of Appeal, in fact the action failed simply because the bank had stamped the words 'without responsibility' on their letter. The observations of the Law Lords were *obiter*.[74]

On the other hand Salmon, L. J., in the same case, whilst recognising the opinions as *obiter*, recognised that they were 'of the highest persuasive authority and I respectively agree with every word of them'.[75] In *W.B. Andersen & Sons Ltd. and Others* v. *Rhodes (Liverpool) Ltd. and others*[76] Cairns J. also dealt with the problem, and the issue, although unresolved, may be left with his opinion:

> When five members of the House of Lords have all said, after close examination of the authorities, that a certain type of tort exists, I think that a judge of first instance should proceed on the basis that

it does exist without pausing to embark on an investigation of whether what was said was necessary to the ultimate decision.[77]

(i) The respondent's arguments in *Hedley Byrne*

Three reasons were given by the respondents why the appellants should not recover damages in *Hedley Byrne*.

1. There was no general duty *not* to make careless statements. The duty was limited to those who could establish some relationship of proximity (as in *Donoghue* v. *Stevenson*). Only by establishing this special duty of care could a remedy be sought for a careless statement and this special duty could only be brought under one of three categories.
   a. Contractual duty.
   b. Fiduciary duty.
   c. Relationship of proximity. The financial loss must flow from physical damage done to the person or the property of the plaintiff. (*Candler* v. *Crane, Christmas* in accord.)
2. If a special relationship could be found under (1) the authority of *Robinson* v. *National Bank of Scotland Ltd.* specifically excluded bankers from such a relationship.[78]
3. The bankers specifically marked their representation 'strictly confidential and given on the express understanding that we incur no responsibility whatever in furnishing it'.[79]

(ii) The appellants' argument

Appellants' case rested upon the premise that, outside contract or a fiduciary duty, where there existed a relationship of proximity (per *Donoghue*) recovery should not be limited to loss flowing from physical damage. Appellants were unable to cite a case in which a defendant had been held liable for a careless statement leading to financial loss otherwise than through the channel of physical damage. In principle such loss ought to be recoverable and that there was no authority did not prevent the House of Lords from acting upon that fundamental principle.[80] The appellants cited American and South African cases to support their premise. Counsel specifically stated that the American cases were significant in that, even though there was no contract, there may be circumstances giving rise to a special relationship. The following cases were cited:[81] *Glanzer, Int. Products,*[82] *Mulroy,*[83] *Doyle,*[84] *Ultramares, Edwards.*[85]

(iii) The main issues in *Hedley Byrne*

It is possible to establish certain fundamental issues from an analysis of the five opinions of the Lords. These issues cover the first argument raised by the respondents outlined above. (The second and third arguments are of lesser significance.)[86] Four main issues listed here are analysed individually below:

1. The extent of *Derry* v. *Peek* with respect to third parties being permitted to bring an action for negligence.
2. The physical/economic damages distinction.
3. The proximity arguments.
4. The creation of a duty of care.

(1) The extent of Derry v. Peek
Each of the Lords discussed the implications of *Derry* v. *Peek* upon the case. It must be recognised that much of the difficulty of the law with regard to establishing a duty outside contract was due to the *implied* authority of this case. The authority was only implied because an action was brought in deceit for fraud and nothing else. In order to establish the exact extent of *Derry* each opinion[87] in *Hedley Byrne* variously cited *Nocton* v. *Lord Ashburton* and in particular the opinion of Haldane, L. C., that:

> . . . the discussion of the case by the noble and learned Lords who took part in the decision appears to me to exclude the hypothesis that they considered any other question to be before them than what was the necessary foundation of an ordinary action in deceit. They must indeed be taken to have thought that the facts proved as to the relationship of the parties in *Derry* v. *Peek* were not enough to establish any special duty arising out of that relationship other than the general duty of honesty. But they do not say that where a different sort of relationship ought to be inferred from the circumstances the case is to be concluded by asking whether an action for deceit will lie. I think that the authorities subsequent to the decision of the House of Lords show a tendency to assume that *it was intended to mean more than it did*. In reality the judgment covered only a part of the field in which liabilities may arise. *There are other*

obligations besides that of honesty the breach of which may give a right to damages. These obligations depend on principles which the judges have worked out in the fashion that is characteristic of a system where much of the law has always been judge-made and unwritten.[88] (Emphasis added)

Thus *Derry* v. *Peek* was no longer to be interpreted as a bar to third party actions in negligence. That is to say *Derry* did not rule that a duty to take care must only be limited to cases of fiduciary relationship.

(2) Physical/economic damages distinction
Each of the Lords analysed the distinction fully.[89] Generally, the various opinions directly supported Lord Denning's dissent in *Candler*, and further examples of illogicality of the distinction were given.[90] Lord Devlin's words in *Hedley Byrne* succinctly abolish the distinction for the first time in English law, and through an example exposes the illogicality of the law since *Derry* v. *Peek*.

> . . . the distinction is now said to depend on whether financial loss is caused through physical injury or whether it is caused directly. The interposition of the physical injury is said to make a difference of principle. I can find neither logic nor common sense in this. If irrespective of contract, a doctor negligently advises a patient that he can safely pursue his occupation and he cannot and the patient's health suffers and he loses his livelihood, the patient has a remedy. But if the doctor negligently advises him that he cannot safely pursue his occupation when in fact he can and he loses his livelihood, there is said to be no remedy. Unless, of course, the patient was a private patient and the doctor accepted half a guinea for his trouble: then the patient can recover all. I am bound to say, my Lords, that I think this to be nonsense. It is not the sort of nonsense that can arise even in the best system of law out of the need to draw nice distinctions – between borderline cases. It arises, if it is the law, simply out of a refusal to make sense. The line is not drawn on any intelligible principle.[91]

Whether the distinction has been totally abolished from the law however is not certain. Recent opinion[92] and cases[93] have again supported the distinction; however, Baxt cites the Australian *Evatt*[94] case which came before the Privy Council in 1970 as pioneering the 'burial of the distinction as far as Australia [was] concerned.'[95]

(3) Proximity and foreseeability

In order to establish a duty of care the Lords considered the question of proximity of the parties in an action. Lord Reid thought that the respondents should have realised the extent to which the information would be used, and therefore he treated the case as if it were one where a negligent misrepresentation was made directly to the person seeking information. He therefore avoided any opinion as to what degree of proximity was necessary before a duty was owed.[96]

Lord Morris considered it unimportant that a person to whom representations would in all probability be passed was unnamed and unknown to the representor.[97]

Lord Hodson discussed the proximity doctrine more extensively,[98] and reviewed the doctrine from *Heaven* v. *Pender* to *Candler*. With respect to authority, previous courts had had to rely upon *Le Lievre* v. *Gould*, which had provided a proximity doctrine only in terms of damage to life or personal property.[99] The majority in *Candler* felt they had to support this view; however Lord Hodson considered Lord Denning's dissent to be valid. Thus in his opinion the relationship may arise where, like the minority view in *Candler*, the third party is actually known to be a reliant party upon information supplied.[100]

Lord Devlin considered that it would be 'a misuse of a general conception' to invite a judge on the facts of any particular case to say whether or not there was 'proximity' between the parties.[101] In this regard the attempt by the appellants in their argument to try and extend the doctrine in *Donoghue* v. *Stevenson* was incorrect, thus implying that the principle of proximity should not be applied to words as well as deeds. *Donoghue*, which involved physical harm, could not be literally applied to a banker's reference. The real value of *Donoghue* to *Hedley Byrne* was that it showed how the law could develop to solve particular problems.[102] Using this argument the common law extension of third party liability for negligent misrepresentation may therefore be said to diverge from a similar development to the law in America. Lord Devlin, quoting Cardozo's words in *Ultramares*, stated that the 'citadel of privity' was being eroded, and cited, in support, cases involving physical damage. In England, on the other hand, the doctrine in *Donoghue* which is comparable with *MacPherson* was *not* applied in *Hedley Byrne*.[103]

Lord Pearce discussed proximity in the context of a party relying upon a representor's skill and care, whether or not a contract exists. He cited in support Lord Denning's dissent in the same fashion as Lord Hodson,[104] and also the 1938 American Restatement.[105]

From this analysis it is evident that no opinion applying the proximity doctrine put it beyond the criteria established by Lord Denning in *Candler*.[106]

(4) Duty of care

The final and probably most significant issue which arose in *Hedley Byrne* was whether there was a duty of care to provide representations to third parties without negligence. In each argument establishing that a duty existed, the Lords expanded upon the various issues outlined in sections 1 to 3 above.[107]

In establishing a common basis of liability the Lords offered a variety of approaches to the creation of a duty of care. However, despite the different paths taken, the same concept of duty emerges.[108]

Lord Reid considered that the creation of a degree of care would arise when a supplier of information ought to have known, or did know, that the information was being relied upon. The supplier of information in this instance is to be judged by the objective standard of what the 'reasonable' man would have done. Outside any contract or fiduciary relationship, a reasonable man who knew that his advice was sought and was to be relied upon should be held responsible (assuming he accepted to supply the information) and he should exercise such care as the circumstances required.[109] To illustrate the principle, Lord Reid cited the example of the accountant in *Candler*.

> It was obvious to the defendants that the plaintiff was relying on their skill and judgment and on their having exercised that care which by contract they owed to the company, and I think that any reasonable man in the plaintiffs shoes would have relied on that.[110]

Lord Morris primarily cited cases where a duty was owing outside privity[111] (a road user had a duty to other road users; other examples included *Heaven* v. *Pender* (scaffolding), *George* v. *Skivington* (hair wash), *Donoghue* v. *Stevenson* (infected drink). Logically he saw no distinction between physical and economic damages and thus it seemed to him that:

> ... If A claims that he has suffered injury or loss as a result of acting upon some misstatement made by B who is not in any contractual or fiduciary relationship with him, the inquiry that is first raised is whether B owed any duty to A: if he did the further inquiry raised as to the nature of the duty. There may be circumstances under

which the only duty owed by B to A is the duty of being honest:
there may be circumstances under which B owes to A the duty not
only of being honest but also a duty of taking reasonable care.[112]

In illustrating his principle Lord Morris relied upon the facts and
decision in *Cann* v. *Willson*. In that case the concept of duty owed to
parties outside of contractual or fiduciary relationship would be
limited to situations where one person issued a document which
required professional skill and judgment in its preparation, and where
he knew and intended that its accuracy would be relied upon by
another.[113] This view again seems to coincide directly with that of Lord
Denning in *Candler*.[114] Lord Hodson agreed with Lord Morris'
assessment of where and to whom a duty may arise.[115]

Lord Pearce considered that the creation of a duty and the extent of
that duty would depend ultimately upon the court's assessment of the
demands of society for protection from the carelessness of others. He
cited developments in the US, namely the position of *Glanzer*,
Ultramares and the 1938 Restatement and concluded with approval
that Lord Denning's assessment in *Candler* was correct.[116]

Finally, Lord Devlin, who had had the chance prior to delivering
his opinion to study the above four judgments, stated that on this issue
he was prepared to adopt any one of them as the general rule. This
would indicate that in his opinion at least there was accord amongst
the Law Lords.[117]

In particular Lord Devlin's opinion may be compared with that in
Glanzer. He stated:

> . . . there is ample authority to justify your Lordships in saying now
> that the categories of special relationships which may give rise to a
> duty to take care in word as well as in deed [are] not limited to
> contractual relationships or to relationships of fiduciary duty, but
> include also relationships which in the words of Lord Shaw in
> *Nocton* v. *Lord Ashburton*[10] [are] *'equivalent to contract'* that is,
> where there [is] an assumption of responsibility in circumstances in
> which, but for the absence of consideration, there would be a
> contract.[118]

This view would seem to correspond exactly with the 'end and aim'
principle in *Glanzer*. If such a doctrine as that of *Lawrence* v. *Fox*[119]
were applicable in England, it would then be likely that the court
would employ it here.[120] In general, however, Lord Devlin was

prepared to adopt the Denning view about the circumstances in which the duty to use care in making statements existed.[121]

VII SUMMARY – THE POSITION IN *HEDLEY BYRNE*

The analysis shows that *Hedley Byrne*, in unanimously adopting Lord Denning's view in *Candler*, provides a fairly firm basis to establish the legal liability of accountants to third parties in negligence. What matters in the present context, however, is the link between *Hedley Byrne* and the American cases. Like *Candler*, it is evident that the effect of *Hedley Byrne* may be equated with the position in *Glanzer*, as endorsed by the First Restatement (1938). *Hedley Byrne* goes no further than that.

A further cause therefore for an increase in litigation in American courts may now be argued to have arisen because US law was extended beyond the confines of the First Restatement position and therefore that of *Hedley Byrne*. Moreover it would be mistaken to infer that *Hedley Byrne* encouraged the creation of the Second Restatement, as has been done by some commentators.[122] If courts in England follow the precedent set in the United States we will see an extension of liability to third parties.

NOTES

[1] See for example V. M. Earle, 'Accountants on Trial in a Theatre of the Absurd', *Fortune*, 227, 228 May 1972. Also C. D. Liggio, 'The Expectation Gap: The Accountant's Legal Waterloo?' *The CPA Journal*, 23, 23 July 1975.

[2] *Hedley Byrne & Co Ltd* v. *Heller & Partners Ltd* [1964] A.C. 465; [1963] 3 W.L.R. 101; [1963] 2 All E.R. 575, H.L. (E).

[3] See R. W. V. Dickerson, *Accountants and the Law of Negligence* (Canadian Institute of Chartered Accountants, 1966) p. 91 and R. Baxt, 'The Liability of Accountants and Auditors for Negligent Statements in Company Accounts' 36 *Modern Law Review* 42, 42 (1973).

[4] *Glanzer* v. *Shepard* 233 N.Y. 236, 135 N.E. 275 (1922).

[5] See text accompanying notes 68 *et seq. infra*.

[6] See L. J. Asquith, opinion in *Candler* v. *Crane, Christmas & Co.* [1951] 2 K.B. 164; [1951] 1 T.L.R. 371; [1951] 1 All E.R. 426, C.A. (2 K.B. 164, 186).

[7] *Derry* v. *Peek* (1889) 37 Ch.D. 541; 14 App. Cas. 337.

[8] See [1951] 2 K.B. 164, 187 note 6 *supra*.

[9] W. M. Prosser, 'Misrepresentation and Third Persons', 19 *Vanderbilt Law Review* 231, 235 (March 1966).

[10] *Nocton* v. *Lord Ashburton* [1914] A.C. 932; 30 T.L.R. 602; H.L.

[11] *Woods* v. *Martins Bank* [1959] 1 Q.B. 55.

[12] *Burke* v. *Cory* (1959) 19 D.L.R. 2d 252 (Ont.App.).

[13] *Cann* v. *Willson* (1888) 39 Ch.D. 39.

[14] *Le Lievre* v. *Gould* [1893] 1 Q.B. 491, 9 T.L.R. 243, C.A.

[15] *Old Gate Estate* v. *Toplis* [1939] 3 All E.R. 209.

[16] [1951] 2 K.B. 164. See Posser, note 9 *supra*, p. 235; also A. S. Goodhart, 'Liability for Negligent Misstatements' 78 *Law Quarterly Review* 107 (1962) and Seavey, note 22 *infra*.

[17] [1914] A.C. 932, 947.

[18] *Low* v. *Bouverie* [1891] 3 Ch. 82.

[19] Ibid., see *Candler*, note 6 *supra* [1951] 2 K.B. 164, 201 (citations omitted).

[20] [1951] 2 K.B. 164, 201. citing Salmond (10th ed.) p. 580. The editor of the text considered the rule as anomalous. The law as applied here was stated also by Winfield on *Torts* (4th ed.) p. 386–7 to be anomalous and was disliked.

[21] [1951] 2 K.B. 164, 202.

[22] See for example W. A. Seavey *Candler* v. *Crane, Christmas & Co.* 'Negligent misrepresentation by Accountants', 67 *Law Quarterly Review* 466, 473 (1951); *Journal of Business Law* 27, 34; J. A. Weir, 'Liability for Syntax. A Note on *Hedley Byrne & Co. Ltd.* v. *Heller & Partners Ltd*', [1963] *Cambridge Law Journal* 216, 219; and R. Steven's, '*Hedley Byrne* v. *Heller*: Judicial Creativity and Doctrinal Possibility' 27 *Modern Law Review* 121, 141 (1964).

[23] Seavey, note 22 *supra*, p. 473.

[24] Ibid.

[25] *MacPherson* v. *Buick Motor Co.* 217 N.Y. 382, 111 N.E. 1050 (1916). See Chapter 4 text accompanying notes 8 to 11.

[26] *Winterbottom* v. *Wright* (1842) 10 M. & W. 109.

[27] *Donoghue* v. *Stevenson* [1932] A.C. 562.

[28] Seavey, note 22 *supra*, p. 470, citing Pollock 'The Snail in the Bottle and Thereafter', 49 *Law Quarterly Review* 22 (1933).

[29] [1951] 2 K.B. 164, 174–5.

[30] [1951] 2 K.B. 164, 187.

[31] *Heaven* v. *Pender* (1883) 11 Q.B.D. 503.

[32] *George* v. *Skivington* (1869) L.R. 5 Ex. 1.

[33] [1951] 2 K.B. 164, 192.

[34] As Seavey, note 22 *supra*, notes ' . . . it is the brilliant dissent of Denning L. J. which makes the case memorable', p. 466.

[35] [1951] 1 All E.R. 426 CA.

[36] [1951] 2 K.B. 164, 174.

[37] [1951] 2 K.B. 164, 176.

[38] Ibid. quoting the opinion of Knight, Bruce L. J. in *Slim* v. *Croucher* (1860) 1 De G.F. & J. 518, 527.

[39] Note 14 *supra*, cases cited in support *Evans* v. *Bicknell* (1801) 6 Ves Jun 173, 183; *Slim* v. *Croucher* (1860) 1 De G.F. & J. 518, 4231; *Brownlie* v.

Campbell (1880) 5 App. Cas. 925, 935–6; *Derry* v. *Peek*, *supra*, *Nocton* v. *Ashburton*, *supra*, and *Donoghue* v. *Stevenson supra*.

40 [1951] 2 K.B. 164, 177.

41 [1951] 2 K.B. 164, 179.

42 Ibid. The reasoning behind this was supported by *Fitzherbert* v. *Natura Brenum* (1534) 94D. (blacksmith); *Shiells* v. *Blackburne* (1789) 1 H.Bl. 159, 162 (clerks in the Custom House); and *Everett* v. *Griffiths* [1920] 3 K.B. 163, 182, 217 (doctors).

43 [1951] 2 K.B. 164, 180–1.

44 [1951] 2 K.B. 164, 180.

45 [1951] 2 K.B. 164, 181.

46 Ibid, emphasis added; supported by *Langridge* v. *Levy* (1837) 2 M. & W. 519, *George* v. *Skivington*, *supra*, *Cann* v. *Willson*, *supra*, *Heaven* v. *Pender supra*.

47 [1951] 2 K.B. 164, 182.

48 Supported by *Everett* v. *Griffiths* [1920] 3 K.B. 163; *Donoghue* v. *Stevenson*, *supra*, and *Humphrey* v. *Bowers* (1939) H.S.T.L.R. 297.

49 [1951] 2 K.B. 164, 183.

50 *Ultramares Corporation* v. *Touche et al* 255 N.Y. 170, 174 N.E. 441 (1931).

51 [1951] 2 K.B. 164, 183. See Chapter 4, text accompanying notes 34 *et seq*.

52 [1951] 2 K.B. 164, 184.

53 Ibid.

54 [1951] 2 K.B. 164, 185.

55 See Chapter 4, text accompanying notes 20 *et seq*. See also 'Note – Torts – Negligent Language – Accountants' Liability to Third Persons', *Rutgers Law Review* 478, 480 (1952).

56 See Chapter 5, text accompanying notes 24–41.

57 As noted *supra* the Companies Act, 1948 ss. 40 and 43 with regard to a prospectus. Cf. with Cardozo in *Ultramares*, who stated that such a measure to extend liability should be brought by legislation and not through the common law courts. The Securities Acts of 1933 and 1934 provided that legislative support.

58 Chapter 5, text accompanying note 94. See also *Rutgers Law Review* 478, 479 (1952) note 55 *supra*.

59 This is supported by Lords Devlin and Pearce in *Hedley Byrne*, note 2 *supra*, at [1964] A.C. 465, 531 and 539.

60 Chapter 5, Table XII.

61 For a further analysis of *Candler* with American precedent see Seavey, note 22 *supra*, especially pp. 476 *et seq*.

62 Stevens, note 22 *supra*, pp. 129–30.

63 See text accompanying note 38 *supra*.

64 Lord Hodson stated: 'So far I have done no more than summarise the argument addressed to the Court of Appeal in *Candler's* case to which effect was given in the dissenting judgment of Denning, L. J., with which I respectfully agree in so far as it dealt with the facts of that case. I am therefore of opinion that his judgment is to be preferred to that of the majority, although the opinion of the majority is undoubtedly supported by the *ratio decidendi* of *Le Lievre* v. *Gould* which they cannot be criticised for following'. [1964] A.C. 465, 509.

65 [1964] A.C. 465, 466. Also Stevens, note 22 *supra*, p. 126.
66 [1964] A.C. 465, 465–6.
67 See Baxt, note 3 *supra*, p. 45; Stevens, note 22 *supra*, pp. 141 *et seq.*;
   R. W. M. Dias, 'Postscript' to Weir, note 22 *supra*, [1963] *Cambridge law
   Journal* 220, 220–1; Hodgin, note 22 *supra*, pp. 28, 30. See also articles by
   Gordon 38 *Australian Law Journal* 39, 79 (1967) and Atiyah 83 *Law
   Quarter Review*, 248 (1967).
68 According to Stevens, *supra*, not3 22, p. 141, *Hedley Byrne* leaves many
   questions unanswered. 'The basic question remains; if the judges are to
   remould common law principles, how far should they seek to direct future
   development? It was said of Carlyle that "he led people out into the
   wilderness and left them there". In terms of law, the House of Lords in
   Hedley Byrne has achieved the same result . . . it is impossible to tell
   whether the effect on doctrine will be fundamental and profound, or
   whether it will be trivial and unimportant.'
69 [1964] A.C. 465, 533.
70 Speech before the Annual General Meeting, Bar Council, 15 July 1963.
   Quoted by Stevens, note 22 *supra*, p. 125 footnote 14.
71 [1964] A.C. 465, 514–32.
72 [1964] A.C. 465, 532–3. 'My Lords, I have devoted much time and thought
   to considering the first reason given by Mr Foster [respondents' counsel] for
   rejecting the appellant's claim. I have done so not only because his reason
   was based on a ground so fundamental that it called for a full refutation but
   also because it is impossible to find the correct answer on the facts to the
   appellants' claim until the relevant criteria for ascertaining whether or not
   there is a duty to take care has been clearly established.' [1964] A.C. 465,
   532 (Lord Devlin).
73 *Rondel* v. *Worsley*, [1966] 3 All E.R. 657 (C.A.); [1967] 3 All E.R. 973
   (H.L.).
74 See Hodgin, note 22 *supra*, p. 28.
75 Ibid.
76 [1967] 2 All E.R. 850.
77 Hodgin, note 22 *supra*, p. 30. Further implications of the *ratio/obiter*
   implications are analysed by Dias, note 67 *supra*.
78 *Robinson* v. *National Bank of Scotland, Ltd.* [1916] S.C. (H.L.) 154.
79 See Lord Devlin's summary [1964] A.C. 465, 514–15.
80 [1964] A.C. 465, 514.
81 [1964] A.C. 465, 470–1.
82 *International Products Co.* v. *Erie R.R. Co.* 244 N.Y. 331 (1927).
83 *Mulroy* v. *Wright* 240 N.W. 116 (1931).
84 *Doyle* v. *Chatham & Phenix National Bank* 253 N.Y. 369 (1930).
85 *Edwards* v. *Lamb* 69 N.H. 599 (1899).
86 Text accompanying notes 71–2 *supra*.
87 [1964] A.C. 465. Lord Reid, p. 484, Lord Morris, p. 500, Lord Hodson,
   p. 512, Lord Devlin, p. 518 and Lord Pearce, p. 535.
88 [1914] A.C. 932, 947.
89 [1964] A.C. 465. Lord Reid, p. 482, Lord Morris, p. 496, Lord Hodson,
   p. 509, Lord Devlin, pp 515–17 and Lord Pearce, p. 534.
90 See Lord Devlin's opinion, [1964] A.C. 465, 516.

[91] [1964] A.C. 465, 517.
[92] See Atiyah, note 67 *supra*, pp. 248–61 and Stevens, note 22 *supra*, p. 241. See also Seavey's comments after *Candler*, note 22 *supra*, p. 473.
[93] *Electrochrome Ltd.* v. *Welsh Plastics Ltd* [1968] 2 All E.R. 205; *S.C.M. (UK) Ltd.* v. *W.J. Whittall & Son Ltd* [1971] Q.B. 337.
[94] *The Mutual Life & Citizens' Assurance Company Ltd and Another* v. *Evatt* [1971] A.C. 793, 378 A.L.J.R. 31.12.1970.
[95] Baxt, note 3 *supra*, p. 51.
[96] [1964] A.C. 465, 482.
[97] [1964] A.C. 465, 494. Baxt, note 3 *supra*, p. 49 has stated that this opinion of Lord Morris meant that a *duty* was owed to anyone unnamed and unknown. However, it may be argued that Lord Morris did not mean this by his opinion. The opinion gave him an opportunity to analyse the duty position and avoid the questions raised by the respondents that the third parties were unknown. In addition Baxt's follow-up sentence does not support his first argument: 'He even went further to suggest that, even though there was no direct dealing between persons, liability would still exist " . . . where one person issues a document which should be the result of an exercise of the skill and judgment required by him in his calling, and *where he knows* and intends that its accuracy will be relied on by another". ([1964] A.C. 465, 497)', p. 49.
[98] A.C. 465, 505–7.
[99] [1893] 1 Q.B. 491, 497. [1964] A.C. 465, 506.
[100] See text accompanying notes 43–62 *supra*.
[101] [1964] A.C. 465, 524.
[102] [1964] A.C. 465, 525.
[103] Note 2 *supra*. This view was supported by Lord Pearce, [1964] A.C. 465, 536.
[104] Note 103 *supra*.
[105] Chapter 5 text accompanying notes 102 *et seq. supra* [1964] A.C. 465, 538–9.
[106] See text accompanying notes 43–62 *supra*.
[107] Unless specifically excluded.
[108] For a contrary view of this opinion see Baxt, note 3 *supra*, p. 49.
[109] [1964] A.C. 465, 486.
[110] [1964] A.C. 465, 487.
[111] [1964] A.C. 465, 495.
[112] Ibid.
[113] [1964] A.C. 465, 497.
[114] See note 108 *supra*.
[115] [1964] A.C. 465, 514.
[116] [1964] A.C. 465, 538–9.
[117] See note 108 *supra*.
[118] [1964] A.C. 465, 528–9.
[119] *Lawrence* v. *Fox* 20 N.Y. 268 (1859).
[120] See Chapter 4, footnote 22 *supra*, re third party beneficiary contract.
[121] [1964] A.C. 465, 530.
[122] See Chapter 5 text accompanying notes 90 *et seq.*

7 SIGNIFICANT DIFFERENCES BETWEEN THE US AND UK LEGAL SYSTEMS AND THEIR EFFECTS UPON ACCOUNTANTS' LEGAL LIABILITY

I INTRODUCTION

This chapter analyses certain major procedural differences in the legal systems of the US and UK. The purpose is to evaluate additional reasons why an increase in litigation has occurred in the US but not in this country.

The class action suit has been a fundamental cause for increased litigation in America. There is no directly comparable procedure in England, although the procedure known as the representative action has some similarities. The chapter discusses the two systems and indicates why the representative action in England is not employed to the same extent and effect as the class action suit in the United States.

The chapter commences with a description of the legal cost systems of the two countries, another area of difference. In America the 'contingent fee' facility which most effectively operates in conjunction with the class action procedure has also been a contributing factor to litigation. In England no contingent fee system is permitted.

II THE LEGAL COSTS SYSTEM IN AMERICA[1]

In any action there are essentially two types of costs[2] which may be incurred:

1. Payments with respect to the actual case in court (court fees and witness fees, for example); and
2. Payments with respect to retaining counsel (and in this respect expert witnesses for the party, such as accountants, investigators, etc.).

The expenditure under (1) is seldom large with respect to the total amount of any claim or when compared to (2), where the main sums are involved and therefore of most significance in any action. It will always be in the interests of either party in a case to reduce the costs of (2) as far as possible because under the American legal system these will almost always[3] be borne by the contracting party whether successful or unsuccessful in an action.[4]

(i) Recoverable costs

In any action, an unsuccessful party will be responsible for certain expenses of his opponent. A party entitled to recover or 'tax' costs may include in his bill only such items of expense as are taxable by virtue of legislative enactment.[5] In some states the legislatures have specifically defined the items of expense which are recoverable as costs by the party.[6] These expenses or costs may include items such as:

1. the cost of serving process on the adverse party;
2. the expense of taking depositions;[7]
3. fees and travel allowances paid to witnesses when subpoenaed;[8]
4. the cost of serving subpoenas on witnesses;[9]
5. filing fees paid to the clerk of the court and copies of required documents;[10]
6. jury fees;[11]
7. fees paid to the sheriff, marshall, etc. on delivery to him of an execution;[12]
8. advertising expenses in cases where such is required.

These (and similar expenses) the prevailing party is entitled to claim in full following a judgment.[13]

The costs which the court does not recognise as recoverable by a successful litigant, there being no right of recovery existing at common law,[14] include:

1. counsel fees;[15]
2. accountants' fees;

3. investigators and other expert witness fees;[16]
4. expenses incurred by the above in the time before and during the trial in connection with the preparation of the case.

Certain costs, termed statutory costs, may be offset against these expenses and are payable to the prevailing party. These costs are determined according to the number of terms of court involved and the length of the trials involved.[17] The total of these statutory costs is generally low, even in a lengthy trial. Therefore a successful litigant can never hope to be fully compensated from this source in an action.[18] The longer the trial, the greater the statutory costs – but also the greater the litigants' counsel fees.

The stringency of the American system of costs, especially against a successful defendant who has been forced to defend his case, has led some commentators[19] to call for reform of the system. However, the facility of the contingent fee has relieved much of the cost burden, at least as far as a plaintiff is concerned.

(ii) Contingent fees[20]

One commentator has written:[21]

> Every American schoolboy knows from the *Pickwick Papers* that fees 'on spec' are not acceptable in England. Contrariwise, in the United States for well over a hundred years[22] contingent fees have found favour as á means of enforcing rights which would otherwise be lost by those not financially able to support long and costly litigation, however meritorious.[23]

In America the validity of the contingent fee system (where an attorney agrees to take on a case on the basis that he will only receive a fee if the action is successful) is bound up with the desire for justice.[24] Contracts for contingent fees are thought to be as much for the benefit of the client as of the attorney, especially in cases where the client has a meritorious cause of action but no means to pay for legal services.[25]

(iii) How the contingent fee system works

By retaining an attorney on a contingent fee basis the plaintiff by prior arrangement agrees to advance or be liable for all necessary disbursements in the litigation. For his part the attorney agrees to serve the plaintiff without any liability on the part of the plaintiff for payment of a fee.

On recovery or settlement of the action the attorney then shares in the proceeds established as damages by the court (this percentage share may be from 10 per cent to 50 per cent dependant upon the damages award).[26]

Courts have recognised that there is potential abuse by unscrupulous attorneys over naive litigants, and have therefore applied strict criteria for the establishment of the relevant fee.[27] For example in New York, certain courts[28] have laid down a strict structure for the establishment of the correct fee for personal injury cases, such that the fee shall not exceed 50 per cent of the first $1,000 of the judgment, 40 per cent of the next $2,000, 35 per cent of the next $22,000, 20 per cent of the next $25,000 and 15 per cent of any amount over $50,000.[29]

Recently it has been feared that a lawyer's self interest in a lawsuit might come between him and his client, not only with respect to the amount of the fee but also with respect to the control of the suit on such questions as whether to accept an offer of settlement. To prevent these possible abuses of the system some courts have attempted limited regulation of contingent fee agreements in the same way as New York.[30]

In the event of the case not being judged in favour of the plaintiff the attorney does not receive a fee and the only costs for which the plaintiff will be liable are the statutory and other costs outlined above.[31]

The contingent fee system may also influence the question of settlement between the parties.[32] The desire for settlement in fact affects all parties to the litigation. The plaintiff attorney is eager to settle so as to avoid extensive preparatory paper and investigatory work; the plaintiffs wish to settle so as to reduce as far as possible his attorney's fees; the defendant may wish to settle not only to avoid extensive and possibly damaging publicity through protracted court action but also because the knowledge of an attorney working on a contingency basis implies an attorney sure of the merits of the case and eager to win the suit.[33] The defendant's attorney[34] may also be eager to settle for the same reason, and in any event he is assured of some fee. The contingent fee basis obviously does not apply to a defendant in an action.

The effects of the class action suit upon costs and the contingent fee systems are discussed at length after an analysis of the English system of costs.[35]

III THE LEGAL COSTS SYSTEM IN ENGLAND[36]

In England, it hardly needs stressing, a litigant rarely brings or defends an action without realising that costs are a major consideration, and that these may greatly exceed the actual sum of recovery. In America, on the other hand, the question of costs does not raise such an issue.[37]

Like the American system, costs in the English system fall essentially under two sets:

1. 'Solicitor and own client' costs. The costs which each party will have to pay his solicitor under the normal contractual relationship.
2. 'Party and party' costs. The costs which an unsuccessful litigant may be ordered to pay his opponent. These costs will be 'taxed' (assessed) by the court; however, they rarely cover the costs the successful litigant will have to pay his own solicitor.

The difference between (1) and (2) above is usually termed 'extra costs' and represents what the litigant must pay from his own resources from the money damages awarded (if such be the case). If the action is one of injunction or rescission of contract, for example, the litigant must pay these extra costs himself as there is unlikely to be any money award.[38]

(i) The make-up of a solicitor's costs[39]

These costs may be divided into two sections following the system of dual representation in the English legal system. The solicitor dealing and contracting directly with the client undertakes the preparatory work on a case, which will usually consist of establishing evidence and negotiating with the opponents in litigation. The solicitor also has direct dealings with the counsel, giving rise to the second division of costs.[40]

The solicitor's costs are established more or less upon a fixed fee system based upon the hours worked, documents prepared, correspondence, etc.[41] The counsel fees however are calculated after negotiation between solicitor and barrister and a brief fee determined, supplemented by a refresher paid to the barrister for every day after the first day he appears in court. Where employed, a junior is entitled to two-thirds of the amount of the leader. The brief fee depends upon the estimated amount of work involved in the case and the standing of the counsel.[42] The amount involved in any case (damages claimed etc.) is not relevant to the calculation of the brief fee. The result is that in a case involving small recovery the solicitor's total cost will be proportionately greater than in a case involving a larger recovery and longer court time. The counsel receiving a percentage of recovery in fees in America in a large case is likely to be considerably better off than his equivalent in England. In a small case the English lawyer is likely to be better off.[43]

(ii) The liability for costs

It is a basic common law right in England that the litigant who is successful will be awarded his costs.[44] Although this right has been weakened through legislation making cost awards discretionary, the normal practice is to award costs when an innocent party is successful and has committed no misconduct.[45] The philosophy ·behind this doctrine is that a totally innocent party should not be subjected to litigation in the first instance; and thus the award attempts to re-establish the financial position of the wronged litigant. Another aim of the system is to make the party to a suit wary of continuing the action when in the wrong. Thus in English law the doctrine applies, that 'costs should follow the event', the event being the judgment of the case in the normal suit.

IV THE EFFECTS OF THE COST SYSTEMS ON LITIGATION

In England, unlike the United States, the cost system is effective as a means of discouraging unfair and unnecessary litigation.[46] At every stage of an action, from summons to final appeal, paramount in the parties' minds is the costs question. The Rules of the Supreme Court rule at length on various aspects of costs, which deter any party from employing the court system to unfair advantage.[47] Goodhart has suggested that one reason why in England there are many less appeals than in the United States is that ' . . . an Englishman does not appeal, unless he thinks that he has a good chance of winning, [this] is based on the fact that if he loses his appeal he will, as a general rule, have to pay his opponent's costs of appeal'.[48] The costs on appeal are comparable to those in the trial court. If a litigant considers a further appeal to the House of Lords, the costs may run into thousands of pounds.[49] In addition, security for costs will have to be paid prior to appeal.

The Rules as to costs not only control actions which are seriously prosecuted, but also prevent persons from commencing or defending a suit without any real intention of bringing it to trial. A plaintiff may, under certain circumstances, discontinue an action but he must then pay the defendant's costs.[50] These will include all the expenses which the defendant has reasonably incurred in preparing his case up to the time of the discontinuance. The same is true if the defendant discontinues.[51]

The Rules favour, as far as possible, settlements of actions before trial so that unnecessary occupation of the court and expense to the parties may both be avoided. The procedure of paying into court is one method of ensuring settlement of action before trial.

Goodhart explains this system:

> The object of this innovation is to provide a medium of compromise for cases where the defendant is willing to pay something for the sake of peace, rather than incur the expense and risk of proving he is not at fault. A defendant before trial may, in satisfaction of the claim or without admitting liability, pay a sum of money into court which the plaintiff is free to accept or refuse. If he refuses it and proceeds to trial, and does not recover more than the sum paid into court, he will, as a rule, be deprived of his costs of the issues as to liability. If he accepts the payment, he receives, under Order 22.r7. the general costs of the action down to the time of payment in.[52]

The English law is practical in the sense that it considers there may be some unscrupulous litigants willing to resort to any lengths or technicalities to avoid a trial. By delaying tactics or extensive appeal some litigants may hope to deter a party from pursuing an action. The system of costs in England attempts to deter such practices by making it financially unprofitable to undertake such a course. The Rules are applied against defendants who attempt to obstruct justice. The fear of substantial costs is the deterrent used by the courts and is one major reason why the English courts are not inundated with cases and appeals to the same extent as in the United States.[53]

Arguably, neither system of costs, the English or the American really provides sufficient remedy for the wronged investor who has suffered financial loss by relying upon negligent or fraudulent misrepresentations. Only when an investor has the facility of the contingent fee will he have some assurance that he will not be out of pocket at the end of a trial – even if it is decided in his favour. On the other hand it is unlikely that a small investor will be able to retain a lawyer on a contingent fee basis because the amount of recovery will be so small.[54]

Both systems are open to criticism. The English system has been criticised because advantages lie always in the hands of the wealthier party. The indemnity system of costs implies that the parties are not afraid to spend large amounts, subject to the Rules enunciated above, in ensuring success and therefore some recovery.[55] The wealthier party can manage to pay the balance of costs he may have to bear whether successful or unsuccessful in the action.

The American system has also been criticised because of a comparable advantage to the wealthier party. The poorer party simply cannot risk a protracted case without a contingent fee contract, because of the considerable attorney fees he will have to pay – win or lose. Even if he is certain that he has been wronged he may not be able to afford to bring an action.[56]

This state of affairs has made the contingent fee system, allied to the class action suit, the panacea for the small investor in America.[57]

V THE AMERICAN CLASS ACTION SUIT

(i) The characteristics of a class action

A class action is one in which one or more members of a numerous class, having a common interest, may sue on behalf of themselves and all other members of the class.[58] The claims of a number of individuals against the same defendant are brought together, yielding considerable economies in time and expense which otherwise each individual would have incurred in order to bring an action himself to obtain relief.[59]

The contemporary class action suit originated in the English Court of Chancery in the seventeenth century, and for approximately two hundred years the procedure was virtually unknown except to the élite group of lawyers who practised exclusively before the Chancellor. Chancery suits, at that time, invariably involved questions of property title concerning numerous people and families.[60]

The American class action procedure has a number of purposes bound up with the desire in the American Jurisdiction to allow justice for all, regardless of wealth.

One purpose is to prevent the multiplicity of suits. Thus when certain tests of adequacy are met, members of the class are saved the cost and trouble of filing and defending separate suits. Moreover, the defendant is freed from litigation in the future by similar plaintiffs pleading the same causes of action.[61] Another purpose is to enhance the cause of justice by ensuring that even the small litigant may seek retribution. Additionally, class actions lessen the possibility of various courts differing in opinion and judgment on essentially similar issues.[62] The class action also enables a case to be brought where the numbers constituting the class are so numerous as to make their joinder as parties impractical under the usual rules of procedure. By establishing a technique whereby the claims of many individuals can be resolved at the same time, the class suit eliminates the possibility of repetitious litigation.[63] This administration point reinforces the economic argument that class suits allow recovery of damages in amounts too small to pursue on their own.

The class action suit, in which all claims are collected together, may also avoid jurisdictional amount limitations imposed by some state courts. There is also the advantage that all parties benefiting from an action will share in the expenses of that action. Originally, it was hoped that the class action would save the court time; in practice, the number of class actions has led to the courts being overwhelmed with cases.[64]

The class action suit has both economic and procedural advantages. It also has psychological advantages.[65] The threat of the class action suit is thought to act as a deterrent to a defendant who has wronged a large class of individuals, even though each individual of the class may have only been nominally injured financially.

(ii) Types of class action

Prior to the 1966 amendment of Rule 23(a) of the Federal Rules of Civil Procedure,[66] three types of class action were defined and recognised by federal and state courts. States may still continue to recognise the three types of suit despite the amendment.[67]

The 'true' class action is one where there is a joint or common right amongst parties. One party having failed to exercise the right, the other parties may sue to recover that right.[68]

The 'hybrid' class action includes suits where the rights sought to be enforced are several, and the object is to adjudicate separate claims against specific property.[69]

The 'spurious' class action includes suits where the rights sought to be enforced are several, and there is a common question of law or fact affecting such several rights and a common relief is sought.[70]

This third type of action will normally be the type which shareholders will bring because there will not be a right to a common fund or common property, but only the right of an indeterminate (prior to trial) damages award. The justification of the spurious class action is its convenience in litigating numerous individual claims in one action. It is really an invitation to all persons similarly situated to join the action and litigate their several claims. However, the suit has no binding effect on the members of the class who are not parties to the action.[71]

Under the Rule 23(a) amendment in 1966 the above classification was re-defined and the Rule gives attention to a class action based upon or involving questions of law or fact common to the class.[72] This would seem to indicate that the spurious class action, defined above, has become the main type of class action because of its facility of permissive joinder. However the new Rule 23(b)(3) suit, although having some similarities to the previous spurious class action, also has more important differences. The present Rule binds all members of the class who do not affirmatively exclude themselves, whereas the spurious class action bound only those who participated in the action.[73]

Most of the recent litigation in the commercial field has occurred under the amended Rule 23(b)(3). This type of action is favoured because it lends itself to cases involving securities frauds and other securities violations – areas of the law in which individual investors or purchasers previously were ill-equipped to seek redress.[74] Another reason the action is popular in the securities area is that the filing of the original action delays the operation of the Statute of Limitations.[75]

(iii) The procedure and management of a class action[76]

The Federal Rules provide that as soon as practicable after the commencement of a class action the court shall determine by order whether it is to be so maintained. This may involve a hearing as in other types of litigation. Having met the basic prerequisites of Rule 23(a), the action may proceed as a class action. The basic prerequisites are that (1) there must be questions of law or fact common to the class; (2) those common questions must predominate over questions affecting the individual members; and (3) the plaintiff must make a preliminary showing that there is a substantial possibility of success in the litigation on the merits of the case.[77] If there is a negative determination by the court then actions will proceed as separate causes.[78]

(1) Notice to class members

In order to satisfy the American jurisdictional requirement of due process in law, a party cannot be bound by a judgment *in personam* in an action to which he has not been made a party, and in the same way absent parties who are part of an action should also be protected.[79] Thus there will normally be a need to serve notice to all the members of the class. This notice should be advertised such that each member is likely to receive notice, and should provide availability for objection to carrying on in the suit.

Subdivision (c)(2) of Rule 23 provides, in addition, that *individual* notice be given to all identifiable members of a (b)(3) class. This provision from the standpoint of cost alone is a great deterrent to the class action's role as a semi-public remedy.[80] The magnitude of the classes in many present day suits is so great as to make the cost of notice prohibitive. In *Eisen*,[81] as one example, where about four million job lot investors were involved the estimated cost of notice was put at $500,000.[82]

It is now generally recognised that if certain reforms[83] concerning the requirement for notice to *all* members of a class, and payment of that notice by the representatives of the class, are made obligatory then the value of the class action suit will dramatically decrease.[84] One class action lawyer has noted:

> The primary value of Rule 23 is that it enables small claimants to seek redress without the prohibitive cost of lawyers. . . . If defendants have their way Rule 23, born of economic necessity, will expire, the victim of economic pressure. . . . [Individual class members] notification, for which defendants contend plaintiff must pay, costs money; if the defendants have their way – lots of it . . . [C]lass action defence counsel have become grim disciples of a back bending due process. . . . There is delicious irony in the wrong-doer's insistences upon a perfectionist notice where the result is not to implement the remedy but to defeat it. If the tactic succeeds, Rule 23 is as dead as the dodo.[85]

In arguing against the need to have any notice, Pomerantz[86] quoted the findings from one case where, after notice had been sent out, only one per cent of the class replied to the effect that they wished to opt out of the suit. However, of this one per cent no member then went on to make his own claim. This would have been the only logical reason for opting out of the class, because exclusion cuts out the member from the benefits of judgment in plaintiff's favour.

(2) Pleading

A suit is usually pleaded by named plaintiffs on behalf of themselves and all others interested or all others similarly situated.[87] One who sues must allege the facts which make the action a proper class action, and must justify representation of the absent members of the class. It must also be shown that:

1. there is a cause of action;
2. there is community of interest between all the class members;
3. the member bringing the action is representative of all the class' interest;
4. the members of the class are numerous;
5. it is impracticable to enjoin them all in the action.[88]

(3) Judgment

Under the present rule whereby all class members are part of the action unless they explicitly absent themselves, the judgment will be binding upon all the members (the so-called *res judicata* doctrine). If a member explicitly opts out of a class action suit, he will not fall within the *res judicata* doctrine and may therefore bring his own action after the original suit has been tried. Defendants are keen therefore to ensure that as many members of the class are included in the one main action, to avoid the expense of numerous subsidiary actions.[89]

(4) Expenses and costs

Unnamed parties who have benefited from a class action, it is generally held, must contribute to the expenses of the proceedings, including the fee for the attorney of the named representatives. In a class action to recover a money judgment, all of the costs and expenses of litigation which are not assessed against the losing defendant should be borne by the members of the plaintiff class in proportion to the amount that each would receive by reason of the judgment.[90] Class action suits are therefore a contradiction to the general rule that only those parties contracting with an attorney are responsible for his fee.[91]

Although the common law rule is that attorney's fees are not ordinarily recoverable as costs from adversary defendants, an award of fees in favour of a plaintiff has occasionally been enforced against losing defendants. This is usually at the discretion of the court and reflects its opinion of defendant's conduct.[92]

The American Law Institute is undertaking a project known as the Federal Securities Code, in an attempt to consolidate the present Federal Securities status, rules and cases.[93] Section 1418(d) of the Code, headed 'Costs: General' states:

> In a private action created by or based on a violation of this code . . . the court, on a finding of bad faith or lack of merit in the action or defences (as the case may be), may (1) assess reasonable costs (including reasonable attorney's fees) against any party, and (2) require any party any time to give an undertaking for the payment of such costs.[94]

According to Jaenicke,[95] this section would permit the award of attorney's fees to the prevailing party, including the defendant. The effect of this would be to effectively discourage 'strike' suits, and thereby class actions, under the present Rule 10b-5.[96] If this code becomes accepted by the courts, the system of costs will become more comparable with the English indemnity system.

(5) Costs, contingent fees and class actions
The Federal Securities Code revision is a direct result of the considerable outcry in legal journals and the press concerning the fees received by attorneys following a class action suit or settlement. The contingent fee system works very closely with the class action procedure for the reason that an attorney, on successful judgment, is assured a substantial fee as the client base is extended from perhaps one or two plaintiffs in a normal suit to a whole class of 'clients' restricted only by the total number of members of that class. The court will take this into account when assessing the fees payable. In addition, the contingent fee attorney will receive his fee, the proportion of the damages fund awarded, prior to the distribution of that fund to the plaintiffs.

In this connection, the class action/contingent fee procedure has been criticised because of its facility for abuse.[97] The fact that a lawyer is able to establish a range of clients restricted only by the size of the class is thought by some to be contrary to the canons of professional ethics.[98] On the other hand, some have defended the system on judicial grounds. Pomerantz notes:

> The class action is born of economics – the economics of the client as well as that of the lawyer. Its premise is simple. When the same wrong is done to a large number of people, no one person generally suffers sufficient damage to justify the expense of hiring a lawyer.

The class action device now solves the problem by enabling any member of the class to get a lawyer for free. The lawyer, by invoking class action principles, is able to sue not just for the few dollars lost by his client but for the often millions of dollars of which the entire class was victimised. The lawyer's motive power is the pot of gold at the end of the rainbow.[99]

Of course, in the class action suit the attorney is taking on a 'semi-public' function. He may be supporting many hundreds of wronged investors who would never normally resort to the courts.[100] He is also bearing all the risk of the action because of the contingent nature of the fee. In addition, the attorney may also underwrite other costs of the action, such as notice requirements, statutory costs, etc., which will be due if the defendant is successful.[101]

VI SOME LIMITATIONS OF THE CLASS ACTION SUIT

Since 1966[102] interest has grown considerably in the possible uses of the class action suit.[103] This interest, inside and outside the US,[104] is due to the fact that the device has been employed in such a wide range of situations, resulting in an explosion of litigation and court settlements. Its use has been seen in securities frauds, anti-trust cases, civil rights and in consumer cases such as malpractice by manufacturers, advertisers employing deceptive trade practices and environmentalist groups.[105] It has also been used to advantage against firms of accountants by third party investors relying upon their reports.

Despite this increase in the use of the class suit, its abilities and purposes should not be over-emphasised. The class action suit is purely a procedural device, established originally to save court time and expense. Enthusiasts of the class action (and even those against it) tend to consider that once a suit is accepted as a class action the plaintiffs are assured retribution.[106] But the conversion of a normal suit into a class action does not ensure plaintiffs any greater likelihood of success in the courts.

Any claim has to be tried on its facts, and any case which is not soundly based on fact and law, regardless of the number of plaintiffs, will not succeed. As Williams notes:

If the law gives no remedy to an individual it does not help to draw on the mantle of a class claim and to sue also on behalf of other persons in the same situation; the multiplication by a hundred or even a thousand fold does not justify an individual claim that has no foundation. . . . Unless the substantive law gives a remedy a class action will be of no avail.[107]

The class action is recognised as having a number of limitations which may act as a deterrent to the introduction of a similar procedural device in countries such as the UK. Although the class action procedure was established to save court time, recently some actions have taken so long to pass through the courts that any previous economic advantages which may have existed were destroyed.[108] The delay has been caused by two aspects of American jurisprudence; the pre-trial discovery process and the due process requirement.

Discovery is the process whereby every party in a civil action is entitled, prior to trial, to the disclosure of all relevant information in the possession of any person. The purpose of the process in the words of the Supreme Court is that: 'Mutual knowledge of all the relevant facts gathered by both parties is essential to proper litigation. To that end either party may compel the other to disgorge whatever facts he has in his possession'.[109] In this way disclosure of factual information and testimony is carried out before the trial, reducing the possibility of surprise during trial.[110] The Federal Rules permit inspection, discovery of documents, and interrogation much as they are permitted in England, but the 'deposition' process is unknown to English law.[111] This process which is part of pre-trial discovery allows either side to examine before the trial the other party under oath, without leave of the court. The results of these depositions may be used as evidence in the trial.

In class actions, the discovery process has been used by unscrupulous litigants to a considerable extent in order to protract the action.[112] The discovery phase in complex litigation 'has become so costly, so time-consuming and so exasperating, that litigants are being priced out of the courts'.[113] On this point, one court has held that 'it is anomalous that the class action rule which began as a device to assure judicial expediency, may become a gigantic burden on the courts' resources beyond its capacity to manage or effectively control'.[114]

Apart from being slow and cumbersome the courts have also been burdened with administrative problems in running the class action. The courts' procedures, whilst for example calculating individual damages awards after trial or in settlement, represent a considerable burden apart from the pure jurisdictional aspects of a case.[115]

A further criticism of the class action device has come from lawyers and accountants against the so-called 'deep-pocket' theory. A corporation's professional advisers are added to a class suit on the basis that, if the corporation is unable to provide sufficient damages, these will be provided by the insurance cover of the professional adviser. This has meant that the action is brought against those who are able to pay rather than against the real tortfeasors. This is an important reason why numerous claims are made against accountants and why insurance premiums have soared.

VII THE ENGLISH 'CLASS ACTION' SUIT

Although a great deal is heard about the American class action suit, very little is reported about its English counterpart. In English law, the term 'class action' does not exist, but the procedure is directly comparable with the 'representative' action from which American law derived the class action suit.

(i) The rules for representative proceedings[116]

Under the Rules of the Supreme Court[117] where numerous persons have the same interest in any proceedings, then an action may be begun and continued by (or against) any one or more of them as representing all or representing all except one or more of them.[118]

Any judgment or order given in proceedings is binding on all the persons whom the plaintiffs sue as representing the class of defendants; but it cannot be enforced against any person not a party to the proceedings, except with the leave of the court.[119]

The basis of the representative action stems from the original practice in the Court of Chancery.[120] That court required *the presence* of all parties interested in a suit in order that a final end might be made to the controversy; but when the parties were so numerous that they never could 'come to justice' the rule was relaxed, and a representative suit was allowed. In such an event, individuals would be selected from the numerous class of litigants to represent the rest.[121]

(ii) Application of the rule

It is an essential condition of a representative action that the persons who are to be represented, and the person or persons representing them, should have the same interest in the same proceedings.[122] In particular it is essential that all the members of the alleged class should have a *common interest*, that all should have a *common grievance*, and that the relief is in its nature *beneficial to all*.[123]

If there exists a common interest and a common grievance, a representative suit may be brought if the relief sought is in its nature beneficial to all whom the plaintiff proposes to represent.[124] However, if some of the class represented by the plaintiff have also adverse interests, or desire to stand aloof, they should be excluded from the action and may, if they are few, be made defendants in the action. In this way they will be bound by the judgment and unable to bring subsequent actions.[125]

In order to bring a representative action, the mere existence of a common 'wrong' will not necessarily suffice if there is no common 'right' or common purpose. Thus in *Markt & Co. Ltd.* v. *Knight S.S. Co. Ltd.* it was held that an action could not proceed when each plaintiff relied on a separate contract, and where the claim of each depended on its own merits.

No representative action can be made where the only relief to be claimed is damages. This is because none of the persons represented in the action has any interest in the damages recovery of the representative(s) bringing the action (thus there is no common interest): *Markt & Co. Ltd.* Take, for example, the case where, by means of similar or identical frauds, a man obtains several sums of money from numerous persons. Although his fraudulent action is common to them all, they do not possess any common object as between themselves, and therefore a representative action would probably not be held maintainable under the rule. However, where in such a case the several persons from whom monies are obtained subscribed those monies with a common object, as for example becoming shareholders of a company, the rule would be held applicable.[126]

If an action is brought for example by shareholders of a company relying upon a company's prospectus, they do not need to prove that the reliance upon the alleged fraud was the case of their advancing money to purchase the shares. The doctrine that there shall be no necessity for any supplementary inquiries prior to adjudging the rights of individuals to an action does not necessarily preclude the bringing of an action.[127]

In tort cases the rule only applies where it is clear that every person to be represented is under the same liability and has the same defences in respect of the claim by which the action is brought. The rule has been held to apply in an action for negligence.[128]

The rule only applies where the persons having the same cause in the proceedings are 'numerous'. In *Re Braybrook*[129] so small a number as five was not held to be 'numerous', unless the amount involved was very small and all the members have expressed a desire for the action to proceed.

Under the rules of the Supreme Court, where an action is brought by one of a class on behalf of the class the court has no jurisdiction to order payment of costs by persons who are not in fact made parties to the action.[130]

VIII THE REPRESENTATIVE AND DERIVATIVE SUIT IN A MINORITY SHAREHOLDER CONTEXT

The representative action is included in most company law texts within the section on minority shareholder's rights.[131] This is because of the facility to use the procedure against the company, directors and others. Protection would be unavailable through general meeting of the company due to the voting power of the majority shareholders. The ability of a minority shareholder to sue a company is, however, constrained within the rules of *Foss* v. *Harbottle*.[132]

(i) The rule in *Foss* v. *Harbottle*

One general principle of company law is that minority shareholders cannot sue for wrongs done to their company, or complain of irregularities in the conduct of its internal affairs. This principle was first established in *Foss* v. *Harbottle* in 1843. Subsequent cases relying upon the principle indicate that the rule rests upon two related propositions: (a) the right of the majority to bar a minority action whenever they might lawfully ratify alleged misconduct; and (b) the normally exclusive right of the company to sue upon a corporate cause of action.

Subsequent cases have also established exceptions to the rule such that it will not apply where an act complained of is either *ultra vires* or constitutes 'a fraud upon the minority', or is unfair and oppressive against the minority.[133] The rule also has no application to any statutory right given to shareholders under the Companies Acts 1948 and 1967.[134]

If any complaint falls under one of the exceptions to the rule, the courts have recognised that the minority may bring an action in a representative form.[135] In discussing this form of action one text states:

> In American law a representative action by shareholders to enforce corporate rights, by seeking the recovery of damages for or property belonging to their corporation, is termed a 'derivative action' (i.e. one derived from the corporation's right of action). Although the English courts have not adopted this usage, they have recognised that certain special rules apply to a minority share-holder's action brought for this purpose.[136]

The representative action in all but name[137] is comparable therefore to the American derivative action. Two types of action may be brought by shareholders in Britain employing the representative action procedure:

1. Actions to recover damages or property for the company.
2. Shareholders' actions to enforce rights against the company.[138]

The procedure, under (1), is therefore of little practical value for a shareholder who has, say, relief upon misrepresentations in a company's financial statements. For under that section the action is brought by a shareholder on behalf of all other shareholders *for the benefit* of the company.[139] The company will be joined as a 'nominal' defendant to the action, even though it is brought for its benefit.[140] The reason for this, and the limited value of this type of action for a shareholder seeking damages, is brought out in one court opinion[141] where the procedure was employed.

> To such an action as this the company are necessary defendants. The reason is obvious: the wrong alleged is done to the company, and the company must be a party to the suit in order to be bound by the result of the action and *to receive the money recovered in the action.* . . . Obviously, in such an action as this, no specific relief is asked against the company; and obviously too, what is recovered cannot be paid to the plaintiff representing the minority, but must go into the coffers of the company.[142]

The action therefore brought for damages by a shareholder representing all other shareholders against, say, the directors and accountants for misrepresentation (or breach of duty) will result if successful in a damages award to the company. Any claim by the plaintiff for wrong done to him individually, such as his loss of investment value, cannot stand.

The procedure would seem to allow a shareholder who considers that auditors have been negligent in an audit which may be thought to represent an act 'oppressive as against the minority', to recover damages for the company.[143] Such an action is hard to conceive.

Under the second type of action, noted above, the shareholder sues as a representative of a class of shareholder *against* the company to *enforce a right*. A shareholder will not normally be entitled to a money judgment in an action against the company, except where for example he is entitled to a dividend which has been declared but not paid.[144] Here again the shareholder relying upon misrepresentations is not aided because his 'right' has already been satisfied (the receipt of the company's financial statements). He cannot expect to recover against the directors, accountants or the company any damage award for the negligent preparation of those statements. Such an action would have to be brought in his own name under a common law action for negligence or deceit which will bring him within the *Hedley Byrne*[145] restrictions analysed in a previous chapter.[146]

IX FURTHER REASONS WHY THE ENGLISH 'CLASS ACTION' CANNOT BE USED TO THE EXTENT OF THE AMERICAN CLASS ACTION

Although English law has a procedure comparable to the American class action suit, it is unlikely ever to be employed to the extent the class suit is used in the US. There are a number of reasons for this.

(i) Costs

By far the most important reason is the question of costs in a representative action. If this country ever wanted the device to take on a greater role in, say, investor protection there would need to be statutory reform of the cost system.

Costs of litigation usually follow the event.[147] A successful litigant can expect to recover from his adversary certain costs after the judgment has been pronounced in his favour. In a representative suit, the successful plaintiff will expect to recover party and party costs from the defendant; however, he may still be liable to the solicitor for his costs.[148] As already seen, there is very often a discrepancy, termed extra costs, between the costs the plaintiff receives and the costs he must pay.[149] Also the representative is not entitled to reimbursement from other class members.[150]

Additionally the successful plaintiff might only receive a small monetary damage award. If a suit is taken out by a shareholder for the loss in value of shares, for example, he will only be entitled to the damages he has actually suffered, the remainder of the award being distributed to the members he represented. The situation arises, therefore, where the representative plaintiff even when winning a case may still be out of pocket financially.[151]

In America, the situation differs because the court may award costs to the plaintiff's solicitor out of a fund awarded for distribution to all the class members, and therefore the plaintiff may expect to recover at least as much as every other class member in the action.[152]

In the event of the plaintiff losing the suit in England, he will have an even greater financial commitment in that he may be ordered to pay the defendant's costs in addition to his own. Again, he will not be entitled to recover any money from the other members of the class, and if the case has been lengthy (which is more likely than in an ordinary civil suit)[153] the costs involved will be punitive.

The contingent fee system in America relieves the plaintiff representative of this risk, by shifting the costs payable to the successful party onto the attorney. In addition, the attorney will not be entitled to any fee if the action is lost.[154]

Costs and the class action consideration underline the different philosophies of the two nations with regard to the procedure. The English system employs a system of cost indemnity to discourage nuisance litigation. In a representative action, where each plaintiff is only likely to recover a small sum, the mechanism works against him. In the United States, however, the class action is recognised as fulfilling this particular need. Its very purpose is to provide a remedy to plaintiffs who have been wronged to a small degree financially, and who therefore would not normally bring an action. In England, even if a number of plaintiffs join the action, all acting as representatives, the recovery is unlikely to be adequate to repay all the necessary expenses. Even if the recovery was likely to be adequate, few will want to bring an action which will result in no benefit, even assuming success, as all recovery will be passed to solicitors in costs.

(ii) Settlements

In the US, the class action suit is recognised as a major reason for settlement by defendants unwilling to risk the substantial damages from plaintiffs' aggregated claims.[155] In England, any procedural device which is likely to coerce a party to settle, regardless of the merits of the case, is regarded with suspicion and unlikely to be encouraged. Although the English court procedure does encourage pre-trial settlement in certain instances,[156] it will frown upon any system encouraging 'legalised blackmail', which is one description of the American class action experience.

The American procedure encourages settlement for a number of reasons. If a company is included as defendant it may not run the risk of defeat as the damages it may have to pay to a large class could destroy the business. This may even be the case if the plaintiff's claim is questionable.[157]

Advocates of the procedure would argue that the business *may* have wronged the class to the extent of the damages being claimed. In a typical class suit in America, the plaintiffs relying upon financial statements may have purchased stock at inflated prices:[158] it is argued that the purpose of misrepresentation was to bolster the stock price.[159]

Settlement is also encouraged because of the adverse publicity a case may generate against defendants. Adverse publicity is damaging to a business, and even more so to defendants such as accountants and lawyers. Whether innocent or guilty, no accounting firm whose existence relies upon professional integrity and respectability wishes to be involved in litigation.

(iii) Administration of a class suit

American class action suits are criticised because of the considerable administrative burden they place upon the courts. One commentator[160] considers that this may be why courts are reluctant to encourage class action suits in other jurisdictions. Williams, when analysing the position in Canada, stated that courts have sometimes refused to grant actions for damages because of possible administration difficulties.[161] In particular respects, administrative problems are increased; for example in the calculation of damages, should the plaintiff class win an action. By having numerous claims for awards and differing amounts payable to individuals, the burden upon the courts is much greater. This need not be justification, however, for discouraging actions. In one Canadian case, the court did not view the complexity of individual calculations as a bar to the maintenance of the claim as a class action, despite the fact that ' . . . there would have to be long, detailed and difficult accountings . . . regarding the sources, amounts and distributions, and specific entitlements of individual members of the class'.[162]

The problems attached to specific administrative difficulties of class actions is receiving some attention in the United States, where the procedural aspects of class action suits have tended to congest the courts. In particular the 'trial lawyers'[163] consider that the small claim actions should be abolished for this reason. In addition, the proof of claim requirement also raises problems. In the *Eisen* case, for example, in order to provide sufficient proof of a damage claim, some six million investor/plaintiffs would have to have obtained certificates from brokers concerning stock purchases over a period of six years. The burden upon the courts would be miniscule compared with that of Wall Street brokers – even assuming the brokers would provide (or could provide) the relevant documentation.[164]

In a more typical class action where investors rely upon a company's misrepresentations, the problem of obtaining sufficient proof of a class and its claims is not so serious. Usually the class in such an event will be those shareholders purchasing shares during a set period of time.[165] If the representations relied upon are financial statements, the period will normally be less than one year. Despite the fact that a considerable number of investors are involved in the claim, the class, and most important, the damages are easily obtained.

In England, the proof of claim and the class would perhaps be obtained even more easily. This is due partly to the fact that there are less markets for the purchase and sale of shares, and also that companies are obliged to maintain a current register of members,[166] it being unlawful for any company to register a transfer of shares unless a proper instrument of transfer has been delivered.[167]

X SUMMARY

The American class action procedure linked with its more favourable cost structure has allowed third parties to recover damages suffered. In England, the representative action has not been allowed to develop as successfully as its counterpart in the States.

Surely no one can condone the situation where a company, acting dishonestly or negligently, is able to obtain £1 from each of one million investors and not be threatened. The same company will however be tried and convicted for making £1 million from one investor.

NOTES

[1] For a full analysis of the American costs system see 20 Am.Jur. 2d ss. 1–85 'Costs'.

[2] The terms 'fees' and 'costs' are sometimes used interchangeably but accurately speaking the terms 'fees' is applicable to the items chargeable by law between the officer or witness and the party whom he serves, while 'costs' has reference to the expenses of litigation as between the parties (20 Am.Jur. 2d 1). Therefore section (i) are costs and section (ii) are fees. See also A. S. Goodhart, 'Costs' 38 *Yale Law Journal* 849, 875 (1929).

[3] Under certain equitable principles counsel fees may be awarded to a successful party in appropriate cases (20 Am.Jur. 2d 2). The courts granting recovery must however be acting within some statutory provision (20 Am.Jur. 2d 8 s. 5). See also 20 Am.Jur. 2d ss. 79 *et seq.* (See note 13 *infra.*)

[4] America is the only major nation which does not award counsel fees to the prevailing party. See: Special Project 'Recent Developments in Attorneys' Fees', 29 *Vanderbilt Law Review* 685, 720 (1976). For an explanation of this see citations in footnote 239, ibid. One reason why the American system of costs differs from the UK for example is that in the early colonial days lawyers were regarded as characters of disrepute and as such the law did not wish to encourage them by awarding costs. It was also felt that a knowledge of law was not essential to the administration of justice. See Goodhart, note 2 *supra*, pp. 872–3 citing Warren, *A History of the American Bar* (1913). Apart from these historical reasons the American system was thought to be more democratic and favoured the poor man. (Ibid p. 874.)

[5] 20 Am.Jur. 2d s. 52, p. 41.

[6] Ibid.

[7] See 20 Am.Jur. 2d ss. 56–9.

[8] Ibid ss. 53–5.

[9] Ibid.

[10] Ibid ss. 60–4.

[11] Ibid s. 68.

[12] Ibid s. 67.

[13] See L. Mayers, *The American Legal System* (rev. ed.) (New York: Harper & Row, 1964) p. 286. Also 20 Am.Jur. 2d s. 14, p. 13. Under the rule stated in numerous cases, the right to recover costs exists only by virtue of statutory authority or a rule of court authorised by statute. Costs are thus 'creatures of statute'. Courts have no inherent power to award costs. They have no power to award costs on merely equitable grounds or as an incident of their power over the parties or the subject matter of the litigation. A

party claiming a judgment for costs against his adversary must bring himself within the operation of some statutory provision. 20 Am.Jur. 2d s. 5, p. 8. Under the Federal Rules of Civil Procedure however the District Courts are given considerable discretion in allowing or denying costs. 20 Am.Jur. 2d s. 8, p. 10.

[14] 20 Am.Jur. 2d s. 72, p. 58.

[15] Ibid, ss. 72 *et seq.* Also *Attorneys at Law* 7 Am.Jur. 2d ss. 203 *et seq.*

[16] 20 Am.Jur. 2d s. 65.

[17] Mayers, note 13 *supra*, p. 287.

[18] In cases the allowance even of costs to the prevailing party is within the discretion of the court. In the case of 'difficult and extraordinary' actions the court may in some states make additional allowance for costs, but this is rarely done. Ibid, p. 287. See also Special Project, note 4 *supra*, pp. 722 *et seq.*

[19] See for example Goodhart, note 2 *supra*; Special Project, note 4 *supra*, pp. 721–2. Note 'Attorneys' Fees: Where shall the Ultimate Burden Lie?' 20 *Vanderbilt Law Review* 1216 (1967); Kuerzel, 'The Attorney's Fees: Why not a Cost of Litigation?' 49 *Iowa Law Review* 75 (1963); Mause 'Winner Takes All: A Re-examination of the Indemnity System', 55 *Iowa Law Review* 26 (1969); McLaughlin, 'The Recovery of Attorney's Fees: A New Method of Financing Legal Services', 40 *Fordham Law Review* 761 (1972); Stirling 'Attorney's Fees: Who Should Bear the Burden?' 41 *Cal. St. B. Journal* 874 (1966).

[20] Canons of Professional Ethics of the American Bar Association Document No. 91 s. 13 allows for contingent fees. 'A contract for a contingent fee, where sanctioned by law, should be reasonable under all the circumstances of the case, including the risk and uncertainty of the compensation, but should always be subject to the supervision of a court as to its reasonableness.' *American Jurisdiction 2d* (Desk Book) (N.Y.: Lawyers Co-Operative Publishing Co. 1962) p. 225.

[21] G. D. Hornstein, 'The Shareholder's Derivative Suit in the United States', [1967] *The Journal of Business Law* 282, 286.

[22] *Ex p. Plitt* 19 Fed. Cas. No. 11, 288 (C.C.E.D. Pa. 1853).

[23] As a footnote to this quotation Hornstein comments that in a public company almost the only investor with a stake substantial enough to finance expensive litigation is the institutional investor, whose principle is well known: 'Sell out and get out', not litigation.

[24] See similar view of Jaenicke, 'The Impact of the Current Legal Climate on the Accounting Profession', a background paper prepared for the Commission on Auditors' Responsibilities, July 1976, p. 44.

[25] *Lipscomb* v. *Adams* 193 Mo. 530, 91 S.W. 1046 (1906), cited by 7 Am.Jur. 2d s. 214, p. 171.

[26] The Supreme Court sanctioned this solution in *Trustees* v. *Greenough* 105 U.S. 161 (1939) and *Central Rail Road and Banking Co.* v. *Bettus* 113 U.S. 116 (1885). See Hornstein, note 21 *supra*, p. 287 footnotes 24 and 25.

[27] See 'Court Rules Limiting Amount of Contingent Fees or Otherwise Imposing Conditions on Contingent Fee Contracts', 77 *A.L.R.* 2d 411.

[28] In *Gair* v. *Peck* 6 N.Y. 2d 97, 188 N.Y.S. 2d 491 77 A.L.R. 2d 390 (1959) it was held within the power of the Appellate Division of the Supreme Court

to adopt a rule of court setting forth a percentage schedule of contingent fees (a 'sliding scale' ranging from 50 per cent etc. see text) 77 A.L.R. 2d 411, 412. (N.Y. App. Div. 1st Dept. Rule 4). See also Special Project, note 4 *supra*, p. 711.

[29] See Mayers, note 13 *supra*, p. 284 and Jaenicke, note 24 *supra*, p. 43.

[30] For example New Jersey, Supreme Court Rule 1:21-7(c) sets out graduated scales of fees. See Special Project, note 4 *supra*, p. 710.

[31] See text accompanying notes 2 and 3 *supra*.

[32] H. P. Hill states: 'I believe the time has come also to limit the proportion of settlements going for legal fees. There have not been any big money judgments against accountants but there certainly have been a number of large settlements.' 'Reponsibilities and Liabilities of Auditors and Accountants', panel discussion in the 1974 National Institute of the Section of Corporation, Banking and Business Law, 30 *Business Lawyer* 169, 179 (1975).

[33] This is especially so in class action suits as discussed below. 'Another aspect of the use of Rule 23 which has caused particular distress and rancour in both defendants and the Professional Bar is the fact that huge recoveries are oftentimes clinched in such a manner that 60 per cent to 80 per cent is distributed thinly among the class members and 20 per cent to 40 per cent (regardless of the amount of work actually performed) goes to the successful attorneys' 94, 135 *Grad* v. *Memorex Corp. et. al*, C.C.H. Fed. Sec. L. Rep. 1194, 029 (1973). Quoted by Hill, ibid, p. 179.

[34] Ibid.

[35] See text accompanying notes 90 *et seq. infra*. For an empirical analysis of the effects of contingent fees on class actions see Elliot 'Auditors' Legal Liability to Third Parties: a Case Law Approach', D.B.A. Dissertation, University of Colorado, 1973.

[36] For a full analysis of the English system of costs, see Walker and Walker 'Costs and the Enforcement of Judgments', Chapter 21 of *The English Legal System* (2nd ed.) (London: Butterworths, 1970) pp. 278 *et seq.* See also Goodhart, note 2 *supra*.

[37] Goodhart, note 2 *supra*, pp. 850–1.

[38] Walker and Walker, note 36 *supra*.

[39] Based upon A. S. Goodhart, 'Judicial Reform in England', 27 *New York University Law Review* 402 *et seq.* (July 1952).

[40] Counsel may be separated into leaders and juniors, the latter being optional to a case. The title junior is something of a misnomer in that the junior may be more experienced than the leader, however, he has agreed to accept a lower fee.

[41] See Goodhart, note 2 *supra*, pp. 856–7.

[42] As Goodhart notes, the eminence of counsel directly affects the brief fee . . . Sir X, Q.C., receiving £500 for work which Mr Y is anxious to do for £50', note 39 *supra*, p. 404. See also Goodhart, note 2 *supra*, p. 858.

[43] Ibid, p. 860.

[44] At a very early date common law costs were not allowed. By 1278, however, the courts of England were authorised to award counsel fees to successful plaintiffs in litigation (Statute of Gloucester, 6 Edw. 1c.┣ (1278)). Since 1607 English courts have been empowered to award counsel fees to defendants in all actions where such awards might be made to plaintiffs. (Statute of

Westminster, 4 Jac.1. c.3 (1607): The award of costs was left entirely to the discretion of the courts by the Surpeme Court of Judicature Acts of 1873 and 1875. See Special Project, note 4 *supra*, p. 720, and Goodhart, note 2 *supra*, pp. 851–60.

[45] *Donald Campbell & Co. Ltd.* v. *Pollak* [1927] A.C. 732, 811–12. As Goodhart writes: 'Where a party successfully enforces a legal right and in no way misconducts himself, he is entitled to costs. On the other hand a party who brings a vexatious or unnecessary action, even if he succeeds to some extent may be ordered to pay the whole costs of the other side.' (Citations omitted) note 2 *supra*, pp. 861–2.

[46] Goodhart, note 2 *supra*, p. 862.

[47] For example, in prolixity, joinder of parties, delay, summary procedure, interrogatories, evidence, estate actions, etc. see Goodhart, ibid, pp. 862–8.

[48] Goodhart, ibid, p. 869.

[49] Ibid.

[50] Rules of the Supreme Court, Order 26, rule 1.

[51] Goodhart, note 2 *supra*, p. 870.

[52] Ibid, p. 871.

[53] Ibid, p. 872.

[54] The use of the contingent fee facility therefore comes into its own when employed with the class action suit. See text accompanying notes 96–101 *infra*.

[55] One commentator has written that 'Proponents of reform [of the American Costs system] usually point to England as furnishing an example worthy of limitation. In its courts a much more severe scheme of costs exists. A severe scale of costs, so goes the argument, tends on the one hand to discourage the institution of unjust suits and on the other to discourage the defense of suits by defendants who have no substantial ground for defense. The difficulty with this view in the minds of many students of the subject is that it makes the litigation of even a bona fide dispute too costly a risk to be undertaken by any but a person of ample means, and this in effect constitutes a denial of justice to persons of limited means.' Mayers, note 13 *supra*, p. 287.

[56] Goodhart states that '[as] long as the cost of fighting a case is merely nominal, as it is under the American practice, the wealthy defendant, especially if the defendant is a corporation, will frequently refuse to pay a first claim on the chance of winning on a technicality or of tiring out the plaintiff. It is the poor man who cannot afford to wait for his money and can, therefore, be forced to accept an unfair settlement by fear of long delay'. Note 2 *supra*, p. 876.

[57] Many American lawyers speaking and writing in England on the subject of the class action and related derivative suits have stated that it is a fundamental right for the small investor. The class action lawyer has been put forward as the defender of the small investor and therefore employs a public duty. See for example Hornstein, note 20 *supra*; Pomerantz, note 106 *infra*; also S. C. Goldberg (ed.), *Expanding Responsibility under the Securities Acts: Transcript* (Law Journal Press, 1973) Conference June 1972. At hearings before the Jenkins Committee on Company Law Reform, certain

American experts stated that the class action suit had a good effect on corporate law because the power of the suit or the ever-present threat of a suit constituted a strong check on improper corporate action. See Hornstein, ibid.

[58] Such suits are variously named creditors' suits, stockholders' suits or representative suits. Cf. with English representative suit, text accompanying notes 116 *et seq. infra.*

[59] See generally Rule 23, Rules of Civil Procedure. Class actions, T.28. U.S.C.A. Rules 17-23.2-19. pp. 289 *et seq.*

[60] Williams, *Consumer Class Actions* (Consumer Association of Canada, July 1974) p. 3. See also 35A C.J.A. Federal Civil Procedure s. 63 p. 115. See text accompanying notes 120 *et seq. infra.*

[61] Ibid.

[62] See 59 Am.Jur. 2d s. 47, p. 408.

[63] *Eisen* v. *Carlisle & Jacquelin* 391 F.2d 555 (1968).

[64] See Pohl, note 73 *infra.*

[65] 59 Am.Jur. 2d s. 47, p. 414.

[66] 18 U.S.C.A. See note 72 *infra.*

[67] Not the federal courts though, who must necessarily follow the Federal Rules of Civil Procedure.

[68] 59 Am.Jur. 2d s. 47.

[69] Ibid.

[70] Ibid.

[71] See text accompanying note 89 *infra.*

[72] See Rules of Civil Procedure, note 59 *supra*, pp. 295 *et seq.*

[73] See M. A. Pohl, 'Developments in Law in Federal Class Action Litigation', 10 *Houston Law Review* 337, 357 (1973). See also supplement to 29 *Business Lawyer* (1974) for a number of articles on the effects of the amended Federal Rule 23, including M. Schwartz, 'The Class Action: Its Incidence and the Eisen Cases, 29 *Business Lawyer* 155 (1974) and J.V. Patrick, Jr., 'The Securities Class Action for Damages Comes of Age (1966–1974)', 39 *Business Lawyer* 159 (1974).

[74] Schwartz, ibid, has calculated that in the Southern District of New York there were 1350 class actions filed over the period 1966–1971.

[75] *Escott* v. *BarChris Construction Company* 283 F. Supp. 643 (1968). Pohl, note 73 *supra*, p. 357.

[76] See generally U.S.C.A. 28, Rule 23 pp. 289–516 on class actions.

[77] See Jaenicke, note 24 *supra*, p. 40. See also text accompanying note 88 *infra.*

[78] The overall action becomes a 'non-class' action.

[79] Subdivision (C)(2) of Rule 23.

[80] See Pohl, note 73 *supra*, p. 372.

[81] *Eisen* v. *Carlisle & Jacquelin*, 41 F.R.D. 147 (S.D.N.Y. 1966); 270 F.2d 119 (2d Cir. 1966), cert. denied, 386 U.S. 1035 (1967); 391 F.2d 555 (2d Cir. 1968); 50 F.R.D. 471 (S.D.N.Y. 1970); 52 F.R.D. 253 (S.D.N.Y. 1971); (1971–2 Transfer Binder) CCH Fed. Sec. L. Rep. 93,371, at 90,922 (S.D.N.Y. Dec. 15, 1971); 54 F.R.D. 565 (S.D.N.Y. 1972); 417 U.S. 156 (1974).

[82] See Schwartz, note 73 *supra*.

[83] The American College of Trial Lawyers, Report and Recommendations of the Special Committee on Rule 23 of the Federal Rules of Civil Procedure. (15 March 1972). See E. E. Pollock, 'Class Actions Reconsidered: Theory and Practice Under Amended Rule 23', 28 *Business Lawyer*, 741, 742 (1973).

[84] See Jaenicke, note 24 *supra*, pp. 40–2.

[85] A. L. Pomerantz, 'New Developments in Class Actions: Has their Death Knell been Sounded' 25 *Business Lawyer* 1259, 1263 1970).

[86] Ibid.

[87] U.S.C.A. 28 Rule 23.

[88] See in addition text accompanying note 77 *supra*.

[89] *Eisen*, note 81 *supra*.

[90] 59 Am.Jur. 2d s. 47, p. 478.

[91] See text accompanying notes 2–19 *supra*.

[92] See 38 A.L.R. 3rd s. 7(a) p. 1401. 'Defendant's conduct' and s. 7(b) 'Defendants' economic condition'.

[93] See a review of the American Law Institute's Proposed Securities Code, Chapter 5 of Jaenicke, note 24 *supra*, pp. 67–81.

[94] Reporters Revision of Text of Tentative Drafts Nos. 1–3 (1974) as cited by Jaenicke, ibid, p. 77.

[95] Ibid, p. 78.

[96] See Chapter 2 *supra*.

[97] See for example Simon, 'Class Actions – Useful Tool or Engine of Destruction', 55 F.R.D. 375; also G. E. Fitzgerald, 'When is a Class a Class?' 28 *Business Lawyer* 95 (1972); also Pohl, note 77 *supra*; S. D. Harlan, 'The New AICPA Audit Commission – Will the Real Questions Please Stand Up?', *Contemporary Auditing Problems* (Proceedings of the 1974 University of Kansas Symposium on Auditing Problems) p. 23; Jaenicke, note 24 *supra*, pp. 43–6.

[98] Ibid.

[99] Pomerantz, note 85 *supra*, p. 1259.

[100] In support see 58 *American Bar Association Journal* 665–7 (1972). Apart from the fact that lawyers get very good publicity by successfully winning a case, another motivating factor of the class action suit combined with the contingent fee is that certain lawyers ('Naiders Raiders') believe they are prosecuting cases which will cause a change for the better for the common man against the 'establishment'. See Fitzgerald, note 97 *supra*, p. 96.

[101] See D. R. Carmichael, News Item, *Journal of Accountancy* (1976).

[102] Rule 23 amendment. Notes 71–2 *supra*.

[103] Patrick, note 73 *supra*.

[104] For example in Canada, see Williams, note 60 *supra*.

[105] Williams, ibid, p. 3.

[106] Williams, note 60 *supra*, pp. 5, 6.

[107] Ibid.

[108] Witness for example the *Eisen* case which took at least eight years to pass from the lower courts up to the US Supreme Court on the question, *inter alia*, of the cost of notice requirements. (417 U.S. 156 (1974)).

178   *Accountants' Professional Negligence*

109 *Hickman* v. *Taylor* 329 U.S. 495, 507 (1947) cited by *Going to Law. A Critique of English Civil Procedure*, Justice Report (London: Stevens Publication, 1974) p. 35 (British Section of the International Commission of Jurists).
110 Ibid.
111 Ibid.
112 Pohl, note 73 *supra*, p. 379.
113 Ibid.
114 *Morris* v. *Bunkard* 51 F.R.D. 530, 535 (S.D.N.Y. 1971).
115 Williams, note 60 *supra*.
116 See generally, *Halsbury's Laws* (4th ed.) paras. 771–2; 50 Digest (Repl) 465–70; also R. R. Pennington, *Company Law* (4th ed.) (London: Butterworths, 1979) pp. 588–90 on Representative and Derivative Actions.
117 Rules of the Supreme Court. 'Causes of Action, Counterclaims and Parties', Representative Proceedings (0.15, r. 12) pp. 202 *et seq*.
118 0.15, r.12(1).
119 0.15, r.12(3).
120 0.15, r.12/1 Application of Rule, p. 203.
121 *Commissioners of Sewers* v. *Gellantly* (1876); 3 Ch. D. 610, 615, ibid, 0.15, r.12/1.
122 A recent case, *Prudential Assurance Co. Ltd.* v. *Newman Industries Ltd.* [1979] 3 All E.R. 507 has outlined the rules for bringing representative actions. See also *Markt & Co. Ltd.* v. *Knight S.S. Co. Ltd.* [1910] 2 K.B. 1021 C.A.
123 *Smith and Others* v. *Cardiff Corporation* [1954] 1 Q.B. 210 C.A. (Emphasis added.)
124 See speech of Lord MacNaghten in *Duke of Bedford* v. *Ellis* [1901] A.C. 1, 8 and cf. judgment of Jessel, M. R. in *Commissioners of Sewers*, note 121 *supra*. See also *Taff Vale Ry* v. *Amalgamated Society* (1901) A.C. 426, 443. Over-ruling this point: *Temperton* v. *Russell* [1893] 1 Q.B. 425; *Wood* v. *McCarthy* [1893] 1 Q.B. 775; *Meker* v. *Denne* [1905] 2 Ch. 538 C.A.; *Mercantile Marine Service Association* v. *Toms* [1916] 2 K.B. 243; *Hardie & Lane Ltd.* v. *Chiltern* [1928] 1 K.B. 663; *Smith and Others*, note 123 *supra*. (Cited in 0.15, r.12/1).
125 *Fraser* v. *Cooper* (1882) 21 Ch. D. 718; *Roy Chowdri* v. *Prasauna Baneiji* L. J. 27 Nov. 1910.
126 *Beeching* v. *Lloyd*, (1855) 3 Drew. 227; *Markt* v. *Knight, supra*.
127 0.15, r.12,2. p. 204.
128 *Campbell* v. *Thompson and Another*, [1953] 1 Q.B. 445; it has not been held applicable though, in cases of conspiracy, libel or trespass, nor for the price of goods sold and delivered, nor for the price of work and labour done. 0.15, r.12/2 A (citations omitted).
129 [1916] W.N. 74.
130 *Price* v. *Rhondda U.D.C.* [1923] W.N. 228; Order 62, rule 2/80 'Entitlement to Cost'.
131 See generally: *Halsbury's Laws of England* (4th ed.) 7 *Companies* paras. 770–2, pp. 460–1; L. S. Sealy, *Cases and Materials in Company Law*, (Cambridge University Press, 1971) pp. 666–8; E. R. H. Ivarmy, *Topham and Ivarmy's Company Law* (15th ed.) (London: Butterworths, 1974) pp.

191–3; A. J. Boyle and R. Sykes (ed.), *Gore-Browne on Companies* (42nd ed.) (London: Jordan, 1972) pp. 790–3; C. M. Schmitthof and J. H. Thompson, *Palmer's Company Law* (21st ed.) (London: Stevens, 1968) pp. 509–10 and Pennington, note 116 *supra*. See also *Prudential Assurance Co. Ltd.* v. *Newman Industries Ltd.* [1973] 3 All E.R. 507 *et seq.*

¹³² *Foss* v. *Harbottle* (1843) 2 Hare 461; 9 Digest (Repl.) 36. See Gore-Browne, note 131 *supra*, p. 783.

¹³³ *Alexander* v. *Automatic Telephone Co.* [1900] 2 Ch. 56 (C.A.); *Hope* v. *International Financial Society* (1877) 4 Ch. D. 327; *Simpson* v. *Westminster Palace Hotel* (1960) 8 H.L.C. 712; *Church* v. *Financial Corporation* (1868) 4 Ch. App. 117. For further cases see Gore-Browne, ibid, pp. 784–6.

¹³⁴ Gore-Browne, note 131 *supra*, p. 785.

¹³⁵ Under the Rules of the Supreme Court, Order 15, Rule 12, *supra*.

¹³⁶ Gore-Browne, note 131 *supra*, p. 790.

¹³⁷ See Hornstein, note 21 *supra*, who relates how little employed the representative action is in the UK when compared with the US. He cites statistics in the US between the period 1932–42 which coincided with the disillusionment and the exposures following the 1929 Stock Market panic. In Manhattan (one of five boroughs in the New York City) 1128 derivative suits were instituted in the state courts and 130 in the federal court for that district, p. 282. These figures perhaps give some indication of the likely extent of the use of the derivative action in present times.

¹³⁸ Gore-Browne, note 131 *supra*, pp. 790–3.

¹³⁹ Ibid, p. 791.

¹⁴⁰ Pennington, note 116 *supra*, p. 563.

¹⁴¹ *Spokes* v. *Grosvenor Hotel Co.* [1897] 2 Q.B. 124 C.A.

¹⁴² [1897] 2 Q.B. 124, 128 C.A. (Emphasis added) cited by Gore-Browne, note 131 *supra*, p. 791.

¹⁴³ No example of such usage has been found.

¹⁴⁴ Gore-Browne, note 131 *supra*, p. 792.

¹⁴⁵ *Hedley Byrne & Co. Ltd.* v. *Heller & Partners Ltd.* [1964] A.C. 465; [1963] 3 W.L.R. 101; [1963] 2 All E.R. 575, H.L. (E).

¹⁴⁶ Chapter 6.

¹⁴⁷ See text accompanying notes 44–5 *supra*.

¹⁴⁸ See text accompanying notes 36–8 *supra*.

¹⁴⁹ Ibid.

¹⁵⁰ See text accompanying note 130 *supra*.

¹⁵¹ For a similar example in the consumer context see Williams, note 60 *supra*, pp. 32–4.

¹⁵² See text accompanying note 90 *supra*.

¹⁵³ This is because of the greater administrative details involved in the running of a representative suit, such as the court time in establishing whether the suit may be fought as a representative suit, establishing facts of common interest, damage awards, etc.

¹⁵⁴ See text accompanying notes 96 *et seq. supra*.

¹⁵⁵ Williams, note 60 *supra*, p. 31.

¹⁵⁶ For example 'paying into court', see text accompanying note 52 *supra*.

¹⁵⁷ Williams, note 60 *supra*, p. 31.

[158] See the Memorex Corporation 'Notice of Settlement', *Wall Street Journal*, 16 May, 1975, p. 19, where under the 'Description of the Litigation' section it states: 'In essence, the complaints in the class action and in the derivative action allege that during the period above mentioned Memorex Securities traded at inflated prices due to the issuance and use of allegedly incorrect or misleading financial statements, press releases, accounting methods and other statements which are alleged to have incorrectly stated Memorex's income. . . . '

[159] In the *National Student Marketing* case as another example the company's very existence relied upon it being able to increase its stock price by meeting its profit predictions. See A. J. Briloff, *Unaccountable Accounting: Games Accountants Play* (New York: Harper and Row, 1972) pp. 116 *et seq.*; also A. Tobias, *The Funny Money Game* (London: Michael Joseph, 1972). See J. Pockson, 'Recent Litigation Against the American Auditor: Its Causes, Effects and Wider Implications', M. A. dissertation, University of Lancaster, 1975, Chapter 4, pp. 40 *et seq.*

[160] Williams, note 60 *supra*.

[161] Ibid, p. 44.

[162] Williams, note 60 *supra*, p. 54.

[163] Note 83 *supra*.

[164] See G. W. Coombe, 'Dialogue on Class Actions' 28 *Business Lawyer* 115, 122, (1973). In the *Eisen* case the District Court has estimated that liability would result in damage to the average class member of $1.30 (estimated attorney fees in the case were estimated at more than $5 million should plaintiffs prevail).

[165] In the Memorex illustration, note 158 *supra*, the relevant class consisted of 'all persons who purchased common stock or 5¼ per cent convertible subordinated debentures of Memorex Corpn., between 31 July 1970 and 14 April 1971'.

[166] Companies Act, 1948, ss. 110–14, 11 & 12 Geo. 6 Ch. 38. 'Register of Members'.

[167] Ibid. ss. 73–9.

8 CAN THE UK ACCOUNTANT EXPECT TO FACE EXTENDED LITIGATION IN THE FUTURE? – CONCLUSIONS

In the past decade there has been an unprecedented explosion of litigation in the United States and numerous cases have been brought against certified public accountants. The objective of this book has been to establish the extent of this litigation, to determine why it was occurring at the present time and most significantly to consider whether it was likely that accountant firms in the UK can expect to face a comparable litigation explosion.

American source data has been used to provide the necessary prediction of likely future events in Britain. In the fields of accounting and law both countries possess distinct similarities. The similarities would even seem to suggest that English accountants were facing comparable litigation problems but this was not found to be the case. Why therefore has there been a substantial increase in litigation in the US and not in the UK?

I INSTITUTIONAL ANALYSIS

The Securities and Exchange Commission (SEC) has been a significant force behind the increase in corporate litigation in the US. It is evident that the SEC is committed to an enforcement policy to ensure fair dealings in the securities markets and to ensure that companies publish reliable financial information. Part of the enforcement policy has been levelled against corporate professionals such as accountants and lawyers.

The number of SEC investigations has increased in the past ten years and many more of the major accounting firms are coming under investigation by the Commission. The important result of an SEC investigation is the likelihood of further civil litigation against parties being investigated.

The SEC recognises the deterrent effect of civil litigation and does not discourage private actions when it has not taken a particular case to the courts itself. Thus the increase in litigation in the US can be directly attributed to the activity of the SEC.

The power of the SEC when compared with the Department of Trade and Industry (DTI) is considerably greater and certainly more effective. The Rule of Practice of the SEC grant it very extensive powers. The Commission has authority to severely restrict the workings of major accounting firms should the situation warrant it.

The DTI has also undertaken many investigations in the past decade in the wake of company failures.[1] Accounting firms have been included in the investigations and criticised in the reports. Unlike the SEC however the DTI does not or cannot pursue effectively its criticisms by commencing litigation. In addition the DTI cannot sanction accounting firms from, say, taking on new clients or suspending them from the audit of publicly quoted companies, powers which the SEC possesses and uses to advantage.

The Institute of Chartered Accountants in England and Wales (ICAEW) and the other accounting bodies have also failed to follow up DTI investigations to ensure that accountants who have been criticised have been disciplined. The majority of the disciplinary proceedings of the ICAEW in recent years have been spent on matters of lesser significance than the criticisms of many recent DTI reports. The research into the American experience has shown that litigation has followed from adverse public opinion; the American profession faced similar public opinion to that currently levelled against the English accounting profession. If the ICAEW does not commit itself to a rigorous policing role then its powers of sanction are likely to pass to a state-run commission comparable to the SEC.

II LEGAL COMPARISONS

The main research for this book has used as its data base a corpus of American cases brought under the common law.[2] These cases formed the basis of comparison with legal developments in this country. In common law there is still a very strong link between the US and the

UK as the Tables of Reliance in the text have indicated;[3] in statute law fewer comparisons exist.

Wherever possible the English equivalent of American statutes have been studied and the relevant chapter[4] shows that in America the statute law affecting accountants liability has been interpreted more liberally by the courts resulting in increased litigation. This is particularly the case with section 11 of the Securities Act of 1933 and section 10b of the Securities Exchange Act of 1934.

III ACCOUNTANTS LIABILITY UNDER THE COMMON LAW

In the past decade in addition to the wider interpretation of statute law certain courts have also weakened common law precedent which had precluded action against accountants. In order to determine whether increased litigation had involved common law cases as well as statutory cases it was necessary to go back to the origins of the law in the US.

The schedules of cases[5] represent in tabular form the significant aspects of negligence actions and indicate how court interpretations have changed with time. The early American law was found to be heavily reliant upon English precedent, but it was discovered that US judges were more willing than their English counterparts to overrule established precedent should the needs of society require it. It is certain that the poor public opinion of the accounting profession and increasing controversy over corporate disclosure policies has tempted the courts to pursue a different approach to the interpretation of established law.

The cases of *Glanzer* v. *Shepard* and *Ultramares Corporation* v. *Touche* were analysed because they reveal important distinctions in the law of legal liability to third parties in negligence currently undergoing change in the US. In the 1930s the law was uncertain with regard to accountants legal liability. The *Ultramares* case decided in 1931 precluded third parties from bringing actions against accountants in negligence because they had no privity of contract. This case remained as precedent throughout the US for at least thirty years.

By the 1960s however courts and legal jurists began to question the logic or validity of the various distinctions made by the Appellate judge in the case. It is contended that the questioning of *Ultramares* has resulted in an increase in litigation against accountants.

The questioning of the *Ultramares* arguments has meant that the current law in the US is divided as to the actual extent of liability for negligence. Various state judicatures have gone beyond the confines of privity to allow actions by third parties. Accountants are recognised as owing a duty, and therefore a legal responsibility, to others apart from the companies employing them. This has made the *Glanzer* case, decided in 1922, very significant because it allowed a third party recovery for negligent misstatements.

Courts in the past decade have needed to find other parameters for assessing liability. With the objective but restrictive measure of privity abandoned, they have turned to the more subjective measures of foreseeability. All the important cases have been examined to evaluate the extent of legal liability. It is evident that recent cases involving accountants have tended to follow the decisions of cases such as *Rusch Factors* v. *Levin*. Writers concur that the extension of liability as outlined in *Rusch* is a sound development from the rigidity of *Ultramares*. If one accepts this, the basis of accountants' legal liability may now extend, *inter alia*, to plaintiffs who are members of a limited class, who have relied upon an accountant's misrepresentation and suffered damage as a result. This view is supported by the Restatement of the Law of Torts (Second), which has major influence in US civil courts.

The law in England needs to be placed in the context of recent American decisions. It is vitally important to establish the position of the law of negligent misrepresentations in England, both in the light of decided cases and also with respect to the recent American cases. The analysis has shown that this law in America has extended beyond the negligence law in England.[6] The extension of the common law itself has led to litigation in the US.

A detailed review of the tort law up to and beyond *Hedley Byrne* v. *Heller*, including a full analysis of *Candler* v. *Crane, Christmas & Co.* shows that negligence law in England has not extended further than Lord Denning's dissent in *Candler*. The position in *Candler* is directly comparable to *Glanzer* and the 1938 Restatement position in the US. Negligence law in England had extended to include situations where information is furnished in the course of a business or profession to a limited class for whose guidance the information was supplied and where it was intended to be relied upon and to influence the person's conduct.

English law therefore has not extended beyond the law decided in the US in the early 1930s, despite the fears expressed at the time of *Hedley Byrne*. Research for this book shows that recent American decisions have increased the liability of accountants beyond English precedent.

IV OTHER FACTORS – COSTS, CONTINGENT FEES AND CLASS ACTIONS

In addition to the institutional differences and the extension of both statute and common law in the US other procedural factors in the law are analysed to show further reasons why extensive litigation has occurred in the US. Although the two countries are comparable in many ways there are significant legal differences that make litigation more likely to arise in the US than in the UK.

In recent years attorneys hired under a contingent fee arrangement have found considerable litigation potential in pursuing actions on behalf of investors against corporations and their professional advisers. Accountants in recent years have been criticised for failing in their duty to inform shareholders of the true situation of a company's financial position. Critics allege that reports by accountants are prepared so as to conceal rather than reveal the true financial position of companies. Lawyers have taken advantage of adverse public opinion to include accountants in legal actions following company failures. The contingent fee facility aids the plaintiff who has been wronged but unable to pay for legal services. The lawyer, under a contingency arrangement, will receive no fee for legal services if the action fails but will be assured a substantial reward if the action is successful. In effect the financial risk of litigation is underwritten by the attorney.

The contingent fee is closely linked with the class action procedure.[7] If an attorney is able to bring an action on behalf of numerous shareholders, as one class, the contingent fee on a successful judgment will be substantially increased as the court will award a percentage from the damages fund payable by an unsuccessful defendant (or in reality, if an accounting firm is involved, by its insurance company).

The reason why the class action and contingent fee facilities have only recently been employed with such effect against accountants is due partly to the public criticism against the profession (connected with litigation in other consumer related fields by third party pressure groups); also because the systems are suited to the corporate/investor situation where there are numerous plaintiffs with identical actions against few defendants; and finally because the class action procedure rules were amended in 1966 – the beginning of the period of extended litigation.

Rule 23(a) of the Federal Rules of Civil Procedure was amended in 1966 with the effect that 'the class' definition binds all members of a certain class who do not affirmatively exclude themselves from the action. Previously class members had to notify their acceptance to be included in a suit brought on their behalf. This meant that the size of the class could be expanded to encapsulate numerous plaintiffs. In corporate litigation the numbers involved will run into many thousands, limited only by the number of shareholders in the company. This has resulted in considerable pressure against accountant defendants; not only because the resultant damages award will be considerably greater but also because of the adverse public opinion which is sure to be generated. Accounting firms whose survival rests upon their integrity cannot afford the risks of protracted class action litigation. All these factors have tended to lead to out of court settlements even when the accounting firms involved consider they have a good chance of winning an action. Since the 1966 amendment the number of actions and settlements against accountants has increased dramatically.

In England, lawyers are not allowed under their ethical rules to retain clients on a contingent fee basis and the costs system in this country makes it financially infeasible for an investor to risk legal action. In many important respects the representative action is comparable to the American class action suit. However, the costs system and other procedural aspects of representative actions makes them ineffective in this country.

One recent case, *Prudential Assurance Co. Ltd.* v. *Newman Industries Ltd. and Others*[8] should be mentioned here because it tends to refute previous arguments. This case is important for two reasons; firstly it was an action brought by an institutional minority investor against directors of a company (Newman Industries Ltd.) and secondly because the Prudential brought the case in a representative capacity on behalf of all members of a class. The institutional investor rarely brings actions preferring to sell the investment rather than incur heavy legal costs; one estimate has put the Prudential's own in-house legal costs in this case at over £300,000.[9] The total damages against Newman Industries in the case has been put at only £450 000. This case could well establish the power of representative action in a minority shareholder context. The cost restrictions, however, will never make it as effective as the American class action.

This book has evaluated five important reasons why it is unlikely that the situation currently occurring in the United States could arise in the United Kingdom, whereby British accountants would be faced with a comparable litigation explosion. In conclusion, these factors are listed here:

1. The influence of the Securities and Exchange Commission in bringing and aiding in litigation.
2. In both common law and statute law US courts have extended the law of negligence beyond the current standing of negligence law in this country.
3. The less stringent costs system in America facilitates actions.
4. The contingent fee system ensures that even the plaintiff without financial means is able to commence litigation. The facility also encourages actions by public interest attorneys.
5. The class action suit, through recent amendment, has made it even more effective in actions by numerous third party plaintiffs against accountants.

V TRENDS FOR THE FUTURE

A study of the legal liability of accountants, and its impact upon the legal and professional environments, leads to the need to evaluate the likely effects upon accountants in the future.

Professional classes such as solicitors, architects and doctors are being sued for professional negligence to a far greater degree. The trends in the law are towards a greater social responsibility on behalf of the professional. The social awareness of the professional accountant in his reporting function to third parties reliant upon his opinion will certainly result in an extension of liability to a wider range of third parties.

The current legal environment has meant greater awareness by the professional institutes of the need to regulate the standards of the members. The Joint Disciplinary Scheme will need to act quickly and publicly in disciplining accountants for malpractice or negligence. Some argue that the professional institutes will never have sufficient jurisdictional power to regulate, because they can only admonish their own members and the Committee of Enquiry approach means that the proper processes of law can never be carried out.

If the professional institutes are unable to police their members then the Department of Trade Inspections must take on a wider role in law. The DTI rarely follows up its Inspectors' reports in court. Revisions to the Companies Act will be needed to give greater powers and responsibility to the DTI. Numerous DTI Inspectors' reports published since 1971 have been critical of accountants. Table XV shows this. Further examples could be quoted, but the point is that if neither the courts nor the profession can regulate then governmental institutions will.

TABLE XV DTI Inspectors' reports

DTI Inspection	Date	Criticism of accountants
1. Pergamon Press	1971	Auditors Chalmers Impey too readily accepted misleading explanations
2. Blanes Bernard Russell	1975	Joint auditors Nyman Libson, Paul & Co and Somers, Baker & Partners were criticised for stock valuations
3. London and County	1976	Harmond Banner criticised at length in the report
4. Vehicle and General	1976	Blease Lloyd were blamed for readily accepting explanations without proper enquiries
5. Lonrho	1976	Peat Marwick Mitchell and Fuller Jenks criticised for not properly verifying claims
6. Roadships	1976	Thompson McLintock found by the inspectors to have acted without reasonable skill and care in the conduct of their audit
7. London Capital Group	1977	Auditors Dixon Ward came under fire from inspectors for being 'slipshod' in certain audits
8. Court Line	1978	Inspectors concluded accounts did not give a true and fair view (auditors were Robson Rhodes)
9. Larkfold Holdings	1979	Turquands Barton Mayhew criticised

SOURCE: DTI Inspectors' Reports (London: HMSO).

We are unlikely to have the type of litigation explosion as has occurred in the United States. The important thing as far as the accounting profession is concerned, and more particularly the practising accountant within the profession, is the need to maintain the highest standards in carrying out professional duties. The accountant must look beyond the contractual relationship with his client. His duty and responsibilities are to any person reading, relying or otherwise acting upon his report. The need for integrity, independence and professionalism have never been greater.

VI FURTHER RESEARCH

The legal liability of accountants is an area of study inadequately researched in England. The dramatic increase in litigation in the US has provoked a number of research studies there but little has been done to evaluate the possible consequences for this country. This book has analysed the topic from the American side to provide the basis for comparison with the UK. Further research should be undertaken to evaluate the consequences of litigation upon the British accounting profession. a number of areas arising out of the research are suggested.

(1) Self regulation
The accounting profession in this country is essentially self-regulatory. The research has indicated that it is ineffective in many respects. The effects of the SEC regulatory process should be studied in depth to evaluate if a comparable body or its regulatory mechanism would be a viable proposition for this country.

(2) Statutory law
Although many cases have been brought under the common law in the US many cases have also been involved with statute law. The leading statutory cases arising in the US of the past decade should be analysed. Initial evidence indicates that a wider interpretation of statutes has been occurring. Further research should evaluate this statutory development and provide indications of how company legislation may be revised in this country.

(3) Implications for the auditing and accounting profession

The cases have provided evidence of the way the accounting profession in the US has needed to revise its practical methods of working. Significant effects have arisen in recent years as a direct result of litigation, for example, The Cohen Commission. Company audits and information disclosure have altered as new standard setting bodies and commissions are set up. The practical developments instituted by these bodies should be researched so as to assess the likely development of the accounting profession in Britain.

(4) DTI investigations

Another significant area which has not been fully researched is the effect of DTI investigations and the subsequent reports upon accounting practice. The present research has shown that there is inadequate follow-up to investigation by the DTI compared with the influence of the SEC investigation. Each of the reports should be analysed and compared with similar SEC investigations to provide indications of the most practical methods of revising the investigatory process to make the company investigation by a body such as the DTI an effective measure against malpractice in this country.

To conclude it is interesting to reflect upon a statement made by Lord Denning in a recent case[10] on the subject of negligent misrepresentation.

> In my opinion the duty to use care in a statement arises, not from any voluntary assumption of responsibility, but from the fact that the person making it know, or ought to know, that others, being his neighbours in this regard, would act on the faith of the statement being accurate.

NOTES

[1] See Chapter 1.
[2] Chapter 4.
[3] Chapter 3.
[4] Chapter 3.
[5] Chapter 4.
[6] See Chapter 6.
[7] See Chapter 7.
[8] [1979] 3 All E.R. 507.
[9] 'Clean sweep by the Prudential', *Investors Chronicle*, 22 Feb. 1980, p. 468.
[10] *Ministry of Housing and Local Government* v. *Sharp* [1970] 1 All E.R. 1009 1018–19.

BIBLIOGRAPHY

I LAW JOURNALS

'Accountants and Accounting: the Responsibilities of CPA's: Imposed by Law and by the AICPA', 26 *Oklahoma Law Review* 383 (1973).

'Accountants Liabilities for False and Misleading Financial Statements', 67 *Columbia Law Review* 1437 (1967).

'Accountants Liabilities to Third Parties under Common Law and Federal Securities Law' 9 *B.C. Industrial and Commercial Law Review* 137 (1967).

'Accountants Liability for Non-Disclosure of After-Acquired Information: Strict Liability Under Rule 10b-5', 22 *Rutgers Law Review* 554 (1968).

'Accountants Liability – For What and To Whom', 36 *Iowa Law Review* 319 (1951).

'Accountants Professional Liability: Expanding Exposure', 22 *Federation of Insurance Council Quarterly* 7 (1972).

Alber, T. A., 'SEC Disclosure Requirements for Corporations' 26 *Business Lawyer* 1223 (1971).

Anderson, A. P., 'Accountants Liability to Third Parties for an Audit', 52 *Marquette Law Review* 158 (1968).

Bagwell, S. D., 'Securities Regulation – Corporate Accountants' Improper Certification of Financial Statement may Result in Rule 10b-5 Violation', 18 *Wayne Law Review* 1675 (1972).

Barr and Koch, 'Accounting and the SEC', 28 *George Washington Law Review* 176 (1969).

Baxt, R., 'The Liability of Accountants and Auditors for Negligent Statements in Company Accounts', 36 *Modern Law Review* 42 (1973).

Baxt, R., 'The Modern Company Auditor – A Nineteenth Century Watchdog?' 33 *Modern Law Review* 413 (1970).

Benston, G. J., 'Accounting Standards in the United States and the United Kingdom, Their Nature, Causes and Consequences', 28 *Vanderbilt Law Review* 235 (1975).

Bergadano, J. A., 'Recent Developments and Perspectives in Accountants' Professional Liability', 42 *Insurance Counsel Journal* 231 (1975).

Blumberg. P. I., 'The Public's Right to Know: Disclosure in the Major American Corporation', 28 *Business Lawyer* 1025 (1973).

Bohlen, F. H., 'Misrepresentations as Deceit, Negligence and Warranty', 42 *Harvard Law Review* 733, (1928–9).

Bradley, E. J., 'Auditors Liability and the Need for Accounting Uniformity', 30 *Law and Contemporary Problems* 898 (1965).

Bradley, E. J., 'Liability to Third Persons for Negligent Audits', [1966] *Journal of Business Law* 190.

Bromberg, A. R., 'Are there Limits to Rule 10b-5?' 29 *Business Lawyer* S-167 (1974).

Burton, J. C., 'SEC Enforcement and Professional Accountants: Philosophy, Objectives and Approach', 28 *Vanderbilt Law Review* 19 (1975).

Chalmers, G. T., 'The Independent Auditor – Guarantor or Guide', 31 *Business Lawyer* 367 (1975).

'Civil Liabilities under the Federal Securities Act', 50 *Yale Law Journal* 90 (1940).

'Civil Liability Under Section 10b and Rule 10b-5: A Suggestion for Replacing the Doctrine of Privity', 74 *Yale Law Journal* 658 (1965).

Clark, J. P., 'Torts – Professional Negligence – Accountants may be Liable to Third Parties for Negligence (Notes)', 50 *Texas Law Review* 411 (1972).

Collier, D., 'Negligence – Accountants are Liable to Third parties for Failure to Exercise Reasonable Care (Case Notes)', 3 *Texas Tech. University Law Review* 210 (1971).

Collins, L. and Livingston, D. K., 'Aspects of Conclusive Evidence Clauses', [1974] *Journal of Business Law* 212.

Cooney, J., 'The Implications of the Revolution in Securities Regulation for Lawyers', 29 *Business Lawyer* 129 (Sp.edn) (1974).

Curran, W. J., 'Professional Negligence – Some General Comments', 12 *Vanderbilt Law Review* 535 (1959).

Dawson, J. P., 'Auditors' Third Party Liability: An Ill-Considered Extension of the Law (Comments)', 46 *Washington Law Review*

675 (1971).

Earle, V. M. III, 'Fairness Myth', 28 *Vanderbilt Law Review* 147 (1975).

'Federal, Criminal and Administrative Control for Auditors: The Need for a Consistent Standard' [1969] *Washington University Law Quarterly* 187.

Fiflis, T. J., 'Current Problems of Accountants' Responsibilities to Third Parties', 28 *Vanderbilt Law Review* 31 (1975).

Fiflis, T. J., 'Views on the Legal and Ethical Responsibilities of Accountants', 30 *Business Lawyer* 186 (Supp. 1975).

Fitzgerald, G. E., 'When is a Class a Class?', 28 *Business Lawyer* 95 (1972).

Folk, E. L. III, 'Civil Liabilities Under the Federal Securities Acts: The *BarChris* Case', 55 *Virginia Law Review* 1 (1969).

Fuerst, H. G., 'Foreseeability in American and English Law', 14 *Cleveland-Marshall Law Review* 552 (1965).

Garrett, R., 'New Directions in Professional Responsibility', 29 *Business Lawyer* 7 (1974).

Gonson, P., 'Disciplinary Proceedings and Other Remedies available to the S.E.C.', 30 *Business Lawyer* 191 (Supp. 1975).

Goodhart, A. S., 'Costs', 38 *Yale Law Journal* 849 (1929).

Goodhart, A. S., 'Current Judicial Reform in England', 27 *New York University Law Review* 402 (1952).

Goodhart, A. S., 'Liability for Innocent but Negligent Misrepresentation', 74 *Yale Law Journal* 886 (1964).

Goodhart, A. S., 'Liability for Negligent Misstatements', 78 *Law Quarterly Review* 107 (1962).

Gormley, R. J., 'Accountants' Professional Liability – A Ten Year Review', 29 *Business Lawyer* 1205 (1973–4).

Green, L., 'The Judicial Process – *Ultramares Corporation* v. *Touche*', 26 *Illinois Law Review* 49 (1931).

Grimsley, G. N., 'Recent Cases – *Hochfelder* v. *Ernst & Ernst* 503 F.2d 1100 (7th Cir. 1974)', 28 *Vanderbilt Law Review* 269 (1975).

Gripp, D. A. and Mitchell, S. G., 'Torts – Negligence – Accountants Held Liable to a Third Party not in Privity', 22 *University of Kansas Law Review* 289 (1974).

Hallet, D. D. and Collins, T. R., 'Auditors' Responsibility for Misrepresentation. Inadequate Protection for Users of Financial Statements', 44 *Washington Law Review* 139 (1968).

Hanson, W., 'Responsibilities of Independent Public Accountants', 22 *Business Lawyer* 975 (1967).

Hawes, D. W., 'Stockholder Appointment of Independent Auditors: A Proposal', 74 *Columbia Law Review* 1 (1974).

Hawkins, C. S., 'Professional Negligence Liability of Public Accountants', 12 *Vanderbilt Law Review* 797 (1959).

Hill, H. P., 'Responsibilities and Liabilities of Auditors and Accountants – An Accountant's View', 30 *Business Lawyer* 169 (Supp. 1975).

Hodgin, R. W., 'The Fortunes of *Hedley Byrne*', [1972] *Journal of Business Law* 27.

Homburger, A., 'State Class Actions and the Federal Rule', 71 *Columbia Law Review* 609 (1971).

Horstein, G. D., 'The Shareholder's Derivative Suit in the United States', [1967] *Journal of Business Law* 282.

Ingalls, E. F., 'Developing and Implementing Higher Professional Standards in Accounting', 30 *Law and Contemporary Problems* 874 (1965).

James, F., 'Limitations on Liability for Economic Loss Caused by Negligence: A Pragmatic Appraisal', 25 *Vanderbilt Law Review* 43 (1972).

Katsoris, C. N., 'Accountants' Third Party Liability – How Far Do We Go?' 36 *Fordham Law Review* 191 (1967).

Keeton, W. P., 'The Ambit of Fraudulent Representors' Liability', 17 *Texas Law Review* 1 (1938).

Kripke, H., 'Book Review of A. Briloff's *Unaccountable Accounting*', 73 *Columbia Law Review* 1681 (1973).

Kripke, H., 'The SEC, the Accountants, Some Myths and Some Realities', 45 *New York University Law Review* 1151 (1970).

Kurland, S., 'Accountants' Legal Liability – *Ultramares* to *BarChris*', 25 *Business Lawyer* 155 (1969).

Levitin, J., 'Accountants Scope for Liability for Defective Financial Reports', 15 *Hastings Law Journal* 436 (1964).

Liggio, C. D., 'The *Ernst* Ruling – Expansion of a Trend', *The New York Law Journal* (14–15 April 1976.)

MacMillan, W. R., 'Sources and Extent of Liability of a Public Accountant', 15 *Chicago-Kent Law Review* 1 (1936).

Marinelli, A. J., 'Expanding Scope of Accountants' Liability to Third Parties', 23 *Case Western Reserve Law Review* 113 (1971).

Mathews, M. H., 'Negligent Statements and Third Party Loss', [1970] *Cambridge Law Journal* 197.

Meek, J. W:, 'Liability of the Accountant to Parties other than his employer for Negligent Misrepresentation', [1942] *Wisconsin Law*

Review 371.

Miller, R. L., 'Public Accountants and Attorneys: Negligence and the Third Party (Notes)', 47 *Notre Dame Lawyer* 588 (1972).

Miller, S. R. and Subak, J. T., 'Impact of Federal Securities Laws, Liabilities of Officers, Directors and Accountants', 30 *Business Lawyer* 387 (1974–5).

Morison, W. L., 'Liability in Negligence for False Statements', 67 *Law Quarterly Review* 212 (1951).

Notes and Comments on Accountants' Liability to Third Parties
   31 *Columbia Law Review* 858 (1951)
   16 *Cornell Law Quarterly* 419 (1931)
   33 *Illinois Law Review* 349 (1938)
   36 *Iowa Law Review* 319 (1951)
   29 *Michigan Law Review* 648 (1931)
    3 *New York University Intra Law Review* 11 (1947)
   16 *New York University Law Quarterly* 436 (1939)
    6 *Rutgers Law Review* 478 (1952)
   13 *St. John's Law Review* 310 (1939)
    6 *University of Chicago Law Review* 127 (1938)
   28 *Columbia Law Review* 216 (1928)
 . 21 *Michigan Law Review* 200 (1922)
   29 *Yale Law Journal* 234 (1919)
   19 *California Law Review* 454 (1931).

'Notes – *Mutual Life and Citizens Assurance Co. Ltd.* v. *Evatt*', 87 *Law Quarterly Review* 147 (1971).

'Overaccountable Accountants? A Proposal for Classification of the Legal Responsibilities Stemming from the Audit Function', 16 *William and Mary Law Review* 71 (1974).

'Overview of Accountants' Duties and Liabilities under the Federal Securities Law and a closer look at Whistle-Blowing', 35 *Ohio State Law Journal* 261 (1974).

Patrick, J. V., 'The Securities Class Action for Damages Comes of Age (1966–1974)', 29 *Business Lawyer* 159 (1974).

Pohl, M. A., 'Developments in Law of Federal Class Action Litigation – Catch 22 in Rule 23', 10 *Houston Law Review* 337 (1973).

Pollock, E. E., 'Class Actions Reconsidered: Theory and Practice under Amended Rule 23', 28 *Business Lawyer* 741 (1973).

Pomerantz, A. L. with Coombe, G. W. Jr., 'Dialogue on Class Actions', 28 *Business Lawyer* (Sp. edn) 109 (1972–3).

Pomerantz, A. L., 'New Developments in Class Actions – Has Their Death Knell been Sounded?', 25 *Business Lawyer* 1259 (1970).

'Potential Liability of Accountants to Third Parties for Negligence', 41 *St. John's Law Review* 588 (1967).

Prosser, W., 'Assault on the Citadel', 69 *Yale Law Journal* 1099 (1960).

Prosser, W., 'Misrepresentation and Third Persons', 19 *Vanderbilt Law Review* 231 (1968).

Rastetter, R. C. Jr., 'Torts – Accountants are Liable to Third Parties for Negligent Misrepresentation when both the Nature of the Transaction and the Group to which the Third Party belongs are known to the Accountant – *Ryan* v. *Kanne*', 20 *Drake Law Review* 411 (1971).

'Recent Developments in Accountants' Professional Liability', 42 *Insurance Counsel Journal* 231 (1975) (*see* Bergadano).

'Recent Developments in Attorney's Fees', 29 *Vanderbilt Law Review* 685 (1976).

'Responsibilities of Professionals under the Federal Securities Law – Some Observations', 68 *North Western University Law Review* 1 (1973).

'The Revolution in Securities Regulation', a seminar published in its entirety in 29 *Business Lawyer* 1 (Sp. edn) (1974).

'Roles and Reasonable Expectations of the Underwriter, Lawyer and Independent Securities Auditor in the Efficient Provision of Verified Information', 52 *Nebraska Law Review* 429 (1972).

Rouse, W., 'Legal Liability of the Public Accountant', 23 *Kentucky Law Journal* 3 (1934).

Ruder, D. S., 'Civil Liability under Rule 10b-5: Judicial Revision of Legislative Intent', 57 *Northwestern University Law Review* 627 (1963).

Schwartz, M., 'The Class Action: Its Incidence and the *Eisen* Cases', 29 *Business Lawyer* 155 (1974).

Scott, D. E., 'The *Hochfelder* and *Herzfeld* Cases', 30 *Business Lawyer* 181 (Supp. 1975).

Seavey, W. A., '*Candler* v. *Crane, Christmas & Co.* – Negligent Misrepresentation by Accountants', 67 *Law Quarterly Review* 466 (1951).

Seavey, W. A., '*Caveat Emptor* as of 1960', 38 *Texas Law Review* 439 (1960).

Seavey, W. A., 'Mr Justice Cardozo and the Law of Torts', 52 *Harvard Law Review* 372 (1939).

'SEC Disciplinary Proceedings against Accountants – A Study in Unbridled Discretion', 27 *Administrative Law Review* 255 (1975).

'Shareholder Derivative Suits: Are they Class Actions?', 42 *Iowa Law Review* 568 (1957).

Sheppard, D. P., 'Accountants' Liability to Third Parties for Negligence', 23 *University of Miami Law Review* 256 (1968).

Sims, R., 'Negligent Misrepresentation – Liability of Accountants to Third Parties – The Privity Requirement. *Aluma Kraft Manufacturing Co.* v. *Elmer Fox & Co.*', 39 *Missouri Law Review* 466 (1974).

Simpson, P., 'The Public Accountants' Professional Liability', 39 *Journal of Kansas Bar Association* 345 (1970).

Solomon, K. I., '*Ultramares* Revisited: A Modern Study of Accountants' Liability to the Public', 18 *De Paul Law Review* 56 (1968).

Sommer, A. A. Jr., 'Survey of Accounting Development in the '60s: What's Ahead in the '70s?', 26 *Business Lawyer* 207 (1970).

Stern, R., 'Accountants' Liability to Third Parties', 17 *Cleveland-Marshall Law Review* 490 (1968).

Stevens, R., '*Hedley Byrne* v. *Heller*: Judicial Creativity and Doctrinal Possibility', 27 *Modern Law Review* 121 (1964).

'Torts; Accountant Liable to Third Party for Negligent Misrepresentation', 53 *Minnesota Law Review* 1375 (1969).

'Torts – Negligent Language – Accountants' Liability to Third Persons', [1952] *Rutgers Law Review* 478.

'Torts – Negligent Misrepresentation – Downfall of Privity', 19 *De Paul Law Review* 803 (1969).

Weir, J. A., 'Liability for Syntax – a Note on *Hedley Byrne & Co. Ltd.* v. *Heller & Partners Ltd.*', [1963] *Cambridge Law Journal* 216.

Wieler, R. L., 'Torts – Negligent Performance of a Contract – Privity. Have the Exceptions Finally Swallowed the Rule?', 33 *Missouri Law Review* 531 (1968).

Wyatt, A. R., 'Auditors' Responsibilities', 12 *St. Louis Law Journal* 331 (1968).

II FINANCIAL AND ACCOUNTING JOURNALS (SELECTED)

'Accountants, Liability for Negligence: Two American Cases', 76 *Accountants Magazine* 340 (1972).

'Accountants' Liability, Three Viewpoints', 128 *Journal of Accountancy* 85 (1969).

'Accountants' Liability to Third Parties – The *Hedley Byrne* Decision', 120 *Journal of Accountancy* 66 (1965).

American Institute of Certified Public Accountants, 'A.I.C.P.A. Brief in *Natelli-Scansaroli*', 139 *Journal of Accountancy* 69 (1975).

Andrews, F., 'S.E.C. Jolting Auditors into a Broader Role in Fraud Detection', *Wall Street Journal* 1 (12 July 1974).

'Arthur Andersen Censured by S.E.C. over Whittaker', *Wall Street Journal* 4 (9 July 1974).

'Arthur Andersen 1974 Report Indicates It Will Keep Growing, Fight Litigation', *Wall Street Journal* 10 (24 June 1974).

'Attorney (Earle) Questions Suits Against the Profession', 131 *Journal of Accountancy* 12 (1971).

'Auditing Standards', 169 *Accountant* 674 (1973).

'Auditing the Auditors', *Economist* 79 (Feb. 1976).

'Auditors' Critics Seek Wider, Faster Action in Reform of Practices', *Wall Street Journal* 1 (15 Nov. 1966).

'Auditors' Responsibility to Disclose Information obtained Subsequent to Publication of Opinion of Financial Statements', Statement in Quotes, 124 *Journal of Accountancy* 56 (1967).

Bab, D. S., 'Current Thoughts About the Legal Liability of the CPA', 41 *New York CPA* 438 (1971).

Bacon, K. H. and L. Gapay, 'S.E.C.'s Top Cops', *Wall Street Journal* 1 (9 July 1973).

Baird, W. M., 'Accountants' Legal Liability: Are the Rules Changing?', 48 *Accountants' Journal* 339 (1970).

Barr, A., 'Accountants and the S.E.C.', 113 *Journal of Accountancy* 31 (1962).

Baxt, R., 'Auditors' Liability for Negligence – *Hedley Byrne* Again', 39 *Chartered Accountant in Australia* 976 (1969).

Baxt, R., 'Liability for Negligent Statements', 48 *Accountants' Journal* 231 (1970).

Baxt, R., 'Liability for Negligent Statements and the Chartered Accountant', 39 *Chartered Accountant in Australia* 881 (1969).

Baxt, R., 'Liability for Negligent Statements: *Evatt* and the M.L.C.', 39 *Chartered Accountant in Australia* 770 (1969).

Bedingfield, J. P., 'Effect of Recent Litigation on Audit Practice', 137 *Journal of Accountancy* 55 (1974).

Benston, G. J., 'Accountants' Integrity and Financial Reporting', 43 *Financial Executive* 10 (1975).

Benston, G. J., 'Financial Reporting and the Stock Market: Evaluation of the Securities Exchange Act of 1934', 42 *Financial Executive*

28 (1974).

Benston, G. J., 'Public (US) Compared to Private (UK) Regulation of Corporate Financial Disclosure', 51 *Accounting Review* 483 (1976).

Benston, G. J., 'Value of the SEC's Accounting Disclosure Requirements', 44 *Accounting Review* 515 (1969).

Blough, C., 'Responsibility to Third Parties', 109 *Journal of Accountancy* 58 (1960).

Briloff, A., 'The "Funny Money" Game', *Financial Analysts Journal* 73 (May/June 1969).

Briloff, A., '*Quo Vadis?*', *Financial Analysts Journal* 34 (March/April 1973).

Briston, R. J., 'The Unacceptable Face?', 84 *Accountancy* 97 (1973).

Burton, J. C., 'A Report on the Symposium on Ethics in Corporate Financial Reporting', 40 *Financial Executive* 28 (1972).

Byrd, K. F., 'Accountancy and the Onslaught of Case Law in North America', 157 *Accountant* 34 (1967).

Causey, D. Y., 'Foreseeability as a Determinant of Audit Responsibility', 48 *Accounting Review* 258 (1973).

Causey, D. Y., 'Newly Emerging Standards of Auditor Responsibility', 51 *Accounting Review* 19 (1976).

'Class Action Suit on Odd Lot Sales will be Reviewed', *Wall Street Journal* 4 (16 Oct. 1973).

Coakley, W. J., 'Accountants' Legal Liability', 126 *Journal of Accountancy* 58 (1968).

Cohen, M. F., 'The S.E.C. and Accountants, Co-operative Efforts to Improve Financial Reporting', 122 *Journal of Accountancy* 56 (1966).

'Court Quotes AICPA Statement in Reversing Lower Ruling', 133 *Journal of Accountancy* 13 (1972).

'CPA's Under Fire', *Financial Analysts Journal* 93 (April 1967).

Daus, E. J., 'Accountants' Liability Today', 37 *New York CPA* 835 (1967).

Dickerson, R. W., 'Allegations of Negligence', 96 *Canadian Chartered Accountant* 265 (1970).

Dickerson, R. W., 'Liability for Negligence', 98 *Canadian Chartered Accountant* 140 (1971) and 284 (1971).

Dickerson, R. W., 'Through the Back Door', 94 *Canadian Chartered Accountant* 408 (1969).

Dohr, J. L., 'Some Reservations on the *State Street Trust Company* Case', 70 *Journal of Accountancy* 218 (1940).

Duncan, R. H., 'Professional Responsibility', 52 *Accountants Journal* 451 (1974).

Duncan, W. S., 'Changing Concepts of the Auditors' Responsibilities', 41 *New York CPA* 372 (1971).

Earle, V. M., 'Accountants on Trial in a Theatre of the Absurd', 85 *Fortune* 227 (1972).

Earle, V. M., 'The Litigation Explosion', 129 *Journal of Accountancy* 65 (1970).

'Fear of Legal Liability is Greater Threat to CPAs', 135 *Journal of Accountancy* 10 (1973).

Gapay, L., 'SEC Moves to Force Corporations to Put More Financial Data in their Annual Reports', *Wall Street Journal* 26 (11 Jan. 1974).

Gapay, L., 'When the SEC Slaps Your Wrist', *Wall Street Journal* 24 (27 Nov. 1973).

Graham, E., 'Malpractice Suits Rise, Leads Doctors to Treat Patients with Caution', *Wall Street Journal* 1 (8 Jan. 1971).

Graham, J., 'The New Takeover Code', 79 *Accountancy* 451 (1969).

Griffin, C. H., 'Beleagured Accountants', 173 *Accountant* 735 (1976).

Hanson, W. E., 'Focus on Fraud', 43 *Financial Executive* 14 (1975).

Heimbuker, C. V., 'Fifty-Three Jurisdictions', 112 *Journal of Accountancy* 42 (1961).

Hershman, A., 'Companies vs. Auditors', 104 *Dun's Review* 33 (1974).

Hershman, A., 'Gumshoe Accountants', 103 *Dun's Review* 29 (1974).

Hershman, A., 'Sue, Sue, Sue: The Angry Stockholders', 102 *Dun's Review* 25 (1973).

Hershman, A., 'The War Over Corporate Fraud', 104 *Dun's Review* 51 (1974).

'High Court Put Big Filing Costs on Class Actions', *Wall Street Journal* 6 (29 May 1974).

Holmes, G., 'Lonrho Board: Uninformed, Misled', 87 *Accountancy* 119 (1976).

Hughes, P. J., 'Auditors' Liability', 80 *Accountancy* 736 (1969).

Hughes, P. J., 'Hazards of Practice – Risks and Remedies', 164 *Accountant* 417 (1971).

Institute of Chartered Accountants of England and Wales, 'Professional Liability Under Scrutiny', 83 *Accountancy* 110 (1972).

Institute of Chartered Accountants of Scotland, 'The Limitation of Professional Liability', 76 *Accountants' Magazine* 445 (1972).

'Investment Advisors, Accountants to Face Tighter SEC Regulation;

Acting Chief Says', *Wall Street Journal* 9 (25 June 1973).

Isbell, D. B. and D. R. Carmichael, 'Disclaimers and Liability – The Rhode Island Trust Case', 135 *Journal of Accountancy* 37 (1973).

Isbell, D. B., 'Rules for Being Sued', 133 *Journal of Accountancy* 84 (1972).

Kenley, W. J., 'Legal Decisions Affecting Auditors: A Review of the *BarChris Construction* and *Continental Vending Machine* Cases in the USA, 39 *Chartered Accountant in Australia* 952 (1969).

'Liability for Negligence', 163 *Accountant* 761 (1970).

Liggio, C. D., 'The Expectation Gap: the Accountants' Legal Waterloo?', *The CPA Journal* 23 (July 1975).

'Loux, Gose & Co., Wichita Accountants is Suspended by SEC', *Wall Street Journal* 5 (5 Sep. 1974).

Martin, R. E., 'Hochfelder – Possible Consequences for the Accounting Profession', *The Arthur Andersen Chronicle* 10 (Jan. 1975).

Metz, B., 'Accounting Profession Vexed by Lawsuits weights Responsibility to Shareholders', *New York Times* 1 (20 Nov. 1966).

Murphy, M. E., 'The British Accounting Tradition in America', 111 *Journal of Accountancy* 54 (1961).

Nash, G., 'Negligent Advice', 41 *Australian Accountant* 127 (1971).

Norgaard, C. T., 'Extending the Boundaries of the Attest Function', 47 *Accounting Review* 433 (1972).

Olson, N. O., 'The Auditor in Legal Difficulty – What's the Answer?' 129 *Journal of Accountancy* 39 (1970).

'On Minimising Liability', 129 *Journal of Accountancy* 39 (1970).

Palmer, R. E., 'Its Time to Stop Talking', 140 *Journal of Accountancy* 60 (1975).

'Peat Marwick is the First Big CPA Firm to Submit to "Quality Review" by Peers', *Wall Street Journal* 8 (17 Apr. 1974).

'Peat Marwick Says it's Got a Good Rating in Quality Review Done by Arthur Young', *Wall Street Journal* 10 (24 Nov. 1975).

'Peat Marwick Submits its Audit Practices to Review by Arthur Young Accountants', *Wall Street Journal* 12 (22 May 1975).

'PMM Agrees to SEC Sanction Barring New Public Clients', 140 *Journal of Accountancy* 10 (1975).

Reiling, H. B. and R. A. Taussig, 'Recent Liability Cases – Implications for Accountants', 130 *Journal of Accountancy* 39 (1970).

Samuels, G., 'Protecting Your Practice Against Liability', 41 *Australian Accountant* 495 (1971).

'Scope of Audit Commission's Work Underestimated: Cohen', 140 *Journal of Accountancy* 18 (1975).

'SEC Bars PMM from Accepting New Publically Held Clients for Six Months', *Wall Street Journal* 3 (3 July 1975).

'SEC Imposes Sanctions on Accounting Firm', 137 *Journal of Accountancy* 10 (1974).

'SEC Moves to Make Accounting Firms More Independent of Corp. Clients', *Wall Street Journal* 6 (14 Oct. 1974).

Seidler, L. J., 'Accountant: Account for Thyself', 135 *Journal of Accountancy* 38 (1973).

Solomon, K. I., C. Chazen and B.S. Augenbraun, 'Who Judges the Auditors, and How?' 142 *Journal of Accountancy* 67 (1976).

Sommer; A. A., 'Legal Liability of Accountants', 42 *Financial Executive* 19 (1974).

'Taming a Legal Monster', *Wall Street Journal* 14 (6 June 1974).

'The Specter of Auditors' Liability', 120 *Journal of Accountancy* 33 (1965).

Trueblood, R. M., 'Legal Liability – A View from the States', 78 *Accountancy* 579 (1967).

Wise, T. A., 'The Auditors have Arrived', *Fortune* 151 (Nov. 1960).

Wise, T. A., 'The Very Private World of Peat, Marwick, Mitchell', *Fortune* 89 (July 1966).

III BOOKS, PAMPHLETS, THESES, ETC.

Bakay, V. H., 'Liability of Certified Public Accountants Related to the Auditing and Accounting Functions as Indicated by a Review of Selected Claims', PhD, University of Michigan, 1970.

Benston, C. J., 'Corporate Financial Disclosure in the UK and the US: a Comparison and Analysis' (Institute of Chartered Accountants in England and Wales) (London: Saxon House, 1976).

Bird, P., 'Accountability: Standards in Financial Reporting' (London: Haymarket Publishing, 1973).

Boutell, W. S. (ed), 'Contemporary Auditing', *Book of Readings*, s. 4 'The Accountants' Legal Liability' (Belmont, Calif.: Dickerson Publishing Co. Inc., 1970).

Boyle, A. J. and R. Sykes (eds.) *Gore-Browne on Companies*, 43rd edn (London: Jordan & Sons Ltd., 1977).

Briloff, A., *Unaccountable Accounting : Games Accountants Play* (New York: Harper & Row, 1972).

Brown, R. (ed), *History of Accounting and Accountants* (London: Frank Cass & Co., 1968).

Burton, J. C., *Corporate Financial Reporting: Ethical and Other Problems* (New York: American Institute of Certified Public Accountants, 1972).

Cain, T. E., *Charlesworth's Company Law* 11th edn (London: Stevens and Sons, Ltd., 1977).

Carey, J. L., *The Rise of the Accounting Profession: From Technician to Professional* (New York: McGraw-Hill, 1971).

Cashin, J. A. (ed.), *Handbook for Auditors* (New York, 1971). Esp. Chapter 4, H. J. Brown, 'Professional Ethics'; Chapter 5, J. Kauffman, 'Legal Liability'; and Chapter 17, N. Kurlander 'Fraud and the Auditor'.

Casler, D. J., 'The Evolution of CPA Ethics' Occasional Paper No. 12 Bureau of Business and Economic Research, Michigan State University, 1964.

Causey, D. Y., 'Duties and Liabilities of the CPA', Studies in Accounting, No. 5 Bureau of Business Research University of Texas (Rev. ed.) 1976.

Causey, D. Y., 'The Growth of Liability of Public Accountants' PhD, University of California Los Angeles, 1971/2.

Clark, J. L., 'Some Aspects of Changing Concepts of the Accountants' Legal Liability', PhD, University of Georgia, 1974.

Cooper, G. and R. J. Gridlan, *Law and Procedure of the Stock Exchange* (London: Butterworths, 1971).

Department of Industry, *London and County Securities Group Limited – Investigation under Sections 165(b) and 172 of the Companies Act 1948* (London: HMSO, 1976).

Dickerson, R. W. V., *Accountants and the Law of Negligence* (Toronto: Canadian Institute of Chartered Accountants, 1966).

Elliot, S. P. C., 'Auditors' Legal Liability to Third Parties: A Case Law Approach', D.B.A., University of Colorado, 1975.

Fiflis, T. J. and H. Kripke, *Accounting for Business Lawyers* (St. Paul, Minn.: West Publishing Co., 1971). Chapter 17 'Legal Liability of Accountants'.

Going to Law, Justice Report (London: Stevens and Sons, Ltd., 1974).

Goldberg, S. C. (ed.) 'Expanding Responsibilities under the Securities Acts: Transcript', Conference transcript, (New York: Law Journal Press, 1973).

Gower, L., *Principles of Modern Company Law*, 4th edn, L.C.B.

Gower, J.B. Cronin, A.S. Easson, Lord Wedderburn (eds) (London: Stevens and Sons, Ltd., 1979).

Guide to the Accounting Requirements of the Companies Acts 1948–1967 (London: Gee & Co., 1967).

Hay, P., *An Introduction to United States Law* (Amsterdam: North-Holland Publishing Co., 1976).

Ivarmy, E. R. H. (ed.) *Topham and Ivarmy's Company Law* 16th edn (London: Butterworths, 1978).

Jaenicke, H. R., 'The Impact of the Current Legal Climate on the Accounting Profession', a background paper prepared for the Commission on Auditors' Responsibilities, 1976.

Jennings, R. W. and H. Marsh, *Securities Regulation, Cases and Materials* (New York: Foundation Press, 1972).

Kane, R. L., 'Legal Responsibility and Civil Liability', Chapter 6 of *The CPA Handbook* Vol. 1 (New York: American Institute of Certified Public Accountants, 1956).

Label, W. A., 'The Accountants' Legal Liability: Its Impact upon the Profession', PhD, University of California Los Angeles, 1971.

Lawson, W., *Company Law – Basic Accounting Principles* (London: Accountancy, 1970).

Lee, T. A., *Company Auditing: Concepts and Practices* (Edinburgh: Institute of Chartered Accountants of Scotland, 1972).

The Legal Systems of Britain (London: HMSO, 1976).

Levy, S., *Accountants' Legal Responsibility* (New York: American Institute of Certified Public Accountants, 1954).

Littleton, A. C. and B. S. Yamey (eds), *Studies in the History of Accounting* (Illinois: Richard D. Irwin, Inc., 1956).

Mayers, L., *The American Legal System* (Rev. edn) (New York: Harper & Row, 1964).

Murphy, C. E., *Significant Differences between English and American Practice* (The Association of the Bar of the City of New York, 1958).

Oliver, M. C., *Company Law* (London: Macdonald & Evans, 1967).

Peat, Marwick, Mitchell & Co., *Research Opportunities in Auditing* (New York, 1976).

Pennington, R. R. *Company Law*, 4th edn (London: Butterworths, 1979).

Pockson, J. R. H. H., 'Recent Litigation against the American Auditor: Its Causes, Effects and Wider Implications', M.A. Dissertation, University of Lancaster, 1975.

Prosser, W. L., *Handbook of the Law of Torts,* 4th edn (St. Paul,

Minn.: West Publishing Co., 1971).

Putnam, C. B. *How to Find the Law*, 4th edn (St. Paul, Minn.: West Publishing Co., 1949).

Rappaport, L. H., *S.E.C, Accounting Practice and Procedure*, 3rd edn (New York: Ronald Press, 1972).

Schmitthof, C. M. (ed.), *Palmer's Company Law*, 22nd edn (London: Stevens and Sons, Ltd., 1976).

Sealey, L. S., *Cases and Materials in Company Law* (Cambridge University Press, 1971).

Solomons, D. and T. M. Berridge, *Introduction and Summary of Recommendations of Prospectus for a Profession* (London: Gee and Co., 1974).

Stamp, E. and C. Marley, *Accounting Principles and the City Code* (London: Butterworths, 1970).

Sterling, R. (ed.), *Institutional Issues in Public Accounting* (Kansas: Scholars Book Co., 1974). Esp. Chapter 3: .C. D. Liggio, 'The Accountant's Legal Environment for the Next Decade', pp. 99–121; T. J. Fiflis, 'The Meaning and Implications of *US* v. *Simon* as to the Legal Role of Accountants', pp. 122–36; and Chapter 7: J. C. Burton, 'The SEC and the Accountants' Profession: Responsibility, Authority and Progress', pp. 265–75 and response thereto.

Stettler, H. (ed.), 'Auditing Looks Ahead', Proceedings of the 1972 Touche Ross University of Kansas Symposium on Auditing Problems, University of Kansas, 1972. Esp. G. Brown and R. Salquist, 'Some Historical Auditing Milestones'; and R. K. Mautz, 'Toward a Philosophy of Auditing'; and A. A. Sommer, 'What are the Courts Saying to Auditors?'.

Street, H. *The Law of Torts*, 6th edn (London: Butterworths, 1976).

Tobias, A., *The Funny Money Game* (London: Michael Joseph, 1972).

Walker, R. J. and M. G. Walker, *English Legal System*, 4th edn (London: Butterworths, 1976).

Willams, N. *Consumer Class Actions* (Consumer Association of Canada, 1974).

Zeff, S. A., *Forging Accounting Principles in Five Countries: A History and an Analysis of Trends* (Illinois: Stipes Publishing Co., 1972).

IV REFERENCE AND OTHER MATERIAL

Legal Digests

American
Sixth Decennial Digest
American Law Reports Annotated (1st, 2nd and 3rd Series)
    Incl.   120 A.L.R. 1253
           77 A.L.R. 2d 411
           38 A.L.R. 3d 1384
           46 A.L.R. 3d 989
    and   15 A.L.R. Fed. 954
Corpus Juris Secundum
    (together with the Shepard Citator)
American Jurisprudence
    Incl.   20 Am.Jur. 2d 1
           59 Am.Jur. 2d 408
Words and Phrases

Legal or quasi – legal publication

American
American Law Institute 'Restatement of the Law, Torts' (1938) and 'Restatement of the Law, Torts (Second), (Tentative Draft No. 12, 1966)
Federal Rules of Civil Procedure – United States Code Annotated
United States Securities and Exchange Commission 'Regulation S – X Form and Contents of Financial Statements' 17 Code of Federal Regulation 210.1–01 (1970) as amended

English
Halsbury's Laws of England, 4th edn (London: Butterworths, 1974).
Halsbury's Statutes of England, 3rd edn (London: Butterworths, 1968).
Rules of the Supreme Court 1965 (S.I. 1965 No. 1776) as subsequently amended.
Stock Exchange *Admission of Securities to Listing* Issued by Authority of the Stock Exchange, London, April 1979.
City Code on Take-Overs and Mergers, Stock Exchange, London (City Working Party) April 1976.

Statutes

American
Securities Act 1933
Securities Exchange Act 1934

English
Companies Act 1948, 11 & 12 Geo. VI c.38
Companies Act 1967, 15 & 16 Eliz. II Part II. c.81
Prevention of Fraud (Investments) Act 1958, 6 & 7 Eliz. II c.45
Protection of Depositors Act 1963, 11 & 12 Eliz. II c.16

Institutional or professional publications

American
United States Securities and Exchange Commission *SEC Docket Series*, Weekly Compilation of Releases from the SEC, including the Accounting Series Releases.
American Institute of Certified Public Accountants *Code of Professional Ethics*, AICPA (New York, 1974).
American Institute of Certified Public Accountants *Codification of Auditing Standards and Procedures – Statement of Auditing Standards No. 1*, Committee on Auditing Procedure AICPA, 1973, as amended.
American Bar Association *Canons of Professional Ethics* ABA
Commission on Auditors' Responsibilities Statement of Issues: Scope and Organisation of the Study of Auditors' Responsibilities, AICPA (New York 1975).

English
Department of Trade and Industry: Investigations under the Companies Acts (London: HMSO).
Institute of Chartered Accountants in England and Wales, London:
  Members Handbook
  Institute Newsletter
  Royal Charter and Bye-Laws.

INDEX